# Really raising standards

## Cognitive intervention and academic achievement

## Philip Adey and Michael Shayer

London and New York

First published 1994
by Routledge
11 New Fetter Lane, London EC4P 4EE

Simultaneously published in the USA and Canada
by Routledge
29 West 35th Street, New York, NY 10001

© 1994 Philip Adey and Michael Shayer

Typeset in Times by Michael Mepham, Frome, Somerset

Printed and bound in Great Britain by
Mackays of Chatham PLC, Chatham, Kent

*British Library Cataloguing in Publication Data*
A catalogue record for this book is available from the British Library

*Library of Congress Cataloging in Publication Data*
Adey, Philip.
   Really raising standards: cognitive intervention and academic
   achievement / Philip Adey and Michael Shayer.
   p. cm.
   Includes bibliographical references and index.
   1. Cognitive learning. 2. Constructivism (Education). 3. Thought
   and thinking – Study and teaching. 4. Cognition in children.
   5. Academic achievement. 6. Learning, Psychology of. I. Shayer,
   Michael, 1928–   .
   II. Title.
   LB1590.3.A35   1993
   371.3–dc20
                                                    93–9022
                                                       CIP

ISBN 0–415–10144–1 (hbk)
ISBN 0–415–10145–X (pbk)

# Contents

# Figures and tables

For a correct version of Figure 2.7
please refer to Figure 3.1 on page 40

**FIGURES**

# Preface

It is a truth universally acknowledged amongst politicians of all persuasions and amongst populist journalists that 'educational standards have fallen'. This is not primarily a book either about philosophical aims of education or about psychometrics, and we do not propose to question closely either the possible meanings of 'standards' or how such standards may be measured with validity. We are, broadly speaking, content to accept public examinations such as the General Certificate of Secondary Education (UK), Scholastic Attainment Tests (USA) or the Baccalaureate (France) as measures of educational achievement which have popular currency and which are the academic goals towards which educational establishments strive.

This does not mean that methods proposed for raising standards, at least in Britain and the United States, are not open to question. One might ask, for instance, whether the setting of standards in the form of instructional objectives can, of itself, lead to a raising of standards. If the teaching force is fundamentally lazy and the materials they are using are grossly ill-designed then setting higher standards may possibly lead to higher achievement through fear of loss of job or loss of sales, but if education is in the hands of professionals whose driving force is the provision of education to the best of their ability then the imposition of specific instructional objectives cannot positively affect the practice of teaching. We may argue thus, but we also have to live with the reality that the popularisation of educational policy often results in rather crude instruments being used to judge educational innovation, from anecdotes about 'when I was at school' to league tables of schools' examination passes.

What a happy circumstance it would be if an innovation which had professional credibility also led to higher scores in the national testing process! The purpose of this book is to describe such a happy circumstance and to investigate its implications for our understanding of how children learn, for the curriculum, for the professional development of teachers, and for educational policy. We will emphasise the psychological foundations of the innovation and contend that no serious progress can be made in improving educational standards without a well-articulated theory which can be tested and described in enough detail to enable replication.

We believe that this book will be of interest to policy makers and parents as well as to a wide range of education professionals including teachers (not exclusively science teachers), administrators, psychologists, and teacher educators. While we naturally would like everyone to read all of it, it may help particular interest groups to focus on those parts of relevance to them if we outline the way that the book is structured. The central story is presented in Chapters 5 and 6, where we describe the innovation called *Thinking Science* and its long-term effect on student academic achievement in a wide range of subjects. The essentially Piagetian model of cognitive development upon which the work is based is described in Chapter 2, especially as it relates to the type of thinking found in the real school population and to typical demands of the curriculum. In Chapter 1 we introduce a distinction central to our argument: that between *instruction* aimed at content objectives and *intervention* in the cognitive development process aimed at raising levels of thinking and so greatly improving children's potential to gain from instruction. In Chapter 3 some intervention programmes which have had significant effects are described, and in Chapter 4 key features are abstracted from these experiences and built into a generalised model for successful intervention.

Chapter 7 is unashamedly psychological, investigating what the results reported in Chapter 6 indicate about the nature of the mind and of learning, while in Chapter 8 we try to answer the questions of those who want to know whether the methods work in subject areas other than science and at ages other than early adolescence. Chapter 9 discusses the professional development of teachers and effective methods of introducing change in classroom practice. Finally, Chapter 10 spells out the implication of what we have learned about possibilities of really raising academic standards for school, school district, and national policies on such matters as selection, streaming, key ages for effective intervention, and remedial teaching. Following case studies of schools which have successfully introduced intervention methods we outline a five-year plan for a school or school system concerned with maximising the intellectual development of its students.

None of these threads can really exist without the other since the methodology is rooted in a theory of cognition, the implications for cognitive science rely on the results obtained in the experiments we report, and application of the methods requires an understanding of how and why teachers change their practice. If this book does no more than restore the faith of politicians and administrators in the ability of educational research to deliver strong, practical messages, we would be content – but our aim has been to do much more.

# Chapter 1

# Learning, development, and intervention

## STANDARDS AND INTERVENTION

Concern with academic standards in schools and colleges has been growing since the end of the Second World War but took on an added urgency after widespread liberalisation of education in the 1960s. As universities in the United States expanded their intake from 1945 onwards professors found that many of their freshman students lacked the intellectual capacity to cope with the courses as then structured. In Britain the Butler Act of 1945 created a three-tier secondary school system of grammar schools for the top 20 per cent in intellectual ability, technical schools for those supposedly gifted in this direction, and secondary modern schools for the rest. Parallel to this state system were the private schools, highly selective in their own way. This system effectively insulated decision makers – themselves exclusively from grammar or private schools – from contact with the intellectual norms of the majority so that when comprehensive schools were introduced in the 1960s and the insulation removed, the writing classes misinterpreted their new experience as a lowering of standards rather than as the revelation of reality. Meanwhile many Third World countries were engaged in massive expansion of their educational systems, aiming for universal primary education and for increased access to secondary education. Again, mean academic performances inevitably fell as those who had previously been excluded from the educational process were exposed to curricula designed for an intellectual élite.

This dawning of realisation of the very wide range of intellectual ability within a population was slow and remained largely a topic of debate within educational circles and parental dinner tables until the lean mean monetarist era of the 1980s when the new business-oriented free marketeers saw in the issue of 'standards' another stick with which a coterie of professionals, in this case education professionals, could be beaten.

There are different planes upon which the educated may address the question of educational standards. There is the philosophical questioning of the meaning of 'standards' and whether setting standards can possibly be the same as raising them; there is the social-ethical plane of discussion of the nature of a just society and rights to education; there is the economic plane of the needs of the body economic for people of different levels and types of education; and finally there is the technical-psychological plane of describing and measuring intellectual diversity and investigating ways of improving performance generally and in particular subject domains. It is quite specifically the last of these planes upon which this book will ride and our aim is to offer a review of the relevant research and some new evidence which will provide an account of possibilities available to policy formers working on the other planes.

In particular the idea of educational *intervention* will be introduced and contrasted to *instruction*. The meaning of instruction is unproblematical: it is the provision of knowledge and understanding through appropriate activities. Instruction can be categorised by topic and by domain, and the end product of instruction can be specified in terms of learning objectives. Generally, its effectiveness can be evaluated by finding out whether or not these objectives have been attained. Effective instruction and its evaluation is the subject of many books on pedagogical methods.

Intervention is not such a familiar term amongst educators. We use it to indicate intervention in the process of cognitive development as in manipulating experiences specifically aimed at maximising developmental potential. Both instruction and intervention are necessary to an effective educational system, but we will claim that while intervention has been sadly neglected it actually offers the only route for the further substantial raising of standards in an educational world which has spent the last 40 years concentrating on improved instructional methods.

To explain this distinction further it will be necessary to spend a little time unpacking possible meanings of the word *development*, and contrasting it with meanings of the word *learning*.

## DEVELOPMENT AND LEARNING

At first sight there is not much danger of confusing the meaning of the word development with that of learning. Development carries with it the idea of unfolding, of maturation, of the inevitable. Learning on the other hand is purposeful, and may or may not happen. Looking a bit more closely, we might agree that some characteristics associated with development are unconsciousness, unidirectionality, and orientation towards natural goals. Let us consider each of these in turn and see where learning fits in, if at all.

### Unconsciousness

There is a point in one's adolescence when one simply cannot understand how a younger child cannot understand something. We 'forget' completely, it seems, the difficulty we ourselves had in understanding that concept only a year or two earlier. It is a characteristic of cognitive development that it is unconscious and that after a particular period of development has occurred we find it very difficult to think again as we did previously. Indeed one of the most important things that teachers in training need to re-learn is the nature of difficulties that children have in understanding. Having unconsciously *developed* beyond these difficulties themselves, student teachers sometimes think that their job will be largely a matter of ordering learning material in (to the teacher) a logical manner, and they fail to appreciate the nature of the difficulties encountered by children whose cognitive development has not proceeded so far. In contrast it is not difficult to imagine what it must be like not to have learned something. A university teacher (knowledgeable but untrained in teaching) is seldom impatient with students who know nothing of a new subject, but becomes exasperated with those who cannot follow his elegant exposition or line of proof.

## Unidirectionality

It is usual to ascribe to development the idea that there is only one avenue down which it may proceed, although that avenue may be broad and may allow for some meandering from side to side. Tadpoles do not develop into anything but frogs and cognitive development inevitably proceeds from the simple to the more complex. The comparison of two states of development carries with it the implication that one is more advanced than the other. As senility approaches, we do not talk of continuing development but of regression, or loss, implying that the process is going into reverse or decaying.

In contrast, learning may proceed in any direction. There is an infinite number of things to learn, grouped in multiply-nested topics, fields, and domains. From a position of knowledge of a few things and ignorance of many, one may choose to set off in any direction to increase learning. Furthermore, consideration of two pieces of knowledge or understanding does not immediately imply that one is more advanced than the other. One cannot say that to understand the nature of atmospheric pressure is more or less advanced than to understand the nature of evil embodied in Iago.

## Orientation towards natural goals

Kessen (1984) discusses the enslavement of developmentalists to the idea of an end-point to development, a goal to which development moves 'steadily or erratically'. Although closely related to the idea of unidirectionality discussed above it does not follow inevitably from it. One can, after all, conceive of an endless road of continuing cognitive elaboration and increase in complexity. The present cognitive developmental state of the developmental psychologist does not necessarily represent perfection! Nevertheless, in most developmental models there is the strong implication of at least an empirical goal, a stage which seems to represent mature adulthood and beyond which no individual has been observed to operate. No such end point is imaginable in learning. However much one knows about a topic there is always more to learn. Learning end points are arbitrary, may be chosen at will, and defined by course syllabuses and examinations.

Both unidirectionality and orientation towards a natural goal (but not unconsciousness) are aspects of *maturation*. There are many biological contexts in which
we think of development as something which happens almost inevitably, given
adequate nutrition and the absence of disease. We speak of the development of a
plant, the development of a mosquito from its larva, and the development of an
embryo from a zygote. The word 'learning' could not be applied in such cases. But
is the word 'development' in the term 'cognitive development' used more than
metaphorically? If it is, then cognitive development is seen as closely related to the
maturation of the central nervous system and the educator is left with little guidance
but to 'wait until the child is ready'. This is an abrogation of responsibility in the
developmental process which is sometimes erroneously ascribed to Piaget. As
discussed by Smith (1987), for Piaget the maturation process interacts with, and is
probably subservient to, the process of equilibration. Equilibration is the establishment of a new developmental state as a result of interaction with the
environment. An event, an observation, occurs which the child cannot assimilate
into her present way of understanding. A possible result is the accommodation of
that way of understanding to the new observation and this accommodation is a
development of the cognitive processing system. It is development in that it is
unconscious and can proceed in only one direction and it is partly under control of
ontogenetic and phylogenetic release mechanisms. And yet, insofar as it requires a
particular type of stimulus from the environment, it can become a learning process.
As soon as one accepts that the environment plays a role in the process of cognitive
development, the way is open for the environment to be manipulated by a parent
or a teacher. If this counts as teaching, and we believe that it does, then the effect
on the child must count as learning. It is this manipulation of the environment to
maximise cognitive development, a very special sort of learning, which is being
described as intervention in the developmental process.

So we see, after all, that while there is a sharp distinction to be made between
extreme characterisations of development and learning, they may also be seen as
shading into one another along a spectrum from 'extreme' learning to 'extreme'
development (Fig. 1.1). Moving from the L (Learning, Left) end of the spectrum
to the D (Development, Dexter) end there is an increasing recognition of the role
that development plays and a decreasing belief in the possibility of influencing
development through external stimuli.

At the L end of the spectrum we find rote learning in which the learner makes
no connection between what is learned and knowledge already held. Whether it be
nonsense syllables, learning a connection between a red triangle and a pellet of
food, or learning that the formula for water is $H_2O$ without any comprehension of
the meaning of the symbols, the new knowledge remains isolated and unavailable
for application to new contexts. Near to this end is simple behaviourism which
conceives of learning as a change in behaviour and of behavioural modification
being brought about by the establishment of new response-stimulus associations.
Although few would now accept that human learning can be satisfactorily described
in such simple terms, behaviourism can provide guidance for the design of effective

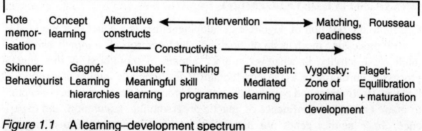

*Figure 1.1*   A learning–development spectrum
(*Source*: Tanner 1978)

instructional methods such as the logical ordering of material, its provision in small steps, frequent recapitulation and repeated testing to ensure mastery. Such methods are appropriate for some types of learning – stereotypically the learning of multiplication tables, foreign vocabulary, or the manipulative skills required to dismantle and reconstruct a rifle. It will be noted that none of these require comprehension.

Moving to the right along the L–D spectrum we come to views of learning which give rise to more sophisticated instructional strategies:

- When new learning can be connected with something already known, we start to incorporate the beginnings of understanding into the learning process. At this point will be found Gagné's (1965) learning hierarchies where the development of each concept is seen to demand the pre-establishment of subordinate concepts or skills.
- Plugging new learning into a network of existing concepts is one of the requirements of meaningful learning (Ausubel 1968). Arising from this is the method of investigating children's current conceptualisations so that new material may be made meaningful by being related to existing understandings. In contrast with the behaviourist approaches there is now some consideration of learners as individuals, rather than simple focusing on the material to be learned. We will have more to say about this approach in Chapter 7.

In the terms of the instruction-intervention distinction, instruction is the most important process taking place towards the left of the L–D spectrum – that end concerned with learning and with domain specific knowledge and understanding.

At the other end of the spectrum, perhaps Rousseau (1762) should be offered the pole position with his belief that Emile should be educated by allowing his natural curiosity to open the world to him with minimum guidance by a mentor – an extreme form of leaving it all to development, or non-intervention. Some interpretations – we would say misinterpretations – of the Piagetian position on cognitive development are not far from this non-interventionist stance and since this will be an important theme throughout the book we should now devote some time to exploring this position further.

## ON COGNITIVE DEVELOPMENT

Central to the position of cognitive developmentalists is a belief in some kind of general processing mechanism of the mind which controls all comprehension. All intellectual activity, in whatever subject domain, is monitored by this general processor. Furthermore, as the term 'cognitive development' implies, it is supposed that the effectiveness and power of the general processor develops from conception to maturity under the influence of genetic programming, maturation, and experience. Since neither genes nor maturation are readily amenable to change by education, the relative importance of these factors to that of experience becomes a critical question for educators.

An elaboration of the developmentalist's position which may, but does not necessarily, follow from the notion of a developing central processor is the idea of distinct stages of development. One could conceive of a cognitive data-processing mechanism which develops by the accretion of more neural connections such that its power increased but without the quality of its processing capability changing over the 15- to 20-year period of its maturation. This would be analogous to an electric motor growing from the 5W toy which can propel a model car to a 3000 kW motor which drives a high speed train. A property of such a model of cognitive development would be that, in principle, any intellectual problem could be solved by a child of any age. The only difference between the abilities of younger and older children would be the rate at which they could deal with the elements of the problem. It is because such a consequence seems to fly in the face of experience about what children of different ages can do, however much time they are given, that most cognitive developmentalists favour a stage-wise developmental process in which at certain ages there is a qualitative shift in the kind of problems that the mind can handle. This was the nature of the theory established by Jean Piaget through 60 years of work with children and reflection on their responses.

There are interpretations of the cognitive-developmentalist position which fall into a deterministic trap: 'Charlie can think only at the level of early concrete operations, so don't waste your time and his by trying to teach him abstract ideas.' This approach represents the crude 'matching' idea, that learning material should be tailored to make cognitive demands which are no higher than the current level of thinking of the learner. Many educators are, quite reasonably, shocked by such a negative view of the teaching and learning process which concentrates more on what children cannot do than on what they can do and views intelligence as a potential with which a child was born and about which nothing can be done by the parent or educator. It may be this sort of interpretation (of which we ourselves have been accused – Shayer and Adey 1981, White 1988) which accounts for the demise in respect accorded to Piaget as a guide for educators. An alternative approach to a model of stage-wise cognitive development whose rate is determined by the interaction of genetic, maturational, and experiential factors is to ask what is the nature of experiences which can be provided which will maximise the potential set by factors over which we have no control? In the pages which follow we propose to show that the strategy of matching the intellectual demand of the curriculum to the current stage of development of the learner is severely flawed. A deliberate policy of challenging learners to transcend their present level of thinking not only accelerates their rate of intellectual development, but also in the long term brings about the achievement which a matching policy on its own would have denied them.

## SOME APPROACHES TO INTERVENTION

Following the realisation of the 'true' range of ability of the population mentioned at the beginning of this chapter the practice, if not the idea, of intervention gradually came out of obscurity during the 1970s to address a variety of populations and age groups. In contrast to the crude matching of material to supposed cognitive level of the learner, programmes which focus on intervention turn attention to the educational environmental factors which may maximally affect the developmental process and so drive on the elaboration of the general cognitive processor. Such programmes and theories will be found in the centre-right region of the L–D spectrum, to the right of theories of instruction which concentrate on the effective presentation of material within specific content domains, and to the left of pure 'leave-it-to-nature' developmental models. All assume that something more general than context-limited concepts can be learned and all implicitly assume that there is one direction in which the development of thinking skills may proceed and either that there is no other direction possible, or that one direction is inherently more valuable than any other. They thus exhibit at least one of the characteristics of development. However, the consideration given to developmental constraints varies widely from one programme to another. Many give little weight to maturational factors in their claims to provide general thinking strategies applicable to a wide range of problems while others are based on the idea of maximising children's developmental potential. In Chapter 4 we will consider in some detail the features and effects of particular intervention programmes which appear to have been most successful in promoting general intellectual development, but here we should illustrate some of the approaches which have become quite widely quoted.

Matthew Lipman's *Philosophy for Children* (Lipman *et al.* 1980) course probably arose from an intuitive feeling that students in American primary and middle schools lacked intellectual stimulation. It was not based on any conscious psychological model but arose rather from a professional philosopher's conviction that the reasoning patterns of argument and discourse lay at the root of effective thinking across all subject domains.

De Bono's work (1976) was addressed initially to improving the thinking of professional adults, and in particular featured exercises designed to promote divergent as distinguished from convergent thinking. As with *Philosophy for Children*, the CoRT (Cognitive Research Trust) (de Bono 1987) is not overtly based on either learning or development theory, but reduces thinking to a set of specific strategies which can be learned and applied in a wide variety of contexts. Insofar as the strategies are learnt the programme is instructional, but their hoped-for general applicability gives CoRT an interventionist flavour.

We turn now to two approaches which are more deeply grounded in psychological models of development and learning and which well illustrate the possibilities of intervention methods.

### Vygotsky: social mediation and development

Vygotsky (born 1896, died of tuberculosis 1934) was described by Michael Cole as 'a Mozartian genius'. He was extremely influential in Soviet psychology but his work was not taken up in the West until the 1960s by, in particular, Jerome Bruner and Reuven Feuerstein. To Western eyes the noteworthy feature of Vygotsky's approach is that from the outset his work integrates aspects of social psychology with aspects of individual and cognitive psychology. In this he differs both from Piaget and current workers in cognitive science who tend to neglect the social dimension. No-one who has worked in a school can be unaware of the importance of this wider viewpoint.

Vygotsky's work on cognition began in part with his dissatisfaction with the use of psychometric tests to predict children's ability to make progress in school learning, in particular with reading. He and his co-workers pioneered *dynamic* testing – 'dynamic' here contrasted to 'static' as a description of the normal use of psychometric tests where the 'objective' form of test items and an emphasis on speed mean that one is discovering only those skills or schemata which the child has readily available for use. A far deeper understanding of the child's potential may be realised by using an individual interview where psychologist and child develop a dialogue with words, pencil, paper, and apparatus. Comparing the child's unassisted responses when discussion is limited to explaining vocabulary and the meaning of the question with final responses obtained following dialogue about the strategies needed for that type of test-item – spatial relations, verbal reasoning, numerical series or whatever – the psychologist can obtain a measure of the child's *potential* to learn. By embodying the mental ability of interest on several different kinds of test-item at different degrees of difficulty the tester conducts what is, in effect, a very short-term intervention delivered in context which allows an assessment of how much further the child can succeed on the test following collaborative help. Vygotsky (1978) showed, in quantitative terms, that the information derived from this mode of testing leads to better predictions of children's progress in school learning over the next two years than did static test scores.

This form of testing was derived from a general theory of the dynamics of development. Part of the model involves *mediation*, the process by which older people or more able peers play an essential part in assisting the child either by effective framing of the world to assist learning or just by specific example. Vygotsky defined the *Zone of Proximal Development* (ZPD) as 'the distance between the actual developmental level as determined by independent problem-solving and the level of potential development as determined through problem-solving under adult guidance or in collaboration with more capable peers' (Vygotsky 1978:86). ZPD describes both what dynamic testing tries to get access to and also the dynamics of mental growth:

> learning which is oriented toward developmental levels that have already been reached is ineffective from the viewpoint of a child's overall development. It does not aim for a new stage of the developmental process but rather lags behind this process.
>
> (Vygotsky 1978:82)

This view is in sharp contrast to the simple matching idea, and rests on the assumption that each child has, in addition to sets of completed skills and strategies which enable her to succeed on conventional test items, a spectrum of half-formed or potential strategies which can be revealed by the technique of dynamic assessment and which the child may turn into complete or successful skills either by chance, by spontaneous effort, or by the mediating influence of an adult or another child.

The Vygotskian description of the social aspect of mental growth casts serious doubt on the notion that improving students' performance in school is just a matter of teaching them more skills and knowledge.

## Feuerstein and the remediation of social disadvantage

The work of Reuven Feuerstein and his large research team in Jerusalem provided another critical experiment in intervention, well supported by falsifiable psychological models. The problem Feuerstein had addressed from the early 1950s was a sociological one. The children of Middle Eastern immigrants to Israel did much worse in school than those from Europe and North America and then were much less successful as young adults competing for jobs. Although Feuerstein and his team of clinical psychologists have worked with children of all ages and with young adults, their main focus came to be on young adolescents. Their Instrumental Enrichment (IE) course was designed to change, over a period of two or more years, the self-concept, motivation, and intellectual processing ability of their target population of disadvantaged students so as to bring them up to the level of the average Israeli by the end of high school.

Feuerstein's experience of working with children traumatised by the holocaust, who had been classified as learning-disabled, convinced him that intelligence is not the fixed quantity of individuals implied by the ascription of an IQ score. He drew a distinction parallel to that we have described as between learning and instruction. He talks of 'general enrichment' as being special instruction in the content and methods of particular subject matter, and of 'instrumental enrichment' as being content-free learning of basic cognitive processes applicable across all subject domains. IE follows the Vygotskyan idea that most effective learning experiences are not available directly to the learner from interaction with his or her environment but must be mediated by an adult or an older child who structures the learning environment, selects and represses experiences, and maximises the attention of the learner to particular features. The Instrumental Enrichment programme is a set of tools to facilitate the role of the teacher in this process of improving students' ability to process data. IE is a metalearning intervention programme in the sense that it teaches students how to learn.

## INTERVENTION AND ACHIEVEMENT

In Great Britain for each major subject in the school curriculum the government directed committees (DES 1988,1991) to draw up detailed lists of desired learning outcomes at ten different levels to fit all years of schooling from 5 to 16 year-olds and with it a programme of testing at ages 7, 11, 14 and 16 years. We propose to question the efficacy of raising educational achievement simply by writing down a list of objectives, calling it a National Curriculum, and writing it into law. It is not, we will maintain, *what* pupils learn, but *how* they learn it that matters. How they learn depends on their cognitive processing capability, and intervention in the process by which this capability develops is the route to fundamentally improved life chances in the population of learners. If by the use of new teaching skills it is found possible to intervene in the course of students' cognitive development so that the incidence of higher level thinking is significantly increased then there would be an automatic increase in the achievement by the students which good instruction from the teachers could deliver. Part of our argument in succeeding chapters is that time taken out from instruction in the early secondary years, devoted instead to intervention activities, pays off handsomely in terms of more effective instruction in the later years. It is also important to note that the teaching skills required really are new and are not generally part of the existing repertoire of good teachers, despite the fact that all of us probably have anecdotal recall of good experiences which feature some of what we shall describe.

In Chapter 2 we will see how cognitive development and intervention in the developmental process may be represented and quantified, and in Chapter 3 we will return to the account of others' experience with programmes designed to 'develop thinking' or 'promote cognitive development' with the aim in Chapter 4 of abstracting some key features from their details.

# Chapter 2

# Describing and measuring cognitive development

## NORMS OF DEVELOPMENT

If we are seriously to investigate the possibilities of intervention in cognitive development as an educational strategy it will be necessary to characterise in some detail the nature of what it is that develops, how that development may be monitored, and how enhancement of the development could be recognised. What the workers mentioned in the last chapter lacked was a quantitative model of their target populations. Part of Feuerstein's model was that of psychometric mental abilities so, implicitly, his model of the population was hidden in the norm-referenced tables of the tests such as Thurstone's Primary Mental Abilities (PMA). Strange as it may seem, by the early 1970s the only worker we have been able to find who looked at the standardisation tables of a major psychometric test – in this case the Stanford-Binet – and asked what model they portrayed of the whole child population was a mammalian brain researcher, Herman Epstein, who was looking for evidence of age-related growth and plateaux phases related to brain-growth evidence. In the Piagetian field we have Piaget as late as 1972 asserting that all people go through the formal operations stage but that maybe some adults only use it in the field of their work life. This notion dies very hard with many people for many reasons.

Without a quantitative descriptive model of the target population the concept of intervention cannot be operationalised or even clearly conceived. To cite one of the international authorities in the medical literature, the work of Tanner (Tanner 1978, Falkner and Tanner 1986) is used very widely in studies of child development.

In Fig. 2.1 typical development curves are shown for boys' height for a representative British population sample. The heavy central curve is that for the average child, at the 50th percentile. The range to be expected in the population is given by curves for the 75th and 25th, the 90th and the 10th, and the 97th and the 3rd percentiles (75 per cent of the population are at or below the 75th percentile; 25 per cent of the population are at or below the 25th percentile, and so on). One can see, for instance, that the average height for a boy aged 11.0 is 146 cm, and that an 11 year-old who is 150 cm tall falls into the tallest 25 per cent for his age group. Further, the range of heights between the 3rd and 97th percentile is about 25 cm.

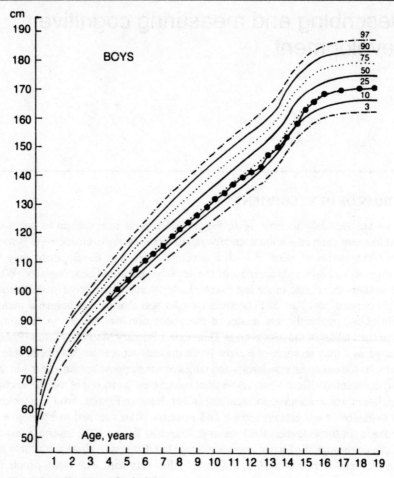

*Fig. 2.1* Growth curves for height
(*Source*: Tanner 1978)

In Fig. 2.2 the way in which such normative data is used to assess the effect of a medical intervention is shown.

The bold line indicates the growth of a boy who at the age of 12 has been treated for thyroid deficiency and has accordingly grown much faster than normal and has moved up to a higher developmental curve as a result of intervention.

Only if normative data such as Tanner's exist can the effect of an intervention stand out and be assessed. Only if the target population can be described in an analogous way in the field of cognitive development can an intervention in the cognitive field be conceived.

While it is true that psychometric tests can be used, as Feuerstein for example used Thurstone's PMA to test whether or not his target population moved up from

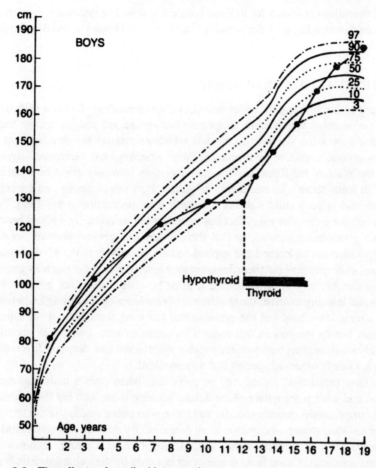

*Fig. 2.2*   The effects of medical intervention
(*Source*: Tanner 1978)

an average of one standard deviation below average (IQ 85) to average (IQ 100) as
a result of the IE intervention, there is one important sense in which this use of
evidence is not analogous to that used in medical intervention. Tanner's curves in
Figs 2.1 and 2.2 are based on a criterion-referenced measure, in this case that
of children's' height. What criterion-referenced measure do we have for a psychological or educational intervention? IQ measures have no developmental theory
underlying them and therefore cannot provide an *explanation* for differences in
item difficulties. The only description of the development of intelligent behaviour
we have which is sufficiently detailed to be related to school learning is that derived
from Piaget. In order to justify this claim it will be necessary to consider the nature
of higher order thinking and to consider how well the Inhelder/Piaget account of

formal operations accounts for it. Even before this it will be necessary to consider the extent to which higher order thinking must be context bound or could be domain general.

## CONTEXTUALISED OR GENERAL?

A feature of the learning–development (L–D) spectrum (Fig. 1.1) is a shift from models of learning which relate to specific knowledge and understandings about particular topics (on the left) to models which emphasise the development of domain general cognitive performance. From a behaviourist viewpoint learning about the Wars of the Roses could not conceivably have any effect on a child's ability to learn about a kinetic theory of gases. 'Pure development', on the other hand, should affect a child's ability to benefit from instruction in any field. Few people believe either that every fact has to be learned individually without benefit of some generalising notions, or that there is any one general problem solving strategy which can be learned and applied equally effectively to the whole domain of human understanding but there does remain a controversy about just how general learning can be, or just how specific it must be. The Ausubelian position that meaningful learning involves the attachment of new learning to existing knowledge about a topic does hold out the promise that knowing something about a topic facilitates further learning in that topic. This seems to accord well with common experience – the expert bird watcher rapidly absorbs the fine detail of differences between a newly observed species and a known bird.

But how broad can 'topics' be? In particular, when does a topic become a domain, and what is the nature of the debate between those who say that learning is, most importantly, domain specific and those who rather emphasise the importance of thinking strategies common to all domains? By *domain* is meant a field of knowledge such as science, social studies, literature, or language acquisition. Domains are distinguished from one another not only by their characteristic body of knowledge, but also by their methods of enquiry. Thus the person who considered himself well-educated in literature would not only be familiar with a wide range of literature, but would also be versed in the art of literary criticism, the evaluation of literature. Similarly, it is supposed that a scientist not only knows a lot of scientific facts, but is able also to employ scientific methods in the pursuit of further scientific knowledge. In other words, each domain has a characteristic body of semantic knowledge (knowledge that . . .) and also a characteristic set of procedural knowledge (knowledge how . . .).

When we talk of domain general knowledge or abilities we may refer to some sort of general problem solving skills which may be applied equally to investigating ways of improving health provision to meet a changing age profile and to why the washing machine has broken down. To put it like this is to make the idea seem ridiculous, which it probably is, although there was an optimistic period (exemplified by the work of Polya 1957 and Newell and Simon 1972, quoted in Nickerson *et al.* 1985) when it was supposed that a general problem solving heuristic applicable across all contexts could be identified, described and codified. The codes produced proved either to be limited in application to specific types of closed problem, generally mathematical in nature, or so blandly general as to be useless in any real situation. ('Consider all elements of the problem; determine your objective; construct your solution in steps such that each step takes you nearer to the solution, remembering that sometimes you may have to move back a step to circumvent an obstacle . . .').

There is, however, another sense in which we can conceive of domain-general abilities, and that is in terms of intellectual processing power. Cognitive-developmentalists, amongst others, consider that the most important determinant in controlling learning in any domain is the general data-processing capabilities of the mind. They concede the existence of fields of knowledge and sets of procedures characteristic of different domains but claim that no amount of training or experience within a domain will lead to expertise unless a person has the fundamental intellectual infrastructure required to master the concepts and procedures of any domain of knowledge.

On the L–D spectrum a border region can be identified between those who consider that learning within topics, or at least domains, is the most profitable way forward for education, and those who seek to put more effort into the development of general processing capabilities. In the early 1990s the mainstream of cognitive psychology (represented by, say, Larkin et al. 1980, Gardner 1983, McPeck 1990, Light and Butterworth 1992) seems to emphasise domain-specific thinking skills and discount the role of general cognitive processes. Some of these writers consider that there are distinctly different intelligences associated with different performances, and others may acknowledge the existence of a general intellectual processor of the mind but consider it not to be amenable to change by educational influence. All believe that the intellectual, social, and linguistic context of a problem plays such a dominant role in finding a solution that it far outweighs the contribution of generalised logical processing. Their message for education is to concentrate on the semantic and strategic knowledge bases characteristic of each of the domains of knowledge considered to be important for social, cultural, or vocational reasons, and not to waste time on attempts to teach general thinking skills.

At the same time, there remains a significant counter-current to (or maybe cross-current in) this mainstream which maintains a belief in the theoretical possibility of teaching general thinking – or at least in the value of pursuing the possibility:

> If [teaching thinking] cannot be done, and we try to do it, we may waste some time and effort. If it can be done, and we fail to try, the inestimable cost will be generations of students whose ability to think is less than it could have been.
>
> (Nickerson et al. 1985:324)

The great attraction of this possibility lies in its potential efficiency. If indeed it proved possible to raise learning potential across all domains by an effort expended on the central processing capability of the mind, then this would offer an enormously efficient use of educational time and effort. In other words, if time spent on developing general thinking skills were to be shown to produce positive effects in learning in a wide variety of domains, then this would represent a handsome pay-off for the effort expended. The evidence for such general development would be the transfer of a training effect from the domain in which it was delivered to domains of a very different nature which lasted long after the training programme. For instance, if a general thinking programme delivered in the context of a science curriculum produced an effect on pupils' language learning, we could say that far transfer had occurred. If the effect persisted for years, we would describe it as a long-term effect. Because of the enormous educational potential of such transfer, the notion of 'long-term far transfer' has become something of a Holy Grail for cognitive psychologists.

One possibility of a model which seems to reconcile general development with domain specificity is offered by Demetriou *et al.* (1992a) who describe five specialised structural systems (SSS). Each SSS differs from the others in (a) the reality domain it interacts with, (b) the reasoning patterns it uses, and (c) the symbolic and representational systems it uses. The five SSSs are the *qualitative-analytic*, covering categorical thinking; the *quantitative-relational,* dealing with applying numbers to reality; the *causal-experimental*, dealing with strategies by which causal relations can be tested by valid experiments and be inferred from information gathered; the *verbal-propositional*, underlying the ability to use language philosophically; and lastly the *spatial-imaginal*, to do with mental operations on images. These five SSSs do have realisations both at the concrete operational level (Shayer *et al.* 1988) and the formal level (Demetriou *et al.* 1993) and go a long way to accounting for individual variability in present levels in the different SSSs. Whereas the domain of literature may require excellence in the qualitative-analytic and the verbal-propositional SSSs, the field of science might better be served by development of the quantitative-relational and the causal-experimental. The SSSs are linked both in terms of relative developmental synchrony and also in terms of metacognitive activity at a higher level by which the contribution of each is accessed appropriately to the task in hand. In effect Demetriou's model combines neo-Piagetian descriptions of development with the differential mental abilities described by the psychometric literature.

It will be clear already that our notion of cognitive intervention is conceived in terms of an effect on domain-general processing and now it is necessary to characterise the nature of such general thinking.

## HIGHER ORDER THINKING

Here is one recent and widely quoted account of higher order thinking:

- Higher order thinking is *non-algorithmic*. That is, the path of action is not fully specified in advance.

- Higher order thinking tends to be *complex*. The total path is not 'visible' (mentally speaking) from any single vantage point.
- Higher order thinking often yields *multiple solutions*, each with costs and benefits, rather than unique solutions.
- Higher order thinking involves *nuanced judgement* and interpretation.
- Higher order thinking involves the application of *multiple criteria*, which sometimes conflict with one another.
- Higher order thinking often involves *uncertainty*. Not everything that bears on the task at hand is known.
- Higher order thinking involves *self-regulation* of the thinking process. We do not recognise higher order thinking in an individual when someone else 'calls the plays' at every step.
- Higher order thinking involves *imposing meaning:* finding structure in apparent disorder.
- Higher order thinking is *effortful*. There is considerable mental work involved in the kinds of elaborations and judgements required.

(Resnick 1987:3)

Lauren Resnick put this list together after consultation with leading psychologists, educators, computer scientists, and philosophers. She makes the point that such thinking is not limited to college students and their teachers but is a necessary part of much intellectual activity at school. Those familiar with Inhelder and Piaget's account of the development of formal operational thinking could see this list of higher order thinking skills as an excellent characterisation of the generality of formal operations although Resnick herself might object that Piaget's formal operations is an adequate account of higher order thinking only as it is expressed in science.

Inhelder and Piaget clearly believed that formal operations are general to thinking in all domains. In *The Growth of Logical Thinking* (1958) they propose that the complete cognitive structure of formal operations includes a set of some 10 *schemata*, or reasoning patterns. Although some of these appear to be more fundamental than and logically prior to others, all do develop together over about the same time-span and one would not find an individual competently fluent with one or two of the reasoning patterns who could not, with very little experience, become fluent with all of them (Shayer 1979, Lawson and Nordland 1976). Some detail of these schemata follows.

**The reasoning patterns of formal operations**

These can be grouped as follows:

*Handling variables*

- control and exclusion of variables

- classification

(Selecting combinations of variables is cited as a reasoning pattern of formal operations by Inhelder and Piaget, but we do not believe that it is.)

*Relationships between variables*

- ratio and proportionality
- compensation and equilibrium
- correlation
- probability

*Formal models*

- constructing and using formal models
- logical reasoning

Each reasoning pattern will now be described in more detail.

## Control and exclusion of variables

Virtually all experiments or critical investigations involve, implicitly or explicitly, the notion of controlling variables. In a simple investigation of a pendulum the weight of the bob, length of the string, and hardness of push are easily understood, easily measured, and equally plausible as factors which may affect the rate of swing. But it is an empirical finding (Shayer and Wylam 1978) that only about 30 per cent of 15 year-olds can correctly answer questions of the type:

> Given a SHORT pendulum with a HEAVY weight and a GENTLE push, what other arrangements would you use to test for the effect of **length** on the rate of swing?

Students commonly change more than one variable, or change two variables and then attribute any effect to both variables. In information processing terms, the solution to this problem requires holding three independent variables and one dependent variable in mind, and considering the possible effects of each independent variable on the dependent variable. Put thus, it can be seen that the demand on working memory space and on executive processing power is considerable, and it becomes less surprising that it is not readily available to students younger than about 12 years.

The exclusion of irrelevant variables requires the identification, from a given set of results, of variables that do *not* have any effect.

In social studies the variable-controlling strategy is more subtle since the variables are not always obvious, they interact with one another, and often are impossible to control. Its importance as a principle remains, however, in the isolation of factors which may possibly have a bearing on an event. To take a relatively isolated example: what are the factors that are causing (at the time of writing) the liberalisation in South Africa? Dreaming up possible factors (sanctions, the church, education, reduction in fear amongst the whites, collapse of the iron curtain, and so on) may need some imagination but it does not require formal operations. However, to consider each in turn and all together and to make rational assessments of their relative contributions to the effect, does require higher level thinking which could properly be described as formal operational.

## Classification

It does not need formal operations to put people or objects into groups according to some given or obvious criterion such as whether they float or sink, or are Catholic or Protestant. What does require higher level thinking is to see that this is only one of many possible ways in which the classification might be carried out, that the categories provided by themselves are inadequate, that one particular criterion does not necessarily allow prediction of others, and that any classification operation may be seen as part of a hierarchical system. These latter abilities require that a person stands outside the process of classification and observes the nature of the process itself. Classification processes are abstractions, and the aspects of classification (hierarchies, multiplication of classification, selection of different criteria for different purposes) are inter-related with one another.

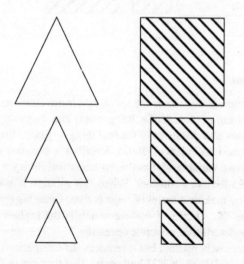

Fig. 2.3

You can see this difference for yourself by looking at the shapes in Fig. 2.3. They differ in size, shape and shading (colour). It can readily be seen, using concrete operations only, that there is a relation between two of the variables: shape and colour. Now imagine that you have in front of you many cards varying in shapes, sizes and colours (Fig. 2.4). You want to demonstrate to a class a set of cards which shows a relationship between size and shape. What cards would you select? This is more difficult because you have to stand outside the classification system itself and invent the classes which will demonstrate a particular relationship. You have to invoke the formal operation of selection of criteria for a particular purpose.

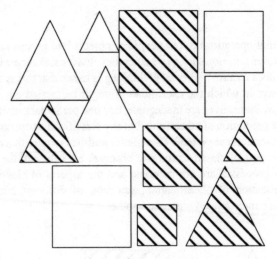

*Fig. 2.4*

**Ratio and proportion**

A *ratio* is a constant number by which one set of data (measurements on a drawing or map, the distance from a fulcrum of a 200 g mass) may be multiplied to give a second set of data (sizes and distances of the real thing or place, distance from the fulcrum of a 100 g mass to balance). Ratio describes a constant multiplicative relationship between two variables. It has the mathematical form $y = mx$. As $x$ goes up, so must $y$ to keep the ratio constant. When this relation is used as a direct operation on reality, by making a series of objects three times bigger, or two times smaller, then one has the schema of scaling which is the highest level number operation still to be a descriptive, concrete operation.

*Proportionality* is closely related, but it requires the comparison of two ratios. For instance, comparing 4:12 with 7:21 and seeing that they are in the same ratio, or seeing that 60 cm³ of gin added to 240 cm³ of tonic makes a drink with a higher concentration of alcohol than one containing 70 cm³ gin in 300 cm³ tonic. Here again handling proportionality can be seen in information processing terms as requiring the mental manipulation of at least four variables independently. A possible consequence of not fully abstracting the proportionality concept from its concrete context is confusion. A potato crisp (chip) manufacturer says his product is healthy because it 'increases the proportion of unsaturated fats in the diet'. This may be true but if the absolute quantity of saturated fats has not changed, you are no better off. In the gin and tonic example the second drink may be weaker, but it contains more alcohol than the first!

Feuerstein among others, regards analogical thinking ('as Paris is to France, so Rome is to Italy') as a lower-level qualitative precursor to proportional thinking (Inhelder and Piaget 1958:66, 314), and Fusco (1983), considers the ability to describe reciprocal relations in a story as an expression of proportional thinking in literature (see Chapter 8).

## Compensation and equilibrium

Compensation, like ratio, involves the relation between two variables, but in this case the mathematical form is $yx = m$. As $y$ goes up $x$ must come down proportionally to keep $m$ constant. At the concrete operational level this is just qualitative and allows a child to see that if a clay block is flattened it remains the same amount and weight of clay since its loss of height has been compensated for by an increase of width or in social terms to understand that compensation should be paid if someone is made redundant. It requires formal operations to express a compensation relationship mathematically and use this expression to calculate exactly how far out a 25 N force must be moved on a lever to exert the same force as a 75 N force closer to the fulcrum.

*Equilibrium* is closely related, but is more complicated because it involves the equating of two compensations. The mathematical form is $ab = cd$. A ruler balanced on a fulcrum, with weights hung on either side, provides a simple example. The rule which predicts what arrangements will balance involves four independent variables: two weights, and two distances of the weights from the fulcrum. As in previous examples, the process of substituting three numbers into a learned algorithm such as

$$m_1 \times d_1 = m_2 \times d_2$$

to obtain a fourth unknown is no more than a concrete operation. But to use the relationship in any non-routine manner does require understanding the compensation principle, a formal operation. In particular, if $m_1$ is increased, then $m_2$ can be increased also to restore the balance, but restoration can also be created by decreasing $d_1$ or increasing $d_2$. Piaget called this *reciprocity* – compensation at a higher, formal level (making a compensatory change on another variable) as distinguished from compensation at a lower, early concrete level, when a child says that the amount of liquid has stayed the same because 'the height is more but the width is less'. If $m_1 = m_2$ then the correlation is only a concrete operation because you do the same to each. But if $m_1 \neq m_2$, then proportionality has to be used to see what to add to $m_2$, so it becomes formal.

Science abounds with examples of equilibrium such as chemical equilibrium (where the entities being balanced are themselves concentrations, that is, ratios) and ecological equilibrium (which may be unstable as well as dynamic). But we talk also of the 'balance of power' and to appreciate why some countries seem to require massive defence spending to maintain their place in the world whilst others appear minimally defended yet economically successful and central on the world stage is to weigh against one another many actual and virtual variables.

## Correlation

If woodlice like wet and dark conditions, what will we see 10 minutes after we put 10 woodlice into a choice chamber with wet/dark wet/light, dry/dark and dry/light conditions? The trouble with living things is that they never conform nicely to expectations, they have too much inbuilt variance. That is why so much 'evidence' we meet with in everyday life is correlational evidence, far removed from the hard, 'proving' type evidence of the school physics laboratory. 'Smoking causes lung cancer.' Well, of course not everyone who smokes gets cancer, and not everyone who gets cancer has smoked, any more than all 10 woodlice move to the wet dark corner, but there is a correlation between smoking and lung cancer, and it is a valid statement that woodlice prefer wet and dark conditions.

Even to understand the nature of correlation between a single pair of variables, say a cream treatment for acne and its effect, one has to consider four possibilities. Those acne sufferers who have been treated and still have acne; those treated whose acne has disappeared; those untreated who still have acne; and those untreated whose acne has cleared up anyway. These are best shown in a $2 \times 2$ table shown in Fig. 2.5.

|  | With treatment | Without treatment |
|---|---|---|
| With acne | A      3 | B      5 |
| Without acne | C      7 | D      5 |

*Fig. 2.5* A 2×2 treatments and effects table

To determine whether or not there is a correlation, one has to compare the numbers that confirm that the treatment has an effect (those in cells B and C) with those that suggest that the treatment has no effect, or a negative effect (cells A and D). The ratio of confirming cases to non-confirming cases is 12:8, not very impressive. It could still be evidence that the cream works, or the difference may be due to chance (which takes us on to the next aspect of abstract thinking, dealt with below). But 'My grandfather's smoked all his life, and he's 85' by itself tells us nothing.

Even with simple problems one often needs the abstract notion of correlation, removed from specific examples, to begin to find out whether or not there is a relationship. Once one does have this schema as a general idea then the apparently far more complicated problems of correlation between two sets of scores, or between smoking and bronchitis with occupation controlled for, become accessible. Can one learn from history by seeking correlations between common events? Unfortunately only at a rather speculative level since conditions change so radically with time. At the time of writing (February 1993) it is extremely likely that any Archduke venturing into the streets of Sarajevo would be killed, but it is extremely unlikely that the event would spark off a world war.

## Probability

In biology, teacher often says that it is no good planting just one pea or bean seed if you want to study the plants' growth. You have to plant half a dozen seeds. Why is this? It is partly to make sure, if there are two or more distinctive forms of the plant, that you take enough seeds to get at least one example of each, and partly to take a large enough sample so that the natural random variation on any one variable such as height can be estimated in terms of an average and a range. Here probabilistic notions underlie simple sampling procedures.

My sister says she can always tell whether milk or tea has been put in first. I give her five cups of tea which I have prepared where she cannot see them, and ask her to taste them. How many must she get right to prove that she always can tell?

One because if she gets 1 right, it proves that she can do it.
Three because she would have more right than wrong.
Four because she could still guess 3 right.
Five because she would have to get them all right to convince me.

These are all answers we have had to this problem from 13 year-olds, and each has its own plausibility. In fact there is no simple numerical answer. Even if she gets five right, there is a 3 per cent chance that she did it by guessing. You can get four out of five binary choices 'right' 18 per cent of the time just by chance. The formal thinking is characterised by loss of adherence to a particular numerical answer, and acceptance of the probabilistic nature of such relationships. This idea is central to the evaluation of much evidence in real life. A person who lived near a nuclear power station gets leukaemia. Until one can see this as evidence which must be evaluated in terms of a probability one is likely to make a snap judgement: nuclear power – no thanks!

**Formal models**

A model is a representation of something else. A working model has different parts which move and which hold the same relationships to one another as in the real thing. A formal model is a working model in which the 'moving parts' are abstract entities which have to be imagined. Scientists are familiar with the kinetic model of matter: solids consist of particles held together in more or less fixed positions; in liquids the particles are still attracted to one another, but move about; and in gases the attraction is lost and the particles fly about all over the place. Since these particles can only be imagined, this is a formal model. It is very useful as it does explain a lot of the behaviour of solids, liquids, and gases, and because the model can be used to predict the behaviour of matter we believe that it does in some respects represent reality.

Far more complex formal models are those which attempt to represent the weather, or the economy. Sociologists, also, have their models which attempt, for instance, to represent the variables in a crowd and the relationships between them, and then to predict crowd behaviour from given values of the variables. To comprehend the principle of such models requires, again, the mental manipulation of many variables together. Once the model has been encapsulated in an algorithm (possibly programmed into a computer) it requires no more than concrete operations to set the values of various variables and read out the prediction. What to do when the prediction fails or how to interpret the significance of the prediction in relation to the evidence requires formal operations.

**Logical reasoning**

Here is described the ability, without necessarily invoking any of the more specialised schemata described above, to analyse the combinatorial relations present in information given. We illustrate this with two items taken from Bond's test of logical thinking (BLOT, Bond 1976). The first illustrates the logical operation of implication, and the second, the denial of implication. Obviously this covers the same ground as Demetriou's SSS verbal-propositional thinking. Performance on the BLOT test is highly correlated ($r = 0.7$ or more) with Piagetian tests derived from *The Growth of Logical Thinking* (Inhelder and Piaget 1958), and fits Piaget's model of formal operations closely (Bond 1980).

> A prospector has found that some rich metals are sometimes found together. In his life he has sometimes found gold and silver together, sometimes he has found silver by itself, every other time he has found neither silver nor gold. Which of the following rules has been true for this prospector?
> (a) Gold and silver are found together, never apart.
> (b) If he found silver then he found gold with it.
> (c) If he found gold then he found silver with it.
> (d) If he found gold then he didn't find silver.

Investigation of the weather records over the last 60 years has led the weather forecasters to claim: 'If it is summer, there will be a cyclone somewhere in Australia.' Which of the following facts would make the forecaster's claim incorrect?

(a) A summer with a cyclone.
(b) A winter with a cyclone.
(c) A summer without cyclones.
(d) A winter without cyclones.
(e) None of these.

## FORMAL OPERATIONS AND GENERAL HIGHER ORDER THINKING

Inhelder and Piaget investigated adolescents' use of the schemata with problems such as the pendulum, the balance beam, and billiard balls bouncing off plane surfaces, all of which have a distinctly scientific look to them. Although this made it easier for them to describe and manipulate the variables and relationships between variables involved, and so to attempt a logical analysis of the reasoning being used by students, they themselves had no doubt that they were describing modes of thinking that influenced every aspect of a person's cognitive life. Nevertheless, the context of their investigations has led many commentators to assume that the construct of formal operational reasoning is of value only within the domain of science, and possibly mathematics. The validity of such an assumption is questioned by the work of, for instance, Peel (1967, 1971) for history and religious education, Biggs and Collis (1982) for mathematics, English, geography and modern languages, Hallam (1967) and Jurd (1973) also in the field of history, and Fusco (1983) in English. All of these authors have used the Piagetian account of formal operations as a basis for investigating higher level thinking in domains other than science or mathematics. In our description of the reasoning patterns we have tried to illustrate each with examples from domains across the curriculum but further examples will be given in Chapter 8 where we consider the work of some of these authors in more detail.

We suggest this effective and broad application of formal operations justifies entertaining the Piagetian account as a comprehensive characterisation of higher order thinking. Further, while it may not be possible to map the reasoning patterns of formal operations point by point on to Resnick's account of higher order thinking skills, there is nevertheless a close correspondence between the two descriptions.

## A DEVELOPMENTAL PROFILE

We are working towards the presentation of a cognitive developmental profile analogous to that given for physical development shown at the beginning of this chapter. We need to be able to say something like:

We found 50 students at 12 years of age close to the mature concrete level. Without intervention these students on average would move up only one quarter of a sub-level by 14 years, and thus would be unlikely to benefit much from subsequent science education. After intervention they all moved up to at least the early formal level providing an irreversible change in their educational prospects.

A combination of the operational and theoretical detail offered by the Inhelder/Piaget model and its common currency make it the most attractive account of general higher order thinking for the purpose of such a profile.

Unfortunately, as late as 1974 there was no general consensus on whether Piaget and his co-workers' account of the development of thinking applied to all children and most books for teachers were still giving a very simple 'age/stage' model of child development. This was such a silly account that anyone with any experience of teaching the whole ability range of primary or secondary students would know it was wrong and this led to a widespread over-reaction: because they knew the age part of the model was wrong people then threw out the stage part as well. One reason that this popular rejection was supported at the time by psychologists was the problem of *decalage*, the apparent inconsistent asynchrony in the attainment of schemata which should theoretically all appear at about the same time. As this is a question that has vexed Piagetian psychology for years, we must address it before we can use Piagetian stages as the measure of development in a cognitive profile. Although the burden of this book is the development of formal operations, this question is best dealt with by looking at an international study of the development of concrete operations. On the way we will add to the plausibility of the hypothesis of a central cognitive processing mechanism of the mind.

**Concrete operations: an international survey**

Longeot (1978) had investigated some details of decalage and confirmed, for instance, that some children advance first on spatial relation tasks while others first develop superior performance on verbal tasks such as classification and seriation. He proposed the idea of *nodes* in the developmental process through which all children pass in order and which act as preconditions for further development in any schema. If evidence were adduced for such nodes then it would only seem explicable on the assumption of a 'central processor' which has to become more complex if children are to begin on the next phase of development.

In a study of children from 5 to 10 years of age in Australia, England, Greece and Pakistan Shayer *et al.* (1988) obtained a wealth of empirical evidence on the development of the concrete operations concerning spatial relations, conservations, and verbo-logical schemata.

Table 2.1 shows the data from the Pakistan survey on 360 children in the age range 6 to 11. From the first signs of concrete operations in 1:1 correspondence through to the concrete generalisation level there are three nodes. The first lies

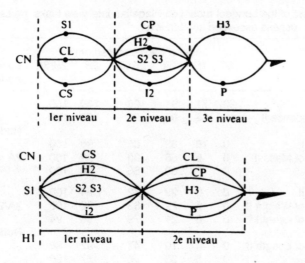

CN = 1:1 Correspondence: S1 corresponds to Pakistan Seriation I;
CL = Conservation of Length; CS = Conservation of Mass;
CP = Conservation of Weight: S2 and S3 correspond to Pakistan Seria-
tion II & III; I2 =Class-Inclusion: H2 = partial success on the Water-
Level task; H3 corresponds to Pakistan Water-Level II, while
P = "Point of (relative) View".

*Fig. 2.6* Two possible nodes and antinodes of cognitive development during the
concrete operations period
(*Source*: Longeot 1978)

directly after 1:1 correspondence, which is a pre-requisite for all the others. The
tasks labelled such as Classification I and Classification II are successive success-
criteria on the same apparatus. In this case the first level is the ability to select just
one criterion, such as colour or shape, by which to sort a collection. The second is
the ability, once one criterion has been used, to find just one other alternative sorting
criterion for the same set. While some children 'get' the conservation tasks first
and others the classification and seriation ones, the success of children in the range
between node 1 and node 2 on tasks in the range between node 2 and node 3 is low
and patchy. In Table 2.1 each child has been given an overall assessment level based
on a two-thirds success criterion on the whole battery.

It can be seen that 93 per cent of the children classified in the 2A range succeeded
on the 1:1 correspondence task, and that those in the 2B range, between node 2 and
node 3, had a greater than 94 per cent success rate on *all* of the previous tasks. Thus

*Table 2.1*   Test of the Longeot model on Piagetian interview tasks: percentage of success assessed at each level

| Task | 1A | 1B | 2A | 2A/2B | 2B | 2B/3A | Location of nodes |
|---|---|---|---|---|---|---|---|
| Seriation I | 20 | 71 | 91 | 100 | 100 | 100 | |
| 1:1 Correspondence II | 10 | 82 | 93 | 97 | 100 | 100 | |
| | | | | | | | Node 1 |
| Classification I | 0 | 18 | 62 | 85 | 98 | 100 | |
| Conservation of Mass II | 0 | 6 | 58 | 89 | 99 | 100 | 2A range |
| Seriation II | 0 | 6 | 60 | 86 | 96 | 100 | |
| Classification II | 0 | 0 | 29 | 72 | 94 | 100 | |
| Conservation of Weight II | 0 | 6 | 22 | 83 | 96 | 100 | 2A/2B range |
| Conservation of Length I | 0 | 0 | 21 | 79 | 95 | 94 | |
| | | | | | | | Node 2 |
| Conservation of Length II | 0 | 0 | 10 | 47 | 92 | 88 | |
| Seriation III | 0 | 0 | 33 | 56 | 77 | 100 | |
| Classification III | 0 | 0 | 21 | 51 | 74 | 100 | 2B range |
| Internal Volume | 0 | 0 | 7 | 49 | 82 | 100 | |
| Conservation of Area II | 0 | 6 | 29 | 44 | 69 | 88 | |
| | | | | | | | Node 3 |
| Mountain I | | | 7 | 14 | 51 | 56 | |
| Plumb Line I | | | 7 | 14 | 65 | 88 | |
| Water Level II | 0 | 0 | 10 | 8 | 26 | 81 | 2B/3A range |
| Displacement Volume | 0 | 0 | 0 | 1 | 17 | 81 | |

Source: Table 4 from Shayer *et al.* (1988:331)

despite the fact that some children may earlier show success on the conservation tasks, it appears that performance synchronises on all tasks at each node and that advance on any of the tasks in the next inter-nodal range is on the basis of virtually complete success on all of the tasks previous to that node.

This data may be explained in terms of a central processor. Children need integrated success on all parts of the psychological spectrum before the central processor makes a qualitative jump allowing the next phase of development to commence. While no study has yet been published which reports in the same detail data for the formal operations period, data reported in Shayer (1978) indicates at least one further node between the early formal (3A) and mature formal (3A/3B) levels.

## The Concepts in Secondary Mathematics and Science (CSMS) survey

Another problem which dogged the Piagetian reports of the ages of development of each cognitive stage was the obvious un-representativeness of the samples of children interviewed. This issue was further clouded by a philosophically grounded party-line by the Genevans that it was wrong in principle to look to representative survey evidence. From Piaget himself it took the form of saying that he was interested only in the development of the 'epistemic subject' – a notion which, in our opinion, was subtle but wrong (at least in the context of describing development), and vulnerable to the Popperian objection of being unfalsifiable. The dilemma could be resolved only by gathering evidence from Piagetian tests on a population sample comparable with those used in medical research. Since this was quite an exacting task, we will describe it here in some detail.

The Concepts in Secondary Mathematics and Science (CSMS) Programme (1974–80) was a large research programme funded by the British Social Science Research Council to look at the many problems involved in educating the whole ability range of students in comprehensive school in intellectually exacting subjects. The first major task tackled was to obtain a good description of the student population. Up to 1973 assessment of levels of cognitive development was, following Piaget's example, achieved only by individual interviews with children. Even had they tried – which they did not for reasons already given – the Genevans may well have been defeated in the attempt to obtain a picture of levels of thinking in a representative population because of the time involved in the Genevan interview which involves a minimum of 20 minutes per child, per task, followed by a longer period of transcription of the evidence gathered.

There was another objection to using the Genevan interview for conducting a survey. This was the problem of ensuring that the same details of behaviour were used for estimating the underlying competence level of all the students surveyed. The virtues of flexibility of the Genevan interview as a research instrument can turn into disadvantages when a student 'misses' some vital clue by following an idea of his own, and therefore fails to show that he could have solved the task had chance not deflected his attention. The way round this dilemma is to produce a structured test situation in which *all* the previous research evidence is used (a) to create a sequence of experiences which ensure that the student 'visits' all aspects of the task, and (b) to produce scoring criteria based on the student's response to each part of the structured task. In this way the grounds of judgement are open to inspection.

The first person to achieve this was the Australian Susan Somerville (1974) whose solution was in structured interview form for the pendulum task from Inhelder and Piaget's (1958) *Growth of Logical Thinking*. The CSMS team took this process one stage further in the case of the pendulum task by writing in the detail, drawn both from Inhelder's original descriptions and Somerville's further evidence, in the form of a 'play' with beginning, middle and end in which up to 30 students can participate at a time. They are shown a number of experiments with pendulums and at each point are asked what they would have done next, given the evidence already shown. In this way their individual design of experiment strategies (control of variables) are shown in detail. As the demonstrations proceed they are then asked specifics on what they can deduce, if anything, until they have been shown all the evidence they need. This yields a 14 item test which takes about 50 minutes to administer. Depending on the items students get right they are then assessed somewhere on a continuum from a minimum of mature concrete through to mature formal. The instrument required for large-scale surveys had been created.

By 1974 the general age/stage picture as presented by Geneva was

| Stage level | Symbol | Age |
|---|---|---|
| Early concrete | 2A | 5/6 |
| Mid concrete | 2A/B | 7/9 |
| Mature concrete | 2B | 10/11 |
| Early formal | 3A | 11/13 |
| Mature formal | 3B | 14/15 |

For a survey which was to cover the age range 10–16 years the CSMS team could not assume this age/stage picture but had to allow for the possibility of a much broader range. Accordingly they needed to produce reliable evidence for students at any level of processing from pre-concrete to mature formal operations. Since the pendulum task only operates between 2B and 3B, two other tests – given the generic name of *Piagetian Reasoning Tasks* – had to be developed. The second, called Volume and Heaviness, was drawn from Piaget and Inhelder's (1974) work on physical quantities and conservations and covers the range 2A to 3A. The third task, drawn from Piaget's work on space (1976) covered the range pre-operational (<2A) to mature concrete (2B) and was called *Spatial Relations*. By giving all three tasks on three different occasions to all students a reliable survey could be performed using a large representative population.

Following advice both on the sample numbers required for standardising psychometric tests and also on the sample numbers required to produce an estimate of the population at large of sufficient accuracy, the decision was made to use opinion-poll sample sizes – that is between 1000 and 2000 – for each year of age sampled, so that in the end about 14,000 students were surveyed from 45 schools. As a check on the representativeness of the sample pupils were also given the National Foundation for Educational Research (NFER)-standardised Calvert Non-Verbal Reasoning test.

This made it possible for the first time to assess a large representative sample of the school population of a whole country. Further work on the scoring decisions resulted in a refinement of the Genevan scale:

| Stage level | Symbol | Scale number |
|---|---|---|
| Early concrete | 2A | 3 |
| Mid concrete | 2A/B | 4 |
| Mature concrete | 2B | 5 |
| Concrete generalisation | 2B* | 6 |

| Early formal | 3A | 7 |
| Mature formal | 3A/B | 8 |
| Formal generalisation | 3B | 9 |

Striking features of the survey carried out in England and Wales were:

- In the population as a whole, fewer than 30 per cent of 16 year-olds were showing the use of even early formal operations (3A). That means that the majority of the population was leaving school using only concrete operations
- The range of levels of thinking within any one age group was far wider than had previously been realised. Cockcroft (1982) wrote of the 'seven-year gap', as the difference between the most able (at the 90th percentile) and the least able children (at the 10th percentile) in the first year of secondary education (year 7/grade 6). The CSMS data showed that the reality is more like a 12-year gap. In ordinary mixed-ability high schools, the most able 12 year-olds were operating at the level of average 18 year-olds or higher and the least able at the level of average 6 year-olds.

Figure 2.7 provides detail of the development of thinking and spread of abilities in the population of England and Wales derived from the CSMS survey of 1974–5 and the international survey just described. Although the CSMS survey was not conducted for this reason, its findings now make it possible both to assess and interpret the significance of an intervention made with the specific aim of changing students' rate of intellectual development. If a sample of students can be given an average location on Fig. 2.7 – say at the age of 12 – then if an intervention had been unsuccessful their average location two years later will have followed up only the percentile curve they were already on. The degree of success of an intervention can be estimated from the extent to which the students have risen up the family of developmental curves. The analogy with medical intervention is now complete.

## CURRICULUM DEMAND

In case there was any question that the profile revealed by the CSMS survey could possibly be described as satisfactory by the normal national standards of expectation it is revealing to look at the cognitive demands made by a recent expression of a National Curriculum, that of England and Wales. Parallels may readily be drawn with other curriculum materials. We will concentrate on science as being the domain in which curriculum analysis has been most thoroughly explored.

Shayer (1972) initially worked out and tested principles for interpreting the interaction between the cognitive level of the student and the level of thinking required for activities in the original Nuffield O-level science courses. This was done by searching the works of Piaget on space, number, probability, physical quantities, causality, and particularly *The Growth of Logical Thinking* (GLT) for relevant descriptions of task behaviour. These were then used, much as a lawyer uses detailed knowledge of relevant cases, to compare as closely as possible like

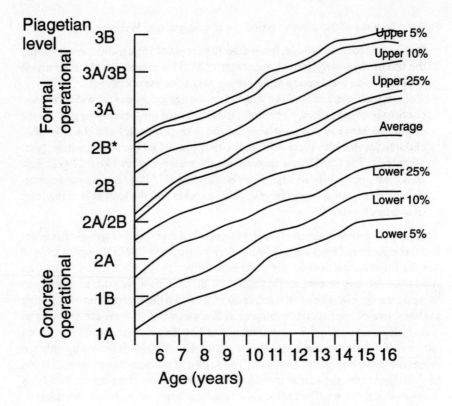

*Fig. 2.7* Cognitive development by age and ability – boys (based on CSMS survey data, 1975–8)

with like in the two domains of (a) Piaget's psychological research and (b) well described science learning objectives. '*Well* described' is stressed because it is notorious how different two different teachers' interpretation of a learning aim – for example, 'formulate hypotheses where the causal link is based on scientific knowledge, understanding or theory' (National Curriculum for Science, Attainment Target 1, level 5a) – can be unless it is broken down into sub-objectives carefully described so as to be unambiguous and testable. This 'case-law' approach was later abstracted and described in two taxonomies published in Shayer and Adey (1981). In Table 2.2 the row headings of these taxonomies are given. In the taxonomies themselves each row is divided into columns containing brief descriptions of behaviours typical of four levels: 2A early concrete, 2B mature concrete, 3A early formal, and 3B mature formal.

It can be seen that Taxonomy 1 focuses on rather general aspects of thinking,

Table 2.2    Curriculum analysis taxonomy headings

| Taxonomy 1 headings | | Taxonomy 2 headings | |
| --- | --- | --- | --- |
| 1.1 | Interest and investigation style | 2.1 | Conservation |
| 1.2 | Reasons for events | 2.2 | Proportionality |
| 1.3 | Relationships | 2.3 | Equilibria of systems |
| 1.4 | Use of models | 2.4 | Mathematical operations |
| 1.5 | Type of categorisation | | (physical science) |
| 1.6 | Depth of interpretation (for | 2.5 | Control of variables |
| | descriptive passages) | 2.6 | Exclusion of irrelevant variables |
| | | 2.7 | Probabilistic thinking |
| | | 2.8 | Correlational reasoning |
| | | 2.9 | Measurement skills |

whereas Taxonomy 2 includes those schemata of concrete and formal operations described in detail earlier in this chapter which are particularly relevant to science. When the curriculum analysis taxonomy (CAT) was originally applied to GCE O-Level science curricula in common use in the 1970s it was found that almost all required that pupils aged 14+ years were expected to have formal operational thinking readily available. As the survey had shown, this was not true for average pupils, but was true for the selective grammar school populations for whom the schemes had originally been devised.

Application of the CAT to the 1991 National Curriculum for Science in England and Wales shows that there is still a significant gap between cognitive demand of attainments expected of 14 year-olds and of 16 year-olds and the levels of thinking currently available in the population (Shayer 1991). A few examples will suffice to illustrate this.

In the National Curriculum document science learning objectives are grouped under four main Attainment Targets (ATs): AT1, Process skill; AT2, Biology; AT3, Chemistry, and AT4, Physics, and further subdivided into 16 sub-headings ('strands'). In each strand the learning objectives, called Statements of Attainment (SoAs), are defined at 10 different levels to cover the whole of schooling from year 1 primary (K, age 5+ years) to the end of secondary (year 11, grade 10, age 16+ years). In each cell of the document there are between one and three SoAs briefly defined, for example:

AT4: Physics
Strand: Forces and their effects.
Level 6 (d) 'understand the relationship between an applied force, the area
over which it acts, and the resulting pressure.'
(e) 'understand the relationship between speed, distance and time.'

In Fig. 2.8 the curriculum analysis taxonomy has been used to make an estimate of
the minimum level of thinking a pupil would need to be able to achieve each of the
SoAs in AT2, 3 and 4. It can be seen that from level 5 or 6 across the board the
SoAs begin to require at least early formal operational thinking.

It is proposed to assess attainment of the National Curriculum objectives by a
series of Standard Attainment Tasks (SATs) to be administered at the end of each
Key Stage, that is at ages 7+, 11+, 14+, and 16+. That the curriculum can be
translated into assessment items which reflect fairly accurately the levels of demand
shown in Fig. 2.8 can be confirmed by inspection of some SAT items used at KS3
(14 year-olds) in May 1992. In the following examples, a Statement of Attainment
is given, followed by a SAT item or part-item which corresponds to that SoA,
followed by our own analysis of the item's cognitive demand, based on the CAT.
We apologise for the acronym-overload, which is part of the price British teachers
must pay for having a National Curriculum.

AT2, *Level 5 (a)*. Be able to name and outline the functions of the major organs
and organ systems in mammals and flowering plants.
*1992 KS3 SAT 5–8, Paper 1 Qu 1e*. Describe in detail the journey of a sperm,
from the time it leaves a testis until it fertilises an egg. Include the names of
the organs and tubes, and explain their function.
*Analysis*: This SoA and the question which assesses it requires students to have
a good descriptive model, in time and space, of the role of the sperm. CAT
1.2 (reasons for events) and 1.4 (models) place this at the concrete
generalisation level because it requires the integration of most aspects of
concrete operations. It does not require formal thinking because it doesn't
require explanatory or hypothetical models. As a Key Stage question this is
fairly well matched to the students because about 60 per cent of 14 year-olds
are at this level or above (Fig. 2.7).

AT4, *Level 6 (d)*. Understand the relationship between an applied force, the area
over which it acts, and the resulting pressure.
*1992 KS3 SAT 5–8, Paper 2 part 1c*. A coin is pushed into some soft clay as
shown in the two drawings. (Drawings of coin edge down, and flat side down
into the clay.) Why is it easier to push the coin into the soft clay in drawing
1 compared with drawing 2? (Four choices given.) The coin in drawing 2 is
pushed down with a force of 60N. The area of the face of the coin is 3 cm$^2$.
What is the pressure of the coin on the clay?

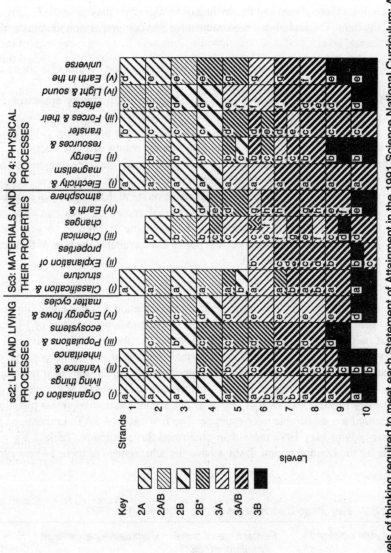

*Fig. 2.8* Levels of thinking required to meet each Statement of Attainment in the 1991 Science National Curriculum; Attainment targets 2, 3 and 4

*Analysis*: Pressure is a compound variable. Comprehension and application of pressure requires the independent manipulation of three variables of force, pressure, and area. CAT 1.3 (relationships) and 2.2 (proportionality) indicate that this requires formal operations. In the case of this item the four-choice format (effectively two choices since two pairs of mutually exclusive 'choices' are given) and the drilling of an algorithm may raise the facility of the item. The underlying requirement for real comprehension remains at the formal level.

*AT3, Level 7 (f)*. Understand the factors which influence the rate of a chemical reaction.

*1992 KS3 SAT 5–8, Paper 3 part 1g*. (Diagram of laboratory apparatus for cracking paraffin is given.) (i) This apparatus is designed to speed up the cracking reaction. State two ways in which this has been done. (ii) Explain in terms of molecules how each of these ways results in a fast reaction.

*Analysis*: Part (i) can be answered from simply learned concrete cause-and-effect schema: rate is increased by heat and by catalyst. Part (ii) however requires understanding in terms of molecule activation through the agency of heat and of catalysts. This requires an abstract (formal) model to provide an adequate explanation. Level 7 is supposed to be attainable by average 16 year-olds. Not more than 32 per cent of such pupils have available the type of thinking required to answer part (ii).

In the original National Curriculum planning the intention was that approximately 50 per cent of all pupils should be at the 5/6 level boundary by the age of 14, that is, that half the pupils should be just into level 6 or above. However, if level 6 achievement in science requires early formal thinking it should be possible to estimate, from Figs 2.7 and 2.8, the proportion of pupils able to attain this. Approximately 20 per cent of 14 year-olds were found by the CSMS survey to be at the early formal (3A) level or above so this predicts that government planning represented a considerable over-estimate. The first national SAT administered to 14 year-olds in May 1992 more than confirmed this prediction. Table 2.3 gives results for the London region. It shows that the achievement of these 14 year-olds

*Table 2.3*   Key Stage 3 science results for London region 1992

| Level obtained | Percentage of pupils (total no. 50,381) | Cumulative percentage |
|---|---|---|
| 5 | 31.8 | 45.8 |
| 6 | 12.9 | 14.0 |
| 7 | 1.1 | 1.1 |
| 8 | 0.02 | 0.02 |

was still well below even what could be predicted to be their potential from the CSMS survey, with only 14 per cent achieving level 6 or above.

This brief analysis reveals that the gap between national expectations and likely outcomes remains much as it was 10 years ago. The case for intervention is essentially that unless the proportion of students having formal thinking capacity by age 14 can be substantially raised, there is little chance of raising standards.

# Chapter 3

# A review of intervention programmes

We were left at the end of Chapter 2 with the problem of whether or not the accessibility of current curriculum material to the school population could be improved by raising the general intellectual level of students. From a cognitive-developmentalist perspective, this translates as: can we enhance, or accelerate, pupils' cognitive development? In 1975 Neimark wrote:

> One of the more surprising gaps in the reported research concerns what Piaget has called 'The American Question': the possibility of accelerating cognitive development through specific training. . . .When more is known about the course of normal development and the variables which affect it, it is quite likely that sophisticated training research will begin in earnest. Piaget's prediction would be that all such attempts are doomed to failure.
>
> (pp. 584–5)

Since then, much of the literature concerned with the promotion of thinking skills talks in terms of 'developing' (as a transitive verb in the active voice) thinking skills, or 'fostering the development of . . .', or 'promoting the development of . . .'. If development is simply a matter of maturation, and thus rather passive and inaccessible to the influence of outside agencies, then 'fostering' or 'promoting' development could have no meaning. It is because we believe that these phrases do have meaning that we propose to explore what meaning they can have.

A theoretical platform has been presented on which one may start to build a mechanism for improving pupils' thinking. Important planks of the platform include:

- Higher order thinking skills can be well described by the reasoning patterns of formal operations.
- The emergence of formal operational thinking is developmental: it occurs in response to a combination of maturation, ontogenetic, and environmental variables.
- The environmental variable includes, importantly, social mediation.
- Formal operations develop as a whole rather than each reasoning pattern developing independently.

- These reasoning patterns are not tied to any particular subject area or domain.

Before trying to build a detailed mechanism on this platform we would do well to take a good look at others' attempts to improve students' general thinking ability. Some attempts to teach thinking can be described as instruction in thinking skills and others as intervention in the development process. In this chapter we will consider a few examples of each and see what can be learned from others' experiences about features which seem to hold promise for our enterprise, and also about ways in which success may be judged.

Thinking skill programmes have been comprehensively reviewed by Nickerson *et al.* (1985), Coles and Robinson (1989), and Nisbet and McGuiness (1990), and we do not intend here to repeat the excellent detail provided in those works. Rather, we will illustrate particular points with a few examples categorised after a scheme proposed by Nickerson and co-workers. This includes programmes based on 'heuristics', 'thinking about thinking', 'cognitive operations', and 'formal thinking'. Where the data is available the effects of each programme described will be given in terms of *effect sizes*. Where an experimental group has been subjected to some treatment and then compared at post-test with an initially matched control group, the effect size is the difference between the mean post-test scores of experimental ($M_e$) and control groups ($M_c$) given in units of the standard deviation of the control group ($\sigma_c$).

$$\text{effect size} = \frac{(M_e - M_c)}{\sigma_c}$$

The relative importance of different effect sizes may be shown in terms of the developmental curves introduced in Chapter 2. An intervention which achieves a modest effect size on cognition of $0.5\sigma$ (one half a standard deviation) will move the mean score from 'average' (the 50th percentile) to that of the top 30 per cent (actually the 69th percentile) of the ability range. An effect size of $1\sigma$ (one standard deviation) is considered substantial, and moves the mean score up to that of the 84th percentile. These shifts are illustrated for students starting at age 11 in Fig. 3.1.

## HEURISTICS

Heuristics are general strategies by which reality may be 'discovered'. In the sense used here, they apply to thinking strategies which generally can be applied to all sorts of problems. Programmes which aim to teach heuristics for better thinking are extreme in terms of being context-free and generally choose not to recognise any possible limits set by ontogenetic development.

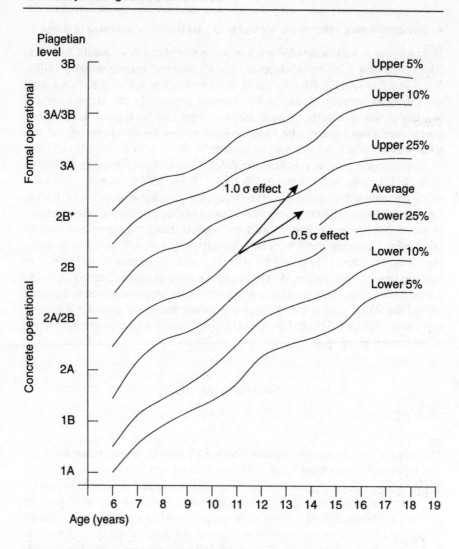

*Fig. 3.1* Cognitive development: effect sizes on 11 year-olds

## CoRT

One of the best known of such thinking skill programmes is de Bono's (1976) CoRT (Cognitive Research Trust). The complete CoRT programme consists of 60 lessons intended to be used with students aged from about 12 years, although CoRT is also used as a management training tool for adults. The materials provide a detailed set of teachers' notes and pupil activities and exercises intended to introduce a set of specific heuristics for thinking. Notes on the 10 lessons of CoRT 1 (Table 3.1) give a flavour of their content. It will be seen that each of the heuristics is given an acronym (PMI, CAF, etc.) and de Bono-trained students are likely to say 'let's do a PMI on that'. The set of heuristics which make up the complete programme thus becomes part of the learner's conscious strategy in tackling new problems.

*Table 3.1* CoRT-1 thinking lessons

| 1 | PMI | *Looking for the Plus points, Minus points, and Interesting points* in any situation to enlarge one's view and by-pass natural immediate reactions to an idea. |
|---|---|---|
| 2 | CAF | *Considering All Factors* in the situation: exploring a situation before closing on a possible solution. |
| 3 | RULES | *An opportunity to practise PMI and CAF.* PMI is used on existing or proposed rules and CAF when making a rule. |
| 4 | C&S | *Consequence and Sequel:* what may happen after a decision has been made. Short term, medium term, and long term consequences are systematically explored. |
| 5 | AGO | *Introduces the ideas of Aims, Goals, and Objectives.* Aspects of 'because' and 'in order to' are investigated. |
| 6 | PLANNING | *An opportunity to practice C&S and AGO*, and to reinforce PMI and CAF. |
| 7 | FIP | A focusing device, *directing attention to First Important Priorities*, after ideas have been generated. |
| 8 | APC | Encourages the student *to develop Alternatives, Possibilities, and Choices* beyond the obvious and satisfactory ones. It is seen as an antidote to emotional and rigid thinking. |
| 9 | DECISIONS | *An opportunity to practise FIP and APC*, and in a more general way, earlier skills. |
| 10 | OPV | *Directs attention to Other Points of View* to provide a balance between one's own point of view and that of others. |

*Source:* Adapted from Edwards (1991:100)

Clearly, this is an instructional approach rather than an interventionist one, although the instruction is in the strategies of thinking and is explicitly content-free. That such an approach is intuitively attractive is shown by the enormous success that de Bono has had world-wide, but up to now the evidence for its effectiveness has been, at best, patchy.

One attempt to evaluate de Bono's CoRT Thinking Program in which de Bono himself had a major hand (Hunter-Grundin 1985) was undertaken under Schools Council auspices in 20 Cambridgeshire primary schools. The differences between experimental and control classes in achievement tests of reading comprehension, arithmetical, and logical reasoning were not only not statistically significant, but averaged zero difference between experimentals and controls for the first year of the study, and 0.17 of a standard deviation for the second year. In terms of tests of creativity – essential in terms of testing the model underlying the intervention – the differences were small and statistically significant only in one out of the 12 tests used for the first year, and three of the 12 tests for the second year. One would expect this number of significant differences by chance sampling variation alone. Thus both in school achievement and on tests of the intervention model itself there was no difference between experimental and control classes. It should be noted that the teacher training programme associated with this evaluation had severe limitations and in fact served to alienate many of the teachers from the programme, so it may be maintained that this does not constitute a reasonable test of CoRT's potential. (In Chapter 9 we explore further the relationship between programme implementation and inservice education for teachers.)

Edwards (1991) has reviewed a number of evaluations of the de Bono approach and concluded that because of substantial weaknesses in design they did not provide a sound basis for a detailed evaluation of the effects of CoRT. Edwards also describes a more recent study which he has conducted using matched experimental and control groups given pre- , post- , and delayed (four weeks) tests. Of the battery of post-tests only scores on a Thinking Approaches Questionnaire developed by the author maintained significant gains at delayed post-test. However, there were statistically significant (Edwards does not quote figures from which effect sizes could be calculated) gains of the experimental group compared with the controls on regular school achievement measures in social sciences and languages, but not in science or mathematics. Edwards quotes de Bono (1976:141) as asserting that CoRT improves performance in language arts 'but that it is difficult to produce gains in knowledge-bound subjects'. Results of a much longer term study by the same author have not yet been published but the initial impression (personal communication) is that impressive gains at the end of a one-year CoRT programme are dissipated one year later.

There is no question about Edward de Bono's creativity in devising exciting materials which have high face validity as promoters of divergent thinking, and which are very popular with teachers and pupils. Although the verdict on their effectiveness so far has to be that of 'non-proven' the de Bono programme addresses important aspects of thinking which no other programme reaches and in our opinion deserves continued experimentation in school implementation and evaluation. It is possible that the evaluations to date have yielded 'type 2' errors – that is have failed to find an effect that is really there. Perhaps not enough thought had been given to the psychological model underlying the intervention in relation to the student sample trained. Liam Hudson (1966) showed that differences in divergent thinking ability only become interesting and useful for adolescents when they have sufficiently high convergent thinking ability to make relevant use of their lateral thinking. Since the CoRT materials are specifically intended to promote divergent thinking, the school population on which the programme might be expected to show an effect would be above-average 14/15 year-olds – at least one standard deviation above average, early formal or above. Notwithstanding de Bono's claims for content-free thinking skills, we suggest that CoRT teachers would benefit from specific training in how to help their students apply what they had learnt in CoRT lessons in their ordinary school learning.

**General problem solvers**

A rather different heuristic approach to the teaching of thinking is to offer sets of rules for solving problems, such as

> Make sure you understand what has to be achieved, the starting conditions, and what operations are permissible.
>
> Try to restate the problem in different terms.
>
> Break the problem down into sub-problems, and try to solve each of these.

The development of sets of such rules was pursued by Polya (1957) with respect to mathematical problems, and by Newell and Simon (1972) who were seeking problem solving strategies which were more generally applicable. From Newell and Simon's work we obtain a twofold insight: better understanding of human problem solving such that a computer could be programmed as a general problem solver (successful within certain limitations), and an understanding of ways in which computers could not, in principle, operate like human problem solvers.

The difficulty with sets of rules, heuristics, or suggestions such as those embedded in the general problem solver lies in applying them to particular cases, and in the disjunction which exists between the logical following of steps or high speed random trial and error by an artificial intelligence and the intuitive, holistic approach which appears to be characteristic of actual human problem solving. Faced with even a mathematical problem with defined, if complex, procedures, what is an average 10 year-old to make of the instruction to 'Try to reformulate the problem' or 'Think of a similar sort of problem and try to solve that'? If it is really similar it will presumably be just as difficult, and if it is not really similar it will not be very helpful. The understanding and putting into practice of the rules is itself a problem. Perkins and Salomon (1989) in an important review of context dependent versus context independent cognitive development note that:

> A number of investigators sought to teach Polya's heuristics for mathematical problem solving with little success. Students exhibited exactly the difficulties expected, given the results of the research on expertise: they didn't know *what to do* with the heuristics. They understood the heuristics in broad terms but didn't seem to understand the mathematics well enough to apply them in the rather complex and context sensitive ways required.
>
> (p. 19)

To have high face validity as general problem solvers the heuristics have to be so general as to be impossible to apply in particular cases. To be practically applicable, the rules have to be particular to specific classes of problems, or at the very least to be re-contextualised each time so that the student can see their application in different domains.

> Schoenfield . . . has demonstrated that heuristic instruction can yield dramatic gains in college students' mathematical problem solving . . . [but] . . . he emphasises that this success requires the teaching of the heuristics in a very contextualised way so the heuristics make good contact with the students' knowledge base in the domain.
>
> (Perkins and Salomon 1989:20)

As this chapter progresses, we will increasingly see the need for the teaching of thinking skills through particular contexts, if the ultimate aim is the development of general cognitive abilities.

## THINKING ABOUT THINKING

Nickerson categorises Matthew Lipman's *Philosophy for Children* under this heading, 'thinking about thinking'. This programme has been actively prosecuted since the early 1970s, and it has earned serious consideration through the consistency of its approach, its foundation in well-established principles of human discourse and rationality, and some evaluation in terms of long-term enhanced student achievement.

*Philosophy for Children* is introduced about grade 5 or 6 (in the UK, years 6 or 7) and delivered through the English or social studies curricula. Its materials include a series of 'novels' which contain dilemmas of rationality, ethics, morals, aesthetics, science reasoning, and civic values, and a teachers' guide called *Philosophical Inquiry* which emphasises the role of the teacher as an intelligent questioner. The dilemmas are set in the context of children's lives and lead into classroom discussions guided by the teacher. There are some particular features of this programme which we shall draw on later: it is delivered over a long time span; it is progressive in complexity so that later materials are suitable for 15 to 16 year-olds; it presents problems which children must puzzle over; the problems are set in contexts familiar to children; and although different novels in the series have subject-specific foci (reasoning in science, reasoning in language arts, reasoning in ethics, reasoning in social studies) these are seen as expressions of domain general reasoning through different contexts rather than as distinctly different types of reasoning. Perhaps the most important feature of *Philosophy for Children* upon which we shall draw is the nature of the discussion between children which is encouraged. The purpose of this discussion is to externalise the reasoning being used so that it can be scrutinised not only by others but by the user herself. Thinking about one's own thinking turns out to be a feature of almost all successful programmes designed to enhance thinking. The process is known as *metacognition*: becoming aware of the strategies of one's own thinking and actions.

In the first evaluation of *Philosophy for Children* (Lipman *et al.* 1980) Lipman himself taught one class for 18 40-minute sessions over nine weeks. Compared with a control group this class made a gain of the equivalent of 27 months in a standard test of logical reasoning. This looks like an effect size of nearly 1σ. More importantly, the experimental group was found to score significantly higher on a standard reading test two years after the intervention, which provides evidence for a long-term effect on the children's ability, at least in language use.

In a larger scale follow-up (Lipman *et al.* 1980), Educational Testing Service (ETS) conducted a study in two schools in New Jersey. Two groups of about 200 children each in grades 5–8 were followed over a year's exposure to *Philosophy for Children*, at the rate of about two and one quarter hours per week. Teachers were given two hours of INSET related to the programme every week during the school year. Two control groups were used to control for the effect of pre-testing and overall the results seem to have been impressive. At post-test experimental groups showed significant gains in aspects of logical reasoning, not surprising after such an intensive course, but also highly significant ($p < .001$) gains in standard assessments of reading and mathematics. These argue for a general effect of the programme on reasoning which leads to better reception of instruction in traditional academic disciplines. Unfortunately we are not given data from which to compute effect sizes, and in this study there does not appear to have been a long-term follow-up to test the permanency of the effects.

These findings are promising, and although the investment of time in teacher training is considerable it does indicate the potential of a method for raising children's reasoning capability which influences achievement.

## COGNITIVE OPERATIONS

Reuven Feuerstein's Instrumental Enrichment (IE) was introduced in Chapter 1 as an archetypal intervention programme. The IE course consists of thirteen instruments, each containing between one and two dozen activities and intended to be taught at a frequency of five hours a week for at least two years. Each activity, or instrument page, may last more than one lesson. Both the psychometric model of mental abilities such as *spatial relations*, *verbal reasoning*, or *numerical abilities* (which Feurestein calls *modalities*) and the Piagetian account of different mental operations were used in the design of the IE course. All parts of the psychological spectrum are addressed more than once in the various instruments by the 'logical multiplication' of the two sources of description. For example, 'as 2 is to 6, so 7 is to 21' is the reasoning pattern of proportion in the numerical modality whereas in the verbal reasoning modality it appears as analogical reasoning, for instance 'as Paris is to France, so London is to England'. In a similar way schemata such as *seriation* and *classification* are manifested in as many different modalities as possible. This part of the Feuerstein model is not shared with the student but is simply used for planning and design purposes.

It is the vocabulary of the *phase parameter*, drawn from information-processing, which is shared with the students. In Table 3.2 the different cognitive functions appearing in the *input*, *elaboration* – or problem solving – and *output* phases become part of the everyday metacognitive discussion by teacher and student and between student and student when thinking about their own strategies of problem solving. Each is given a simplified name such as 'two sources of information'. In contrast to courses such as de Bono's CoRT where heuristics like 'doing a PMI' are actually the vehicle for students' thinking, in IE the cognitive functions are the names given by students to strategies which assist them to design their own context related heuristics for solving each problem in hand. Thus IE aims to provide the necessary mental tools putting students in a position where they have to construct for themselves the higher level thinking required. This could be described as meta-constructivism – the construction by the learner of learning strategies.

*Table 3.2*   Instrumental enrichment cognitive functions

*I Gathering all the information we need (Input)*
1   Using our senses (listening, seeing, smelling, tasting, touching, feeling) to gather clear and complete information (clear perception).
2   Using a system or plan so that we do not skip or miss something important or repeat ourselves.
3   Giving the thing we gather through our senses and our experience a name so that we can remember it more clearly and talk about it (labelling).
4   Describing things and events in terms of where and when they occur (temporal and spatial referents).
5   Deciding on the characteristics of a thing or event that always stay the same, even when changes take place (conservation, constancy, and object permanence).
6   Organising the information we gather by considering more than one thing at a time (two sources of information).
7   Being precise and accurate when it matters (need for precision).

*II Using the information we have gathered (Elaboration)*
1   Defining what the problem is, what we are being asked to do, and what we must figure out (analysing disequilibrium).
2   Using only that part of the information we have gathered that is relevant, that is, that applies to the problem, and ignoring the rest (relevance).
3   Having a good picture in our mind of what we are looking for, or what we must do (interiorisation).
4   Making a plan that will include the steps we need to take to reach our goal (planning behaviour).
5   Remembering and keeping in mind various pieces of information we need (broadening our mental field).
6   Looking for the relationship by which separate objects, events, and experiences can be tied together (projecting relationships).
7   Comparing objects and experiences to others to see what is similar and what is different (comparative behaviour).
8   Finding the class or set to which the new object or experience belongs (categorisation).
9   Thinking about different possibilities and figuring out what would happen if you were to choose one or another (hypothetical thinking).
10  Using logic to prove things and to defend your opinion (logical evidence).

*III Expressing the solution to a problem (Output)*
1   Being clear and precise in your language to be sure that there is no
    question as to what your answer is. Put yourself into the 'shoes' of the
    listener to be sure that your answer will be understood (overcoming
    egocentric communication).
2   Think things through before you answer instead of immediately trying to
    answer and making a mistake, and then trying again (overcoming
    trial-and-error).
3   Count to 10 (at least) so that you do not say or do something you will be
    sorry for later (restraining impulsive behaviour).
4   If you cannot answer a question for some reason even though you 'know'
    the answer, do not fret or panic. Leave the question for a little while and
    then, when you return to it, use a strategy to help you find the answer
    (overcoming blocking).
5   Carrying an exact picture of an object in your mind to another place for
    comparison without losing or changing some details (visual transport).

Feuerstein makes a point of the fact that IE is free of all traditional school subject matter which he claims is often associated by learners with previous failures, but users are encouraged to bridge the cognitive operations developed by the instruments to more conventional school subject matter so that learners can see the application of the thinking processes in many contexts.

The original evaluation of IE in Israel (Feuerstein *et al.* 1980) contrasted the effects of a two-year IE intervention on 90 disadvantaged students with 90 similar students receiving a General Enrichment (GE) programme. This study is critically reviewed in detail in Shayer and Beasley (1987). On the Thurstone Primary Mental Abilities test (testing crystallised intelligence) the mean effect-size was $0.35\sigma$ in favour of the IE group. On eight tests of school achievement the mean effect-size was $0.15\sigma$, and only two of the differences were statistically significant. On the Embedded Figures test, testing for field-independence and hence fluid intelligence, the mean effect-size was $0.89\sigma$ in favour of the IE group. On a Classroom Participation test related to collaborative work-life capacity the mean effect-size on the three parameters tested was $0.62\sigma$. On the other hand, on two other test batteries related to ability to profit from schooling, there was a vanishingly small difference between the IE and GE groups.

While these initial effects are comparatively modest, valuable further evidence was provided by Feuerstein's co-workers in a follow-up study (Rand *et al.* 1981). Two years after the end of the intervention the students involved entered the Israeli army on compulsory service. On a test of general intelligence derived from the American Army Alpha the IE group were then $0.85\sigma$ ahead of the controls. Whereas they had originally been about three years behind in their schooling, now they were on a par with the average Israeli population in, for example, their promotion possibilities. Feuerstein attributed this to the effects of IE continuing to increase the difference between the groups after the intervention. We will return later to a technical consideration of the best way to evaluate the effect of cognitive intervention

and will see that some immediate post-tests underestimate the effects of interventions. In the IE evaluation probably the Field Independence test measuring fluid
intelligence was a better estimator of the intervention effects than the other tests
used.

An over-ambitious replication of Feuerstein's IE study was undertaken in North
America following the initiative of Carl Haywood at Vanderbilt University. A
detailed summary of project evidence is given in Shayer and Beasley (1987). With
five major sites in the project and associated problems of control it was difficult to
make valid comparisons between experimental and control groups. With sample
sizes of the order of 200, the weighted mean effect-size on the Lorge–Thorndike
non-verbal IQ test was $0.45\sigma$. On Raven's Matrices (fluid intelligence) the effect-
size was $0.61\sigma$ and on the Thurstone PMA (crystallised intelligence) the mean
effect-size was also $0.61\sigma$. On the CTBS Academic Achievement test the mean
effect-size for seven school activities was $0.51\sigma$ but this was only for one class of
10 students, and only three of the seven differences were statistically significant.

Two projects in the UK apparently finding little effect of IE (Weller and Craft
1983 and Blagg 1991) are not reported here, as we believe that neither replications
were properly supported, and they will be discussed in Chapter 9 under the heading
of inservice training. Unlike the Vanderbilt study above where the evaluator also
organised the training of teachers, Blagg's meticulous evaluation was of a project
not under his administrative control.

Notwithstanding one or two unpromising reports, the reported evidence on IE
was sufficiently encouraging to persuade Shayer and Beasley (1987) to undertake
a small-scale study designed to estimate the potential effects of IE under optimal
conditions and also to look at more of the variables relating to Feuerstein's
intervention models. A single class of 20 pupils in a special school (described in
the UK as ESN(M), that is a school for pupils who are educationally sub-normal
with moderate learning difficulties) initially aged between 12 and 13 years, were
randomly assigned to the experimental or to the control group. The experimental
group were withdrawn from the class for three hours of IE each week for the 20
months of the experiment, while the control group received a variety of general
enrichment material which their teacher dubbed 'Think-Tank' after a children's
television series of the time. The IE lessons were conducted by a teacher trained by
Shayer, and also supported by one or two collaborative visits to her lessons per
week for two terms in order to ensure that the underlying theory was realised in her
teaching practice. This is more support than is possible in a larger study but was
necessary to ensure that the maximum effect could be estimated.

A 12-task individual interview battery previously used to conduct a survey in
Pakistan (Shayer *et al.* 1988) was used as pre- and post-test for the Piagetian aspect
of IE. Thurstone's PMA was used to test mental abilities. The phase parameter was
tested by using Feuerstein's Learning Potential Assessment (LPA) test in a form
developed by Beasley (1984) to give quantitative results. In addition to giving
information on the relative use by experimental and controls on 13 of the most
relevant cognitive functions (Table 3.2), Beasley's test also used incidentally

Raven's matrices providing an additional test of fluid intelligence. Lastly, school achievement was tested by standardised tests of reading, mathematics, and basic skills from the Richmond battery.

*Table 3.3*  Pre- to post-test mean differences (experimental – control)

| Class of test | Test | | Signifi-cance level | Effect-size (σ) | Mental age difference months |
|---|---|---|---|---|---|
| Fluid | Piagetian battery | | 0.001 | 1.22 | 20.1 |
| intelligence | Raven's matrices | | 0.01 | 1.07 | 11.6 |
| Crystallised | Thurstone's | Verbal (w) | 0.02 | –0.37 | –3.8 |
| intelligence | PMA | Verbal (p) | n. s. | 0 | 0 |
| | | Spatial | 0.1 | 0.23 | 8.2 |
| | | Reasoning (w) | 0.001 | 0.98 | 9.6 |
| | | Reasoning (p) | n. s. | –0.26 | –6 |
| | | Perception | 0.1 | –0.35 | –13.6 |
| | | Numbers | n. s. | 0.07 | –0.6 |
| Achievement | Neale reading | Accuracy | 0.2 | 0.36 | 1.8 |
| | | Comprehension | n. s. | 0.26 | 0.4 |
| | | Rate | 0.2 | 0.47 | 3.5 |
| | NFER maths achivement | | 0.2 | 0.21 | 1.4 |
| | Richmond basic | Map reading | 0.1 | 0.57 | — |
| | Skills | Graphs/tables | 0.1 | 0.46 | — |
| IE Phase | LPA Cognitive functions | | 0.005 | 0.72 | — |

*Source:* Shayer and Beasley 1987

In Table 3.3 the main findings of the study are reported in terms of pre-post mean differences between the experimental and control groups. The mental age differences for the Piagetian battery were estimated using the norms of the CSMS survey reported in Chapter 2. On the Raven's matrices and Phase parameter it should be said that the LPA modification was only operationalised by May of the first year of the intervention so that for these measures the pre- and post-test cover only the last 12 months of the intervention, and so are probably underestimates.

The way in which Raven's Matrices was used throws light on Vygotsky's theory of the Zone of Proximal Development (ZPD) (Beasley and Shayer 1990). The items in one of the LPA tests used – LPAD variations – were closely related to those in Raven's matrices. The children were first taken through the Raven's matrices items in order of difficulty for each section until they started to fail. They were then given the dynamic assessment interview in which structured observations were taken in terms of the cognitive functions, and mediation was also given and recorded. At the end of the interview they were then taken back to Raven's matrices to the point where they had started to fail, and the extra items on which they then succeeded were recorded. The difference between pre- and post-mediation scores then estimates their learning potential. These results are shown in Table 3.4.

*Table 3.4*    Means (and standard deviations) of pupils' mental ages in years on Raven's matrices during LPA

|  | Experimental | | | Control | | |
|---|---|---|---|---|---|---|
|  | Mean age | Unassisted | Post-mediation | Mean age | Unassisted | Post-mediation |
| Pre-test 5/83 | 13/0 | 7.7 (0.65) | 9.5 (1.8) | 13/1 | 8.3 (0.43) | 10.5 (2.1) |
| Post-test 5/84 | 14/0 | 9.6 (2.4) | 11.2 (2.2) | 14/0 | 9.3 (2.0) | 10.7 (2.2) |

It can be seen that the experimental group realised, at unassisted post-test, the mental age level which at pre-test had been estimated as their potential and now had a new, higher, potential. The control group had not realised their predicted potential and, more importantly, their potential estimate (post-mediation) had hardly changed. The magnitude of the ZPD is about two mental age years.

Finally, the effect-sizes reported in all three studies are summarised in Table 3.5.

*Table 3.5*    Effect-sizes (experimental – control) of IE on various measures

| Study | Type of measure | | | | |
|---|---|---|---|---|---|
|  | Crystallised intelligence | Fluid intelligence | School achieve-ment | Piagetian operations | IE cognitive functions |
|  | σ | σ | σ | σ | σ |
| Israeli | 0.35 | 0.89 | 0.15 | — | — |
| North American | 0.61 | 0.61, 0.45 | 0.51 | — | — |
| British | 0.04 | 1.07 | 0.39 | 1.22 | 0.72 |

The data reported on fluid intelligence, on the Piagetian measures, and on the cognitive function element of Feuerstein's phase parameter all estimate here-and-now competence which should be in place at the end of the intervention and require no further experience for their realisation. Our view is that the Israeli and British studies were probably conducted in optimal, and the North American in far from optimal, conditions and that the only shortcoming of the Israeli study was the restricted nature of the testing. The best view of all the evidence is that effect-sizes on underlying thinking ability of the order of one standard deviation – or an extra two years of development in mental age terms – are achievable as a result of two years' use of IE. This is the equivalent of pushing a target population up nearly 30 percentile points on the curves shown in Fig. 2.7. It should be born in mind, given the target population, that in Piagetian terms the main effect of IE is to bring students to the concrete generalisation level rather than to develop formal operations. This can be seen by imagining a start from the line representing the lower 20 per cent at 12+ in Fig. 2.7.

## Applied Feuerstein IE: Context-delivered versus context-independent intervention

Both Feuerstein and de Bono have in common that they deliver their intervention in special thinking lessons which are not related to the context of ordinary school learning. In Feuerstein's case this was quite deliberate, in order that the students would not associate IE lessons with students' previous experience of failure. However, context-independent interventions give both the student and the teacher the further problem of how to use their new-found thinking expertise in the context of their ordinary school learning. The principle of context-delivered interventions is that a psychological intervention model is delivered within the context of a school subject with which the students are already familiar. Two examples of context-delivered IE will be described.

Mervyn Mehl (1985) taught physics to first-year medical students at the University of the Western Cape, a creation of apartheid South Africa with an exclusively coloured student intake. Resourcing of secondary schools for coloured and black students was so poor that students were ill prepared for university science and 50 per cent of the students regularly had to drop out of medical school because they failed their first year physics. Mehl was convinced that these results did not reflect the underlying ability of his students but rather their lack of any previous teaching challenging them to think within the context of their learning.

In the discussion of IE it was seen that Feuerstein draws from the psychometric model of mental abilities, from Piaget, from information-processing and cognitive psychology, and also on the idea of mediated learning with its origins in Vygotsky's psychology. In the application of IE to physics the mental abilities and the Piaget operations part of the model is fixed already by the context and content of the physics learning to be addressed. On the other hand the language by which the IE teacher thinks about the learning deficiencies of the student, which he may also share with the students, is drawn from the 30+ cognitive functions shown in Table 3.2. Mehl first set out to describe his students' typical deficient learning in terms of these cognitive functions, but expressed in negative form, as shown in Table 3.6.

Mehl investigated these deficiencies through individual interviews based on the dynamic testing of Vygotsky as further developed by Feuerstein. The interviews gave information mainly on the input and output phase, so it was supplemented for the elaboration aspect by a written test on problems involving the application of Newton's laws, given to all 200 new entrants to the physics course.

He categorised the most frequent deficient cognitive functions responsible for his students' deficient learning strategies under headings from Table 3.6. For example, when students were asked to make sketches of the dynamics task in order to help their thinking, typically they only used part of the numerical information given and the sketches showed that they had not used the verbal information in order to get a clear picture of what was happening. While none of the detail which Mehl describes is anything that a good physics teacher might not have noted, the further description in Feuerstein's terms – in this case under the heading of *blurred and sweeping perception* – allows for an analysis which can be the starting point for remediation, instead of being merely a description of student behaviour to be deplored.

On the basis of his analyses, Mehl developed a new style course for his students. There were two elements in this. The course itself was re-presented in nine structured booklets in which the deficient learning strategies were addressed by the provision of specific input and elaboration algorithms (Landa 1974, 1976) showing, for example, how to extract the salient information from the data given in the problem, and also drawing students' attention to concepts which are relevant. Secondly, the strategies underlying the booklets formed part of the language of the tutorial discussions between student and teacher. It is easier to see the second aspect as being shared with IE than the first, and it is important to note that the 'algorithms' are not physics algorithms giving instant rote access to solutions, but rather problem solving algorithms which are developed as an intrinsic part of the presentation of the concept.

Mehl's original aim was realised on the experimental group: the average student failure rate of 50 per cent at the end of the first year was cut to zero. There was a very convenient control, in that approximately half the students received their instruction in Afrikaans, and half – the experimental group – received it in English. In previous years the failure rate was the same for both groups, and in the intervention year the failure rate of the Afrikaans speaking group who did not receive the intervention was the same as usual. Furthermore, on six of the quarterly physics tests the effect-size (experimental–control) ranged from $2.0\sigma$ to $4.1\sigma$, with a mean of $2.7\sigma$. This corresponds to a difference of about 30 per cent between the groups for the test scores reported as percentages (for example, 62 per cent versus 35.5 per cent for a test where the effect-size was $2.59\sigma$). On the other hand, when the two groups were compared on part of the course which had not been 'Feuer-steinised', there was no difference at all in the groups' performance. Although no test was given to see if there had been any general effect of the intervention on the students' thinking ability, the fact that the strikingly large effect did not even generalise to other aspects of physics suggests there probably was no effect.

Juliet Strang (Froufe 1987, Strang and Shayer 1993) replicated Mehl's study on a below-average year 9 class in a London comprehensive school. She took a six-week introductory chemistry course featuring chemical reactions, thermal and

Table 3.6   The nature and locus of cognitive impairments

*I The Input Phase*
1   Blurred and sweeping perception.
2   Unplanned, impulsive and unsystematic exploratory behaviour.
3   Lack of or impaired receptive verbal tools that affect discrimination.
4   Lack of or impaired spatial orientation.
5   Lack of or impaired temporal concepts.
6   Lack of or impaired conservation of constancies.
7   Lack of or deficient need for precision and accuracy in data gathering.
8   Lack of capacity for considering two or more sources of information at
    once.

*II The Elaboration Phase*
1   Inadequacy in the perception of the existence and definition of an actual
    problem.
2   Inability to select relevant vs. non-relevant cues in defining a problem.
3   Lack of spontaneous comparative behaviour or limitation of its application
    by a restricted need system.
4   Narrowness of mental field.
5   Episodic grasp of reality.
6   Lack of or impaired need for pursuing logical evidence.
7   Lack of or impaired interiorisation.
8   Lack of or impaired inferential thinking.
9   Lack of or impaired strategies for hypothesis testing.
10  Lack of or impaired planning behaviour.
11  Non-elaboration of certain cognitive categories because the verbal
    concepts are not part of the individual's repertoire on a receptive level or
    are not mobilised at the expressive level.

*III The Output Phase*
1   Egocentric communication modalities.
2   Difficulties in projecting virtual relationships.
3   Blocking.
4   Trial and error responses.
5   Lack of or impaired receptive verbal tools for communicating adequately
    elaborated responses.
6   Lack of or impaired need for precision and accuracy in communicating
    responses.
7   Deficiencies in visual transport.
8   Impulsive acting out behaviour.

*Source*: Feuerstein *et al.* 1979

electrolytic decomposition, elements and compounds, and atoms' valency and symbols for the conduct of her intervention. She used individual interviews with students from another class to analyse typical learning errors in terms of the cognitive functions listed in Table 3.6 such as conservation of constancies, hypothetical thinking, and relevance. This description was then used both to write structured worksheets and to create lesson plans which would direct students'

attention selectively to different aspects of the chemistry module which the interviews had shown them unlikely to achieve on their own.

The class of 21 students was taught by the Head of Department (a chemist). For
this module the class was divided into two in terms of the science section of an
NFER test of cognitive abilities so that the ability and gender composition of the
groups was similar. Strang, a biologist, taught 11 of the students in a separate
laboratory. At the end all students were given the usual end-of-module test to
compare their achievement. The effect-size was $1.15\sigma$ in favour of the experimental
group corresponding to a mean score difference of 59 per cent compared with 38
per cent.

It can be seen that very large effects on the results of *instruction* can be obtained
by applying some of the principles of an *intervention* to analysing students' learning
difficulties, and modifying teaching strategies accordingly. In this case both Mehl
and Strang have sacrificed the metacognitive aspect of IE by not sharing with the
students the vocabulary of Feuerstein's cognitive functions, but using it instead
both to structure learning experiences for the students and to gain insight into how
to assist them to learn.

### Somerset Thinking Skills

The Somerset course originated in the Schools Council IE project in the early 1980s
(Weller and Craft 1983; Blagg 1991). Nigel Blagg was the chief educational
psychologist for Somerset at the time and undertook the evaluation of the use of IE
which will be discussed in Chapter 9. Following this experience he and a team of
experienced teachers produced a course which in part used IE principles but
embedded them as far as possible in recognisable contexts of school learning. The
Somerset Thinking Skills Course (Blagg *et al.* 1988) is an intervention programme
which lies mid-way between the context-independent and context-delivered type
described earlier, and is designed to be used with a broader ability range than IE.

## CAN FORMAL OPERATIONS BE TAUGHT?

We will consider now just a few of the studies which have attempted, directly or
indirectly, to encourage the growth of formal operational thinking in school or
college students. As the quote from Neimark at the beginning of this chapter shows,
there used to be a construal of the Piagetian position which emphasised the
maturation aspect of development to such an extent that some educators were apt to
take a rather passive view of what teachers could do to promote the developmental
process. This interpretation ignores the central role of equilibration which Piaget
had propounded as the driver of development. Equilibration involves a response to
events in the environment and to the extent that parents and teachers can structure
a child's environment they are able to have some influence on cognitive development, within limits allowed by the equilibration–maturation interaction.

Adey (1988) and Goossens (1989) have reviewed cognitive acceleration studies based on the Piagetian paradigm, and here we will look at just a few key examples from which we learned much.

**Teaching reasoning patterns**

In the United States in the 1970s the problem of the widening ability range of freshman students, especially in science, produced a crop of generally short-term Procustean intervention studies, mainly Piaget-based, to improve the thinking and learning of the new students. Valuable outcomes of this work included the establishment of some ground rules for the evaluation of intervention in terms of the transfer of cognitive skills from the context in which the training occurred to remote domains, and also the discovery that intensive programmes designed to 'teach' higher order thinking are not, in general, productive. For example, McKinnon (Renner *et al.* 1976, ch. 7) showed that the percentage of freshman students using formal operational thinking ranged from 61 per cent in a four-year private university through 46 per cent in a five-year public teachers' college down to 12 per cent in a five-year public university. He describes a one-semester course, 'Forum for Scientific Enquiry', intended to promote formal operational thinking in the context of science. Although first-year students seemed to have benefited from it, the actual effect-sizes on Piagetian tests were only $0.24\sigma$ mean difference from the pre- and post-test scores of a control group.

Likewise at the University of Nebraska in the mid-1970s a freshman programme called ADAPT consisting of courses each tailored to the subject choice of the students was taught. The intention of the course was to increase the proportion of students showing formal operational thinking by the end of the year, so that their subsequent scholastic progress would improve. Tomlinson-Keasey (1976, 1977) monitored the success of this course using Piagetian and other tests for two successive years. For the first year the effect-size was $0.22\sigma$, and for the second it was $0.14\sigma$. Both of these, and the 'Forum' results above, were statistically significant differences but in relation to student learning the actual effect-sizes were so small as to be trivial compared with the effort involved. What can be said of the ADAPT course, however, is that on the Watson–Glazer test of critical thinking skills the experimental group started the year a whole standard deviation behind the control group and had fully caught up with them by the end of the year. Unfortunately, given the relative difficulty of operationalising the notion of critical thinking, and the current emphasis on academic achievement, it seems that knowledge of these attempts has dropped below the horizon of fashion.

Many studies in the 1970s attempted to train students in one or two of the reasoning patterns for formal operations. For instance, Siegler *et al.* (1973) trained 10 and 11 year-olds to control variables in the pendulum problem. The children were given a framework of words such as 'dimension' and 'level' (value), and some instruction in measuring and thinking in terms of algorithms such as 'If one level of the dimension is always higher on the measure than the other level, then that is the important dimension.' They were then taken through a set of experiments analogous to the pendulum, and given successive hints until they succeeded. Finally, they were introduced to the pendulum problem, but with explicit linking to the words and strategies they had previously used. This study could be regarded, in fact, as a dynamic test on the Vygotsky pattern and to provide an estimate of the *learning potential* of the students over the next two years or so, although the authors could not at the time have been in a position to interpret their evidence in this way.

The same view can be taken of a study conducted by Lawson and Wollman (1976). Their training was in four sessions over two weeks with immediate post-tests. Thirty-two students in grade 5 (10/11 year-olds) and grade 7 (12/13 year-olds) were trained on the flexible rods problem and on three other problems involving control of variables. The style of intervention – both interactive and with provision of framing and specific relevant language – resembles strongly some aspects of the dynamic assessment procedures of Feuerstein. In effect that which is in the zone of proximal development is invoked and added to by the mediating action of the researchers. While this is all in quite recent memory the children are then given three sets of post-tests: flexible rods, on which they have been trained; pendulum and spheres which also involve control of variables, and the balance beam task which involves the different schemata of proportion and equilibrium. For both groups the effects on flexible rods were large: over 2 standard deviations compared with controls. For the near-transfer tasks – pendulum and spheres – the effect-sizes were about $0.8\sigma$ for the grade 5 children, and $2.2\sigma$ and $1.3\sigma$ respectively in grade 7. However, on the far-transfer task of the balance beam the differences were not statistically significant. If this is viewed as a dynamic assessment rather than an intervention, then the lack of transfer to the balance task is less surprising. Through Lawson and Wollman's procedures, one can infer the potential – not necessarily to be realised – of the children to develop to at least the early formal level over the subsequent two years.

Lawson and Snitgen (1982) at Arizona State ran a one-semester programme called 'Biological science for the elementary school teacher' which incorporated specific instruction in many, but not all, of the reasoning patterns of formal operations. These reasoning patterns were introduced in the context of biological science but given expression in many other science and 'everyday' contexts. The experimental design had no control group, but two experimental groups only one of which received pre-tests of levels of cognitive development and fluid intelligence (Raven's matrices). Both groups were given post-tests of fluid intelligence, field dependency (group embedded figures test) and formal operations. Only the last concerns us here. The programme resulted in highly significant (effect-sizes pre-to post-test from $0.4\sigma$ to $1.2\sigma$) gains in scores on those formal schemata which were explicitly included in the instructional programme, but the groups showed no improvement in performance on formal operational schemata which were not included in the instruction. In other words, no transfer had taken place and it could not be claimed that the general development of formal operations had been achieved.

The overall conclusion of such short-term approaches to training in the reasoning patterns of formal operations cannot be claimed as evidence of generally enhanced cognitive processing. It does seem that attempts to instruct students directly in the use of formal reasoning patterns are not successful in developing generalised strategies which can be applied to novel situations, let alone in the general development of formal operational thinking which would show itself as transfer to facility with other, non-trained, reasoning patterns. Such a conclusion could be predicted from the model of formal operations as a developmental and unified entity outlined in Chapter 2.

## Using equilibration

There were, however, some rather different intervention studies. Kuhn and Angelev (1976) designed a study intended to test the validity of Piaget's integrated model of formal operations. They argued that 'specific teaching, modelling of, or exposure to higher-stage structures is not a necessary part . . .' of the process by which individuals construct for themselves the higher structures. A feedback loop consisting solely of knowledge of success or failure should be sufficient to induce the necessary cognitive conflict. Moreover, if the 'structured whole' model of Piaget were valid then the result of a non-intrusive intervention should show up not only on a test of control of variables (the pendulum task), but also on a test of combinatorial thinking (the chemicals task). A 15-week intervention was designed in which the tasks given to above-average 9 to 11 year-olds had the same underlying structure as the pendulum problem. Children were told that they could open a certain number only, out of 27 black boxes, in which they would find either white or blue tokens. The white tokens could later be exchanged for prizes. Differing values of three variables – size, colour and shape – were displayed on the box-lids, and were related to the presence of white tokens inside. 'For all problems, one variable was operative and one particular level [value] of this variable corresponded to the presence of white tokens.' The number of choices allowed for success on each problem was one more than the minimum logically necessary to solve it. If the rule was 'all green boxes contain white tokens', then they were allowed to inspect four boxes from a sub-set in which size was constant. The subject's task, then, was to generate a hypothesis as to the relevant variable and variable level (value), test this prediction by opening a box, and then revise his or her hypothesis as necessary.

There were four experimental groups with 15 children in each who received: (a) one session every two weeks, (b) one session a week, (c) two sessions a week, and (d) one session a week with explicit demonstration of control of variables strategy. The interesting aspect of the design was the possible contrast of the post-test results for group (d) with those of group (c). In Table 3.7 the mean differences (experimentals minus controls) have been calculated for each of the four groups on the two tests, as estimates of effect-size. (It was not possible to estimate the standard deviations from the F-tests provided so here we have converted the scale used by Kuhn and Angelev to match the scale used in Chapter 6 for reporting effect-sizes on Piagetian tests. On this scale the standard deviation of the CASE samples was approximately 1, so the values in Table 3.7 can be treated as estimate of effect-sizes.)

*Table 3.7*   Mean differences (experimental – control) on Piagetian tests

|  | Pendulum | Chemicals |
|---|---|---|
| Once in 2 weeks | 0.32 | −0.14 (n.s.) |
| Once a week | 0.76 | 0.38 |
| Twice a week | 0.95 | 0.66 |
| Weekly with demonstration | 0.87 | 0.09 (n.s.) |

If Piaget's 'structured-whole' account of development is valid, then group (d) might show an effect on the pendulum task requiring control of variables, but without the children's active work of construction there might be no effect on the 'structured-whole' – i. e. there would be no change in their underlying thinking ability as tested by a test of a different reasoning pattern. As can be seen, the twice-a-week group showed effect-sizes of the same magnitude on the pendulum task (testing control of variables) and the chemicals task (testing combinatorial thinking). The once-a-week plus demonstration group had a post-test effect on the pendulum task ($0.87\sigma$) between the weekly and twice-weekly group but only a small, and statistically non-significant, effect on the chemicals task (testing a different reasoning pattern). At the time (1980) this seemed a small but important piece of evidence suggesting that direct teaching of thinking skill strategies might be self-defeating.

Further evidence was available from an Australian study with above-average 11 year-old girls. Rosenthal (1979) provided two different intervention styles related to control of variables in scientific and geographical phenomena set in the context of school science. In fact the 'training' in both styles featured active pupil discussion and dialogue between teacher and children, but whereas with the group who were given 'method training' the focus was specifically on the confusion which could result from not controlling variables when collecting evidence, the 'dimension-trained' group were encouraged to abstract from particular values like 'long' and 'heavy' for a pendulum to think of the underlying variables of *length* and *weight*. As with the Kuhn and Angelev study, the girls were given Piagetian pre- and post-tests one of which related directly to controlling variables, and the other testing combinatorial thinking in a logical context (the 'Butch and Slim' test from the British ability scales prototype). As can be seen in Table 3.8, both methods were effective.

Rosenthal divided the girls for testing in each group according to whether they were initially just at the early formal (3A) level or at the end of the concrete operational stage (2B). It can be seen that both groups showed substantial effects at post-test two months after the intervention on the flexible rods task, testing control of variables, and that there were smaller transfer effects to the logical thinking test (Butch and Slim). There is also just a suspicion of evidence that the explicit approach on controlling variables suited better those already with some formal thinking ability, whereas the indirect emphasis on abstracting the concept of a variable was more effective with those at the mature concrete level. Rosenthal's work falls into the category of a context-delivered intervention since she planted a Piagetian intervention aimed at increasing pupils' thinking ability within the context of ordinary school science lessons.

Table 3.8   Effect-sizes for Rosenthal (1979) in relation to intervention style

| Group | Pre-test level | Post-test effect | |
| | | Flexible rods σ | Butch and Slim σ |
| --- | --- | --- | --- |
| Method trained | Early formal | 1.44 | 0.88 |
| | Mature concrete | 0.94 | 0.43 |
| Dimension trained | Early formal | 1.07 | 0.46 |
| | Mature concrete | 1.41 | 0.70 |

These studies do suggest that some generalisation can be produced, not by direct instruction in particular reasoning patterns, but by putting students into a position where first they have mastered all of the necessary concrete precursors, and secondly they find that concrete thinking is inadequate to solve the problem in hand. As with Feuerstein's Instrumental Enrichment, students have to construct for themselves higher level methods of thinking. In constructing for themselves, say, the control of variables schema pupils also develop higher levels of reasoning across other schemata. Again this is a case of metaconstructivism, where pupils construct not only their own knowledge but also their own methods of processing data.

# Chapter 4

# Features of successful intervention

In our enterprise of designing an intervention programme for promoting cognitive development, we are now in a position to abstract lessons from the successes (and some failures) of others' work detailed in the last chapter. We will describe a list of features which seem to hold real promise for cognitive stimulation, and where appropriate illustrate each description with examples of classroom activities. These features, which should form the basis of a cognitive intervention programme, are:

- duration and density
- concrete preparation
- cognitive conflict
- construction
- metacognition
- bridging

And since our characterisation of higher order thinking is that of Piaget's formal operations, the schemata of formal operations described in Chapter 2 will provide the context for the development of activities.

## DENSITY AND DURATION

Both Lipman's and Feuerstein's work suggests that to have a permanent effect on the way that people think an intervention programme must be allowed to operate over a sufficiently long time period to make a permanent difference to the way in which students process fresh learning and approach problem solving.

This empirical result should not be surprising to anyone who sees the development of thinking as a special case of development in general. If your model includes some central processing mechanism of the mind which is supposed to develop under the influence of maturation as well as environmental stimulation, then it seems inevitable that any environmental influence will be slow acting and should be maintained for long enough to be effective. Short sharp exercises, however intellectually intensive, will not do. In fact, there is little theoretical or empirical reason to suppose that a cognitive intervention programme needs to be very intensive provided that it is maintained at a steady rate over a long period. On the basis of Feuerstein's experience and our own pilot study we took 'long period' to mean two years.

## CONCRETE PREPARATION

Formal operations only operate on a situation that has first been described by the subject in terms of descriptive concrete models. Put another way, a problem does not even appear as a problem worthy of attention if its terms have no meaning. To someone who has never seen a hat or a rabbit, it is not interesting to see a rabbit pulled out of a hat. For all he knows, hats are precisely the place where rabbits live.

Concrete preparation means establishing familiarity with the vocabulary, apparatus and framework in which a problem situation will be set. Rosenthal (1979) got her pupils to consider the dimensions of the variables of a problem. Being able to recognise variables and the possible values of those variables is a concrete operation, but it is a necessary precursor to the formal operation of understanding more complex relationships between the variables. Part of the process of concrete preparation is to give pupils practice in using the terminology. Thus a teacher may display a selection of books on the table: 'In what ways are these different from one another?' she asks. Answers typically include 'colour', 'size', 'hard- or soft-back', and so on. 'These are ways in which the books *vary* from each other. We call colour, size, etc., *variables*. The *values* of the variable colour include red, green, blue, . . .'. Practice is provided in identifying variables and values in other situations, and at the same time the idea of *relationships* may be introduced in a simple qualitative way: 'All the triangles are blue, and the squares are red. So there is a relationship between the variables' colour and shape' (see Fig. 2.3, p. 19).

In establishing the idea of a relationship it is necessary also for students to encounter examples where there is *no* relationship. For example, a set of loaded but opaque coloured jars are explored and the following table of data established by investigation:

| Jar no. | Colour | Size | Weight (g) |
|---------|--------|-------|------------|
| 1 | blue | small | 155 |
| 2 | blue | small | 220 |
| 3 | red | large | 155 |
| 4 | red | large | 220 |

There is a simple relationship between colour and size (big jars are red, small ones are blue). However, in discussion pupils find that they cannot predict what the weight a new red jar, or a new large jar, will be because the weight of the jars bears no relationship to either colour or size.

An important principle for the teaching of new technical vocabulary, drawn from the Piagetian 'matching' model discussed in Chapter 2, is that the context for the practice examples given should require processing at no more than the mature concrete level. In this way something like 90 per cent of the students can gain confidence in the use of the vocabulary before they, later, are asked to use it as one of their tools for investigating an activity which requires formal operations. This may seem so blindingly obvious that we have to ask the reader here to consciously search their memory for how, for example, they were taught science or mathematics themselves, and how these subjects feature in school practice today. He/she will find that exactly the opposite is the rule: new vocabulary is *never* introduced until the subject-matter which requires it for its successful interpretation is first met. Usually this is a good principle for instruction, for the motivation of the student to learn is enhanced by their seeing the relevance of the more powerful vocabulary, concept, or interpretative tool. But for intervention the usual practice works the other way, by guaranteeing that only the more able get to use the new vocabulary – maybe only 40 per cent of the students in a mixed-ability class as contrasted with 90 per cent, if the context where application is made requires formal processing.

## COGNITIVE CONFLICT

This is the term used to describe an event or observation which the student finds puzzling and discordant with previous experience or understanding. All perceptions are interpreted through the learners' present conceptual framework. Where current conceptualisation fails to make sense of an experience, cognitive conflict can lead to constructive mental work by students to accommodate their conceptual framework to the new type of thinking necessary. Cognitive conflict is a feature both of Piaget's account of the impact of environmental stimulus and children's constructivist response on cognitive growth, and of cognitive acceleration programmes which are effective in raising levels of thinking.

The provision of cognitive conflict is also a characteristic of much teaching that would be considered 'good' by expert observers. An example is provided by Nordland's description of two classes in an Australian High School which were the subject of detailed observation by a research team over a three-month period (Tobin *et al.* 1990). The teachers professed a commitment to 'individualised and self-paced teaching and learning' which they believed 'produced higher-level cognitive outcomes than more traditional approaches did' (p. 136). However, observers noticed exactly the opposite in the classes. In order to be individualised the students' curriculum was driven by workbooks, but the workbooks made only low-level recall demands, often directing them to particular pages in the textbook where answers would be found without any mental construction or re-interpretation required. Nordland, rather politely, condemns the teaching as being seriously under-demanding especially as Piagetian interviews with the grade 10 students reveal that the great majority are already capable of formal operational thinking. It is not surprising that, lacking the stimulus of cognitive conflict, many students are bored and disruptive.

Fensham and Kass (1988) have provided a useful account of the potential and limitations of what they term 'discrepant events' in the promotion of conceptual change. They note that everything which a subject finds surprising does not fulfil the potential of cognitive conflict. Probably the majority of surprising experiences are shrugged off as inexplicable or as uninteresting, or possibly given a magical or miraculous explanation. The message is that the conflict situation must be carefully judged by the teacher or curriculum developer (a) to be within a context which is somewhat familiar to the students, and (b) while making a real cognitive demand on the student, not to be so far ahead as to be incomprehensible.

Kuhn *et al.*'s (1988) investigation of the co-ordination of new evidence with existing cognitive schema confirms that instances of cognitive conflict do not automatically produce a 'Road to Damascus' conversion to a new conceptualisation. Children and adults confronted with evidence which they find difficult to explain often produce a series of irrational or self-contradictory statements in an attempt to 'explain away' the evidence without fully engaging with it. This explains the importance of the concrete preparation phase: for the dissonant event to have any effect on the student's cognitive structure she or he must first be prepared carefully either to expect one thing, or to be ready to weigh what happens against certain possible alternative explanations. The conflict requires careful management by the teacher.

Examples of well-managed situations for the establishment of cognitive conflict abound in the materials of the Children's Learning in Science Project (CLISP, 1987). These are founded in the notion that to develop scientific concepts the teacher must first expose the 'alternative conceptions' which pupils currently hold. Discussion of alternative explanations of observations lead to the design of critical tests. When these are carried out, the predictions based on misconceptions are confronted with evidence from reality. Note that in this case the cognitive conflict which arises concerns a particular concept and the aim of activities is the construction by the pupils of this concept, an essentially instructional and relatively short-term aim. Important though such instructional aims are within the total educational process, they are quite distinct from the interventionist goals with which we are concerned. If our concern is with the development of the schemata of formal operations then the cognitive conflict provided should be such as to help pupils construct these reasoning patterns for themselves. This is a somewhat higher risk strategy than the construction of specific science concepts, but one which potentially has far wider generalisability. An example, shown in Fig. 4.1, of an activity designed to induce conflict with the development of higher order thinking in mind will make the distinction clear.

Two sets of jars are prepared. Five jars, A–E, are all the same size but are loaded to have different masses. Six jars, 1 to 6, are each successively smaller than the one before but they all have the same mass. Jar 1/A is common to both sets. The jars are opaque, and labelled only with their number or letter. Students are invited to

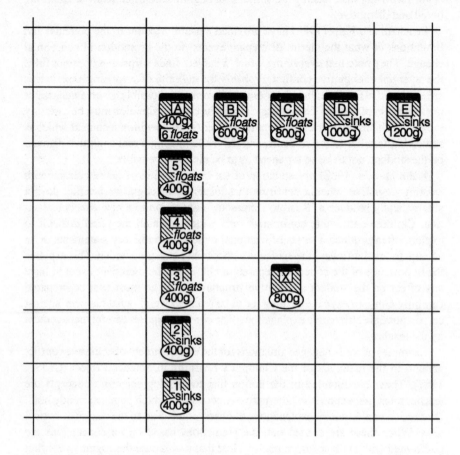

*Fig. 4.1*  Floating and sinking jars

weigh each jar and then drop it in a large bowl of water to see whether it floats or
sinks. Considering jars A–E first, only two variables are involved: mass and
buoyancy. Students can develop a concrete model relating the two: 'heavy things
sink, light things float'. A focus on jars 1–6 leads to another concrete model: 'small
things sink, big things float'. Now, jar X is produced. It is the same size as jar 3, a
floater, and the same mass as jar C, also a floater.

Application of the concrete models established so far leads to the prediction that
jar X will float. When it is put in the water, it sinks. There is conflict between
perceptual experience and the concrete operations used thus far which causes
students to puzzle and seek an explanation for the surprising result. There is nothing
in the terminology or apparatus which is strange, it is simply that the concrete

operations will not provide an explanation for the sinking of jar X because a three-variable, formal, model is required employing the notion of 'weight-for-a-certain-size'. The intention is that a series of experiences of this type over a sufficiently long period will actually induce the development of higher orders of thinking. Our expectation here is not that after the floating and sinking activity pupils will all have a grasp of density (some do, some do not) but that they will develop their repertoire of general ideas – in this case that of compound variables – which provide explanatory power in a wide range of situations.

Another aspect of the good management of conflict situations is the maintenance of conflict in the face of a student's attempt to resolve the conflict inadequately or prematurely, as observed by Kuhn *et al.* (1988). Consider the following dialogue (simplified to make a point, but similar to many we have heard). The pupil has a number of tubes, and has been investigating the possible effects of length, width, or material of tube on the note produced when you blow across the top of it:

T: What affects the note when you blow across a tube?
P: The wider the tube, the deeper the note.
T: Show me.
P: (Blows across wide long tube and narrow short one.)
T: How do you know the width affects the note?
P: Wide one gives a deeper note. (*Perceives no conflict.*)
T: How do you know it is not the length that affects the note? (*Conflict established.*)
P: Both the length and the width affect the note. (*Conflict resolved to the satisfaction of the pupil.*)
T: How can you tell whether it is length or width, or both? (*Conflict re-established.*)
P: ...

One can see the student coming up with a series of 'explanations' which are not explanations at all and the teacher not letting him off the hook but continuing to push for the construction of an adequate control of variables schema.

It will be clear that the management of cognitive conflict is in the hands of the teacher, and no printed or other hard expressions of the curriculum could ever by themselves adequately encompass the process. Activities may be designed and described in detail which provide excellent opportunities for the generation of conflict, but unless the teacher has professional ownership of the methods she or he is unlikely to produce the intended effect. The same is true for all of the key features of intervention methods which are described in this chapter, and in Chapter 9 we will return to the issue of changing practices in classroom through effective inservice staff development.

## THE CONSTRUCTION ZONE

We have briefly touched on the notion of 'construction', and now must pay more attention to possible mechanisms by which well managed cognitive conflict can lead to the construction of reasoning patterns by the student.

Newman *et al.* (1989), drawing on Vygotsky's concept of the zone of proximal development, have described as 'construction zone activity' mental activity, often collaborative but not exclusively so, which is specifically devoted to *going beyond* children's present limits of assured competencies. The 'construction zone' is nicely described by Sheldon White, in his foreword to Newman *et al.*'s book as: 'a magic place where minds meet, where things are not the same to all who see them, where meanings are fluid, and where one person's construal may preempt another's'.

If cognitive conflict upsets a student's equilibrium feeling of understanding as much as he needs to, construction is the process which follows and which re-establishes equilibrium through the development of a more powerful and effective way of thinking about the problem. Our colleague Carolyn Yates has proposed a 'jig-saw puzzle' analogy for this process. Sitting around a table collaboratively completing a jigsaw, one person fitting in a piece often stimulates another: 'Ah! now I see where this piece goes.' If one of the players is a teacher who actually knows pretty well how the puzzle goes together she can ask framing and focusing questions to aid the process and occasionally add a piece herself, but unless the students construct much of the puzzle themselves it will not be their own and (to come out of the analogy) they will not have gone beyond their present level of reasoning.

Here is an example of construction zone activity: dialogue and action which leads to the construction of a reasoning pattern, in this case of the schema of control of variables in a multi- and interacting-variable situation. The problem concerns optimal conditions for fermentation using yeast.

| *Dialogue* | *Commentary* |
|---|---|
| T:   What do you know about yeast? | |
| P1:  It's a fungus. | |
| P2:  In beer and wine. | Pieces of knowledge contributed more |
| P3:  In water it bubbles. | or less at random, until the teacher |
| T:   Air bubbles? | lights on one and asks for more |
| P4:  Carbon dioxide. | information. |
| T:   How could we catch the gas? | T refines the language, insinuating the |
|     (Fingers a balloon.) | word 'gas', while hinting at the answer |
| P:   Put a balloon on the flask. | to his question. |
| T:    What does yeast need to make | |
|     gas? | |
| Ps:  Water, yeast, sugar. | |

P4: You don't put sugar in bread.

P5: You use dough though.　　　　Ps explore possibilities and T resolves

T: We will add some sugar to　　a factual conflict.
start it working.

P: You need heat as well.

T: What are the variables?　　　Ps are familiar with the meaning of

P: Water, sugar, heat.　　　　　variables, and T wants them to use the

T: Explain.　　　　　　　　　　proper terminology.
　　　　　　　　　　　　　　　Now he pushes for justification.

P: Because if you change them
you get more or less gas.

T: We are going to use the same　Simplifies the situation, making the
amount of water in each flask,　experimental design more manageable
so it will not be a variable.　（this is a learning situation, not a real
　　　　　　　　　　　　　　　laboratory!)

Ps: Now complete table in　　　The construction becomes individual
worksheet asking which　　　and can be individually tailored to
combination of the variables　pupils' needs.
they want in each flask.

T: (Circulates asking probing
questions and seeking
explanations for choices
from individuals.)

In Chapter 7 we will explore further an information-processing model of the mind in which the schemata of formal operations are seen as ready-made procedures which can be accessed by short-term memory in the process of problem solving. By promoting mediating strategies of class management by teachers in the construction zone, we are seeking to maximise the opportunities each pupil has for building up, bit by bit, the reasoning patterns which will do more powerful work of thinking for them. Cognitive acceleration would consist of significantly reducing the period during which the schemata are constructed. This is the reason that in our work the decision was made to structure each lesson around one or more of Piaget's formal operational schemata as they occur implicitly in varied science contexts. In this way the 'central processor' in children's minds may be modified, without their having been taught new strategies explicitly.

## Metacognition

In the simplest interpretation of the word, metacognition means thinking about one's own thinking, becoming conscious of ones' own reasoning. It is a feature of the development of higher order thinking which seems to carry almost universal support from cognitive psychologists. In an important paper reviewing the state of the domain-specific versus domain-general debate (see Chapter 2), Perkins and Salomon (1989) claim that metacognition is likely to be an essential element of any programme which is successful in improving general thinking skills. Analysing Schoenfield's success in developing students' mathematical problem solving ability, they note:

> At the same time an important thrust of Schoenfield's approach is fostering a seemingly quite general level of control or problem management. Students learn to monitor and direct their own progress, asking questions such as 'What am I doing now?', 'Is it getting me anywhere?', 'What else could I be doing instead?'. This general metacognitive level helps students to avoid persevering in unproductive approaches, to remember to check candidate answers, and so on.
>
> (p. 21)

Karmiloff-Smith (1991) believes that it is this very ability to be reflexive, to become conscious of our own thought processes, which lifts human learning to a plane so far beyond animal learning: 'The human system's capacity to re-represent recursively its internal representations allows us eventually to become grammarians, poets, philosophers, physicists, and so forth' (p. 182). Donaldson (1978), a strong critic of much of the Piagetian position, quotes with approval Piaget's finding that children's reflection on problems and consideration of possibilities before acting are important aspects of cognitive development:

> What is now at stake, however, is the child's more general awareness of his own thought processes – his self-awareness. For as Vygotsky rightly says: 'control of a function is the counterpart of one's consciousness of it'. If the child is going to control and direct his own thinking, in the kind of way we have been considering, he must become conscious of it.
>
> (p. 94)

Feuerstein's emphasis on the role of adults as mediators of learning can be seen as the most effective way to encourage metacognition. In practice a teacher can ask pupils to talk about difficulties and successes they have with problems, both with the teacher and with each other – not just 'that was difficult' but 'what was difficult about it, and how did I overcome the difficulty?' Students are encouraged to reflect on the sort of thinking they have been engaged in, to bring it to the front of their consciousness, and to make of it an explicit tool which may then be available for use in a new context. Using the words to describe reasoning patterns is a special application of what Vygotsky (1978) describes as the use of language as a mediator of learning. The language of reasoning mediates meta-learning.

In fact it turns out that there is a great deal of confusion over the actual recognition of metacognition, and this is a reflection of a confusion in the literature in the meanings and uses of the word. The authors found this out to their cost when viewing some video material being prepared to train teachers in the use of cognitive acceleration methods. The producer, an expert in her field but not versed in our jargon, asked us simply to view the material shot and to identify examples of concrete preparation, cognitive conflict, metacognition, and so on. 'That's meta-cognition', shouted one of us at a particular point. 'No it isn't', shouted the other. The producer reasonably looked askance and wondered silently if we ourselves had any idea what we were talking about. After a couple of weeks of exposing our own meanings and testing them against the literature we were able to reach a position where, at least, we could agree on terminology to be used in our INSET tapes.

Von Wright (1992) draws on the history of 'reflections on reflections' and distinguishes two levels of reflection, the confounding of which we believe to be the origin of our own and others' confusion. At the lower level, von Wright's subject is

> capable of reflecting about many features of the world in the sense of considering and comparing them in her mind, and of reflecting upon her means of coping in familiar contexts. However . . . she is unlikely to be capable of reflecting about herself as the intentional subject of her own actions.
>
> (p. 60–1)

Von Wright's comments on the development of self as a social construct are important but not immediately germane to our present concerns. His higher level of reflection is what we have come to describe as metacognition:

> Reflecting about one's own knowledge or intentions involves an element which is absent from reflections about the surrounding world. Self-reflection presup-poses, in the language of mental models, a 'metamodel': in order to reason about how I reason, I need access to a model of my reasoning performance.
>
> (p. 61)

He concludes, 'The distinction between these two levels of reflection has often been made by developmental psychologists such as Vygotsky, who draws the line between "soznanie" or consciousness on the broader sense, and "osoznanie" or conscious awareness.'

Ann Brown (1983, 1987), in a resolute attempt to clarify this confused field, describes four strands in her discussion of the metacognition literature: (a) verbal reports as data (self-knowledge of cognitive processes), (b) executive control within an information processing framework, (c) self-regulation within the Piagetian framework, and (d) other-regulation, a Vygotskian notion. As she points out, the trouble with verbal reports as data is that either the children are far away in time from the phenomena – in which case there are problems of distortion or irrelevance – or the children are on-task, and the demand for additional verbalisation uses up some of the processing space the child needs for the task itself. Information-processing models (b) and Piagetian research on self-regulation (c) come much closer to descriptions of here-and-now behaviour. Indeed, they begin to look like exemplifications of the parable of the villagers of the blind giving accounts of the elephant: very much as alternative descriptions of the same thing. The other-regulation literature (d) adds detail to these of the social mediation of thinking by others.

Brown puts her finger on a major problem, unresolved either in (b) or (c):

Confused in the metacognitive literature, even lost in some versions of the concept, is this essential distinction between self-regulation during learning and knowledge of, or even mental experimentation with, one's own thoughts. Whatever distinctions must be made to render metacognition a more malleable concept, this one is a fine candidate for inclusion in the list.

(Brown *et al.* 1983:122)

The distinction here, which maps on to that of von Wright, is between self-regulation which may be an unconscious process and the conscious attention to one's own thinking – *going-above*, as it were, and looking down on one's own thinking. This latter meaning is well illustrated by Nelson *et al.* (1990). They speak of metacognition as constituting 'self-awareness judgements . . . which refer to the monitoring and control of one's own cognitive processes', which may be 'frontal lobe activity'. We interpret this as describing a conscious reflection and naming – for some process of decision or transfer – of strategies and concepts which the subject has *previously* developed, and now wishes either to deploy or relate to some other context. Gregory Bateson (1983:139, et seq.) calls this 'deutero-learning'.

Clearly the self-regulation meaning of metacognition as it relates to individual internal processes is the same as Brown's (b) and (c), while the Vygotskian part (d) is also related to the same thing, but describes the inter-personal aspect of the development of executive control. We suggest now that this 'same thing' is what we have described above as construction zone activity (CZA) – going-beyond one's present repertoire of reasoning. So we have two senses of 'meta': higher level abstraction about learning behaviour – *going-above*, and a *going-beyond* the present learning behaviours. Now that CZA has been distinguished and described it becomes possible to follow Ann Brown's advice and restrict our use of the word metacognition to going-above activities.

Perhaps the reason that the two senses of metacognition had been confused with each other is that unless learners have recently gone beyond, they do not have anything to be reflective about, or to abstract at a higher level. All of us involved in intervention research will intuitively have been involved in promoting both going-beyond and going-above, so any attempt to describe the abstractive side of metacognition brings in its train an associated set of going-beyond behaviours. Note that the contrary does not necessarily apply: children may have been given many and rich opportunities for going-beyond activities but they may not spontaneously proceed to a going-above step, and can very easily lose the bulk of what they have precariously achieved unless a mediator provides them with the time and occasion to abstract as well.

At this point it is possible to sound a note of caution about the Perkins and Salomon work cited above. It does run the danger – probably not in the hands of its originators (see Salomon *et al.* 1989) – of trying to make metacognition do the work much of which may better be promoted by construction (CZA). Bateson, in three classic papers collected in *Steps to an Ecology of Mind* (1983:133, 250 and 402) spells out some of the obvious reasons:

> The television screen does not give you total coverage or report of the events which occur in the whole television process . . . because to report on any extra part of the total process would require extra circuitry . . . . Each additional step towards increased consciousness will take the system farther from total consciousness. To add a report on events in a given part of the machine will actually *decrease* the percentage of total events reported.

He also tells the story of the centipede who, on being asked on which foot he intended to set out with, hesitated and then fell over on his side.

Case (1985) relates this idea to the specifics of different stages of cognitive development in terms of the crucial importance of using short-term storage space as effectively as possible. Piaget writes paradoxically of thought as being the *unconscious* activity of the mind, with a similar proviso implicit. In finding a place for metacognition in the intervention process it is necessary to avoid the mistake of believing that the expanded consciousness of metacognitive activity is the driving force of better cognition.

In summary, it seems best at this point to restrict the meaning of 'metacognition' to the going-above aspect of the distinction made, stressing conscious, reflective awareness about strategies – 'thinking about-thinking (and action)'. The other aspect: the going-beyond activities which were collapsed under metacognition are better considered under the heading of construction zone activity (CZA), or 'construction' for short.

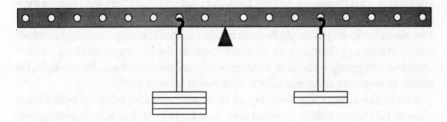

*Fig. 4.2*    Balance beam

Here is one example of spontaneous metacognitive dialogue observed in a CASE lesson. Two girls were working with a balance beam which had eight hooks on either side of the fulcrum. It was balanced with a 400 g mass on hook 2, and a 200 g mass on hook 4 (see Fig. 4.2). The worksheet asked the question: 'If the 400 g mass is moved out one hook, how will you have to move the 200 g mass to make the beam balance again?' One girl said to the other, 'If you move one out one hook, you must move the other out one hook also'. The other girl initially agreed, then hesitated, then said 'No, I don't think so. Because the 200 g mass is half as heavy as the 400 g, we will have to move it out twice as far. If it's half the weight we must move it twice the distance.' Then she added: 'I didn't even know that until I said it!' Here is a student who first goes beyond, constructs a reasoning pattern of compensation for herself, and then goes above, becoming conscious of the rule she has just invented.

In moving on to the next feature of successful intervention programmes we will find that we cannot leave metacognition behind, since it is intimately involved in the process of bridging.

## Bridging

Explicit bridging to other contexts is the final link in the chain of developing, abstracting, and generalising reasoning. In the earliest days of cognitive psychology, it was believed that there were certain 'faculties' which students could develop with training in much the same way that muscles can be developed. Unfortunately for the faculty psychologists the experimental evidence against the idea became overwhelming. 'Memory-training exercises' on lists of nonsense syllables had precisely no effect on the students' subsequent ability to learn irregular French verbs. Transfer only occurred if a specific effort to transfer was built into the teaching programme. We might now explain this finding in terms of a learning strategy which could be abstracted and applied to new material.

The term 'bridging' itself is taken from Feuerstein's Instrumental Enrichment, and describes a feature of every IE lesson. Sometimes in the initial discussion, always in the final part of working on an IE instrument page, students are encouraged first to summarise how the successful strategies they used helped them solve the problems (metacognition), and secondly to use their imagination to see how the same strategies might be used in other school learning contexts, or outside school (bridging). Bridging in IE often requires the divergent thinking skill of seeing or imagining some quite different everyday context where, for example, the ability to sequence tasks mentally in time might be very useful.

One of the authors was finishing an IE lesson on spatial relations with a small class of 12/13 year-olds in a special school, at 12.40 p. m. It was early closing day, and his next research proposal had to be in the post that day, and that meant by 1 p. m. He told his students, 'I am in your hands. I don't know the way to the post office, and as I leave about six minutes to one, unless I know exactly where to go at each point in my car, I won't do it!' They used all the strategies they had just been using and talking about in the IE instrument page, successfully, and took him through all the decision points. All were so pleased, the next day, to be told that the letter was posted with a minute to spare. Thus in IE the two ends of the bridging connection are in principle context-independent. The power of the bridging activity in IE is the promotion of integrated concrete thinking, and so the more the variety of contexts the more is concrete generalisation promoted.

By contrast, when bridging is designed for the generalisation of formal operational schemata from specific activities in, say, science, the process increases the depth of insight the student has into chemistry, physics or biology as the case may be. This may be achieved in two ways: (a) the development of new contexts specifically for the practice of a reasoning pattern first met in a special 'thinking' lesson, and (b) the recalling, while in a regular school lesson, of the applicability of a reasoning pattern previously developed. In this latter sense, after practice with a reasoning pattern and naming it, bridging means seeking examples of its use in other lessons and in everyday life. The schema of proportionality may be introduced through an academic lever exercise, brought to consciousness through use of the terms *ratio* and *proportion*, and then applied to such topics as the strength of orange juice or comparing the price of records in terms of amount of music per penny.

Many examples of the (a) type use of bridging have been generated by teachers with whom we have worked, directly or indirectly, over the past few years. Some examples will be given in the next chapter.

The distinction between our use of bridging and its use in IE may be simply the distinction between its use in a context-independent intervention (IE) and within a context-delivered intervention such as *Thinking Science*.

By now it will be clear why the idea of bridging cannot be divorced from that of metacognition, even using our restricted definition of metacognition. If bridging is the conscious transfer of a reasoning pattern from a context in which it is first encountered to a new context, then the transfer is most likely to be effective if the reasoning pattern has previously been made conscious and verbalised.

## Perkins, Salomon, and transfer

This relationship is made quite clear in the analyses of transfer given by Gavriel Salomon and David Perkins (Salomon 1988, Salomon *et al.* 1989; Perkins and Salomon 1989). First, their review of relevant research convinces them that

> transfer is possible, that it is very much a matter of how the knowledge and skill is acquired and how the individual, now facing a new situation, goes about trying to handle it. Given appropriate conditions such as cueing, practising, generating abstract rules, socially developing explanations and principles, conjuring up analogies . . . and the like transfer from one problem domain to another can be obtained.
>
> (Perkins and Salomon 1989:22)

They distinguish three types of transfer, describing spontaneous transfer, where the student her/himself retrieves a thinking strategy developed previously and applies it to the new situation, as 'the strongest case'. Then there is transfer when a teacher suggests the use of a strategy developed in a different context. Finally, quicker learning in a new context because of generalisable strategies mastered previously in a different context is considered the weakest form of transfer. Curiously, we are inclined to view the last named as a rather deep-seated form of transfer. The fact that it is unconscious argues for its effect being due to a fundamental change in the central processing mechanism of the mind, rather than to strategies learned consciously as a result of instruction.

Salomon distinguishes between the *low road* and the *high road* to transfer. He argues that the gist of the low road is

> the automatic triggering of well-practised routines in circumstances where there is considerable perceptual similarity to the original learning context . . . [it] trades on the extensive overlap at the level of the superficial stimulus among many situations where we might apply a skill or piece of knowledge which has been mastered to near-automaticity.

Whereas for travel by the high road

> one learns something by means of *mindful abstraction,* that is by means of a deliberate, volitional process through which a central idea, principle, rule, generalisation or strategy becomes decontextualised and available for far reaching transfer to entirely novel situations. . . . Facing a new situation, one abstracts key elements from it and starts searching back into memory for cases that match the new one in essence or principle.

This high road will be recognised as the same as Nelson *et al.* (1990) describe as 'frontal lobe activity', the conscious naming of reasoning for later use. Brown *et al.* (1983) see this as 'late-developing information that human thinkers have about their own cognitive processes' (p. 107) which begs the question: If conscious metacognition is a feature of mature cognition, how can we use it as a strategy for the purpose of promoting the maturation of thinking? In using metacognition as one of the features of a programme designed to promote formal operations, we are perhaps limited initially to the mimicking of a characteristic of higher order thinking until the mimicking becomes the reality.

This contrasts with some aspects of Salomon's High Road. The burden of their argument for transfer rests on the notion of mindful calling up of strategies used in the past, and the necessity for these strategies to have been made conscious at the time that they were first encountered. We noted above that this is to make metacognition do all the work of cognitive acceleration. We would rather aim for an even higher road, the unconscious development of a central cognitive processor that would produce far-transfer effects by a mechanism invisible to the learner (perhaps we should say 'developer') herself and thus far more powerful and generalisable than anything restricted to conscious processing. The implication of this argument is that, of the processes we have posited as central to cognitive acceleration, cognitive conflict and construction zone activity are at least as important as metacognition and bridging.

We will conclude this section with a last quote from Perkins and Saloman which shows how close we are to agreement:

> The approach that now seems warranted calls for the intimate intermingling of generality and context-specificity in instruction . . . . We forecast that wider-

scale efforts to join subject-matter instruction and the teaching of thinking will be one of the exciting stories of the next decade of research and educational innovation.

(p. 24)

Amen to that.

## Putting it together

These are the features which we have identified as prime candidates for inclusion in any programme designed to promote higher order thinking:

- Concrete preparation to introduce the necessary vocabulary and clarify the terms in which a problem is to be set.
- Cognitive conflict at a level to set the students' minds a puzzle which is interesting and attackable.
- Construction zone activity in which the conflict is at least partially resolved as students' minds go beyond their previous thinking capability.
- Metacognition in the sense of conscious reflection on the problem solving process and naming of reasoning patterns developed, for future use.
- The bridging of these reasoning patterns to new contexts in order to (a) generalise them and (b) consolidate their use.

It appears that Feuerstein's IE lessons do a lot of the work of integrating these elements. They have well defined time-lines, with $10 \pm 5$ minutes devoted to what we have described as concrete preparation followed by $20 \pm 5$ minutes' individual work on IE tasks (instrument pages) and then about 15 minutes' class discussion. During these phases there are opportunities both for cognitive conflict and the 'construction zone going-beyond' activity. At the end is a summary, $5 \pm 2$ minutes. This last phase, often conducted mainly by the students, is their opportunity both for reflective abstraction and inventing examples for bridging. IE teachers have realised that, however good and varied the constructive thinking in a lesson has been, it is necessary also to give its achievements a name and provisional locations for further use, and their mediation is devoted to getting this done by the students themselves.

Figure 4.3 represents one attempt at displaying the integration of the elements. The aspects (a) and (b) of concrete preparation apply to introductory lessons where something like a mastery learning approach is taken to the learning of new technical vocabulary. Aspect (c), selection of relevant verbal tools, would often be at the reception end of the bridging process, where pupils are presented with a problem and asked what ideas or technical terms they have met before that might have some application. Here they may select as relevant the new vocabulary they have previously mastered and which here may be called upon to help them in a more exacting task. If class discussion is now focused on the specifics of the problem (d), class management can now begin construction zone activity. The less the

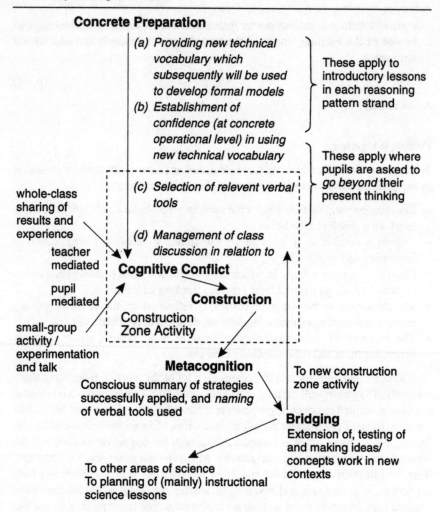

**Concrete Preparation**

(a) *Providing new technical vocabulary which subsequently will be used to develop formal models*

(b) *Establishment of confidence (at concrete operational level) in using new technical vocabulary*

These apply to introductory lessons in each reasoning pattern strand

(c) *Selection of relevent verbal tools*

(d) *Management of class discussion in relation to*

These apply where pupils are asked to *go beyond* their present thinking

whole-class sharing of results and experience

teacher mediated

**Cognitive Conflict**

pupil mediated

**Construction**

small-group activity / experimentation and talk

Construction Zone Activity

**Metacognition**

Conscious summary of strategies successfully applied, and *naming* of verbal tools used

To new construction zone activity

**Bridging**

Extension of, testing of and making ideas/ concepts work in new contexts

To other areas of science
To planning of (mainly) instructional science lessons

*Fig. 4.3*  Summary of the features of a cognitive acceleration programme

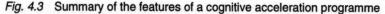

teacher short-circuits construction by supplying the ideas herself the better. If the investigation has been well designed there will be many opportunities within the CZA for students themselves both to take their strategies further and also to encounter (pupil mediated) cognitive conflict as they do so. Alternatively, the teacher may come to a group working in the laboratory and induce the cognitive conflict him/herself. A teacher-mediated example was given earlier in the chapter in the lesson on tubes where the teacher confronts the pupil with an alternative interpretation of the evidence he has presented.

Later in the lesson the teacher may call the whole class together, and invite them to share all the insights and difficulties students in different groups have encountered. This is the occasion where metacognition is doubly helpful. Reflective abstraction and collaborative summary of what has been (just) achieved helps all students to retain and later recall what worked in that context. It is necessary to give things a name so that, later, that name will help students recall the procedure in a new, possibly relevant situation. In both CASE and IE this is where some bridging is also helpful, and would be the other face of metacognition, the mindful abstraction from the immediate context to other possible contexts of application. This is an application of Salomon's High Road.

Finally, in the bottom right hand corner of the diagram is something more specific to the teacher: whether or not the students have achieved bridging, the teacher needs herself to invent and record possible other science learning applications of the output of a CASE lesson, so that when she comes to plan an ordinary instruction lesson she can modify its structure to utilise bridging opportunities offered by the reasoning patterns it involves. On this account, metacognition is not given the role of *producing* enhanced thinking ability, but rather the semantic role of facilitating later access to a strategy that has been achieved (convergent thinking), and assisting in the invention of other applications (divergent thinking).

Now we must turn to the working out of this model in practice.

# Chapter 5

# CASE: The development and delivery of a programme

In this chapter we will describe how the theoretical conclusions to which we have been led were translated into a working curriculum. The project through which this was achieved was called Cognitive Acceleration through Science Education (CASE), funded by the British Economic and Social Research Council (Grant no. C00232179) from September 1984 until August 1987. Michael Shayer was the Project Director, and the full-time researchers were Philip Adey and Carolyn Yates.

## AGE AND SUBJECT CONTEXT

We saw in Chapter 2 that the original Genevan age/stage model of cognitive development appeared to have been rather optimistic in putting the age of the start of formal operational thinking at about 11 years. The CSMS survey (Fig. 2.7) suggested that in fact not more than 5 per cent of 11 year-olds exhibit early formal operational thinking. Nevertheless, this is the age at which secondary schooling starts in Britain and it may be seen as the threshold to higher level thinking for the majority of pupils. Later we will show that there is some physiological justification for believing this, but at the time our choice of age range was as much pragmatic as theoretical. To work with younger pupils would have meant going to 9 year-olds, since a two-year programme was planned and at the end of their 10+ year most pupils transfer from primary to secondary schools. On the basis of the CSMS evidence we were not confident that we could have a marked effect on the promotion of formal operations with 9 year-olds, although the prospect of working in the less constrained atmosphere of primary schools was certainly attractive.

The decision to run the intervention in secondary schools with their separate subject teachers brought us to another decision point. Where would the intervention fit in the school timetable? In approaching a high-school principal with a proposal to introduce a set of activities which might, or might not, help pupils to develop higher order thinking skills one does not want to create extra difficulties by asking him or her to re-write the entire timetable to provide a new space for 'thinking lessons'. This has been a stumbling block for many enthusiasts wishing to introduce into schools general cognitive intervention programmes such as Instrumental Enrichment. A way around this problem is to embed the intervention programme in an existing subject. This is not simply a matter of micro-political expediency. The strategic decision to deliver the intervention through a specific context reduces the initial unfamiliarity factor for teachers and students enabling them immediately to apply new thinking skills within a familiar context. Following successful context-related application, the further step can be taken of generalising (bridging) the reasoning patterns to other contexts.

Accepting that the intervention programme was to be set in a secondary school subject domain, the particular choice of science requires justification. Neither an emphasis on the domain generality of formal operations nor the features which theoretically informed our proposed curriculum materials argued for preference to be given to a particular subject. In Chapter 2 we rejected the notion that science might claim a unique position for the development of general thinking skills but recognised that the work already done in a science context gave it certain pragmatic advantages over other subjects. Adding to this our own familiarity with the foundations of science teaching and the fact that the world of science education has traditionally been rather sympathetic to psychologies of learning, the choice of science as the doorway through which to explore the development of general thinking became a reasonable one.

## DEVELOPMENT OF THE MATERIALS AND EXAMPLES

The CASE project materials were designed to address individually each of the schemata of formal operations and incorporate the principles of concrete preparation, cognitive conflict, construction zone activity, metacognition, and bridging into a set of activities whose context was overtly scientific. The use of the principles in CASE and their origin is shown in Table 5.1.

Table 5.1  Origin of CASE parameters

| CASE parameter | Piaget | Vygotsky/Feuerstein |
|---|---|---|
| Schemata of formal operations | ✓ | |
| Concrete preparation | ✓ | ✓ |
| Cognitive conflict | ✓ | |
| Construction | ✓ | ✓ |
| Metacognition | | ✓ |
| Bridging | | ✓ |

The strategy of selecting activities in the context of science which represent all the formal operational reasoning patterns derives from the view that the probability of affecting the central processor is much increased by using all parts of the psychological spectrum, rather than just one at a time as in the case of some of the research summarised in Chapter 3.

Activities were initially drafted by the research team. The first two activities are devoted to establishing the ideas of *variables*, *values* of variables, and *relationships* between variables. These activities are mainly concrete preparation. For each of the remaining activities we would consider a formal schema, choose a practical problem which could be a source of cognitive conflict, and then devise the necessary concrete preparation. The following examples indicate how the psychological foundations of the course were incorporated in a variety of ways into activities. In references below 'TS' stands for *Thinking Science*, the name under which the activities have been published (Adey *et al*. 1989).

*TS1, Variables*, is based on seeking relationships between variables in simple situations such as the coloured card shapes described under classification in Chapter 2 (p.19). Students discover different sorts of relationships and, importantly, examples where no relationship exists (see Chapter 4, p. 61)

In *TS3, Tubes*, pupils are given small tubes which vary in length, width, and material. They are asked to find out what factors effect the note made when one blows across the tube. A worksheet encourages them to test the tubes in pairs. So far there is no great demand on cognition. As soon as anyone has a hypothesis they bring it to the teacher. Perhaps, 'Thickness makes a difference'. 'Show me!' The student blows across two tubes of different thickness and gets different notes. But the tubes are also of different length. 'What makes you sure it is thickness that effects the note?' Here is the conflict. The simple concrete strategy of comparing two tubes does not, by itself, produce the right answer. The student is encouraged both to try again, and to discuss his findings with others and compare notes (in both senses! ). The discussion encourages metacognition.

In *TS8, The wheelbarrow*, the focus is the schemata of proportionality. Students have a 'wheelbarrow' made of a notched stick. One end of the wheelbarrow rests on a table edge, and a load is hung from one of the notches. The other end of the wheelbarrow is hung from a force meter to measure the lift effort required.

They record and tabulate the *lift* as successive *loads* are added. With about six pairs of values completed, they use a given grid to draw the straight line graph relating lift to load. From this they are asked to make predictions about what the force would be with extra loads which are not available. The first predictions can be read off by simple extrapolation of the graph, but then the graph paper runs out and a concrete strategy is no longer available. This is the point of conflict, where a more sophisticated view of the relationship – that involving the constant ratio of load to effort – has to be invented. Students have to go beyond the concrete support of the graph and construct a more general mathematical model through which they can extrapolate. Cognitive operations on the data must be formalised to achieve a successful solution to the problem.

Metacognition is more a feature of the teacher's strategy introduced through inservice courses than of the printed materials and one example of metacognitive dialogue was given in Chapter 4 (p. 71). Here, one example illustrates how a worksheet can act as a starting point for metacognitive speculation, although in prosecuting the activity the teacher plays an essential role in building on this starting point.

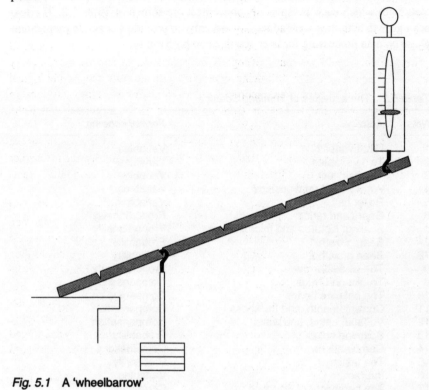

*Fig. 5.1* A 'wheelbarrow'

In *TS21, Classification*, students go through a set of six exercises such as putting animals into groups (according to their own criteria); arranging a variety of foodstuffs on the shelves of a larder, and sorting chemicals by colour and by solubility. Finally, they are asked to consider the classifications that they have done and to reflect on which was the most difficult for them, and why, and which was the easiest, and why. They compare their feelings with other groups, and discuss why some groups found some activities difficult and others found the same ones easy. These are the types of questions which encourage students to reflect on their own thinking strategies, and so helps to externalise them and make them more generally available.

After drafting the activities the researchers themselves taught each of them to two classes of 12 year-olds in a London comprehensive secondary school. This experience helped us to check on timing, apparatus, language, and to some extent on the conceptual appropriateness of the draft material. Following this pre-trial in the 'laboratory' school each activity was revised and duplicated for the main trial. A total of 30 activities, each designed to last about 60–70 minutes, were originally devised, pre-trialed, revised, and duplicated. Titles of the activities, and the schemata with which each is especially concerned, are shown in Table 5.2. The two bean growth activities were added subsequently to provide a concrete preparation phase on data processing for later activities on probability.

Table 5.2   The activities of Thinking Science

| No. | Activity | Formal schema |
|---|---|---|
| 1 | What varies? | Variables |
| 2 | Two variables | Variables |
| 3 | The 'fair' test | Variables |
| 4 | What sort of relationship? | Variables |
| 5 | Roller ball | Variables |
| 6 | Gears and ratios | Proportionality |
| 7 | Scaling: pictures and microscopes | Proportionality |
| 7A | Bean growth 1 | Probability |
| 7B | Bean growth 2 | Probability |
| 8 | The wheelbarrow | Proportionality |
| 9 | Trunks and twigs | Compensation |
| 10 | The balance beam | Compensation |
| 11 | Current, length, and thickness | Compensation |
| 12 | Voltage, amps, and watts | Compensation |
| 13 | Spinning coins | Probability |
| 14 | Combinations | Combinations |
| 15 | Tea tasting | Probability |
| 16 | Interaction | Variables |
| 17 | The behaviour of woodlice | Correlation |
| 18 | Treatments and effects | Correlation |
| 19 | Sampling: fish in a pond | Probability |
| 20 | Throwing dice | Probability |
| 21 | Making groups | Classification |
| 22 | More classifying: birds | Classification |
| 23 | Explaining states of matter | Formal models |
| 24 | Explaining solutions | Formal models |
| 25 | Explaining chemical reactions | Formal models |
| 26 | Pressure | Compound variables |
| 27 | Floating and sinking | Compound variables |
| 28 | Up hill and down dale | Equilibrium |
| 29 | Equilibrium in the balance | Equilibrium |
| 30 | Divers | Compound variables |

The structure of the Thinking Science course can be seen in Fig. 5.2. The circle enclosing the TS activity number indicates the Piagetian level at which most of the lesson proceeds. The vertical lines indicate our estimate of the range from the minimum Piagetian level at which a student is likely to find the lesson profitable, to the upper level towards which the activity is designed to begin moving the student. The bulk of the lesson operates at a lower level than this because of the concrete preparation element when new vocabulary is introduced or previously used vocabulary extended and students become familiar with the apparatus of this activity. The intention is that 90 per cent of the class should understand this phase of the lesson. When cognitive conflict is introduced and the student's attention is directed to a higher level of formal thinking we build on the confidence already established to stretch all students and also to make an only partial understanding at the last phase tolerable. It will be seen that as the course develops, the level at which the lessons operate rises gradually.

In addition, in Fig. 5.2 the structure of the course can be seen in terms of the main strands corresponding to the Piagetian schemata or reasoning patterns. Probability involves both sampling and the use of ratio or proportion where appropriate. Control of variables and correlation are related both to the design of experiments and to interpreting the data gathered in well-designed experiments. These two strands relate more obviously to biology, whereas the strand of ratio, proportion and equilibrium has a more immediate application to the context of the physical sciences. The three lessons labelled 'formal models' are set in the context of chemistry – atoms in relation to changes of state and binary reactions – but are meant to introduce the student to the realisation that many of the models they use in biology, chemistry and physics have a hypothetical, formal, character, even if they are not immediately analysable in terms of reasoning patterns.

## THE MAIN TRIAL SAMPLE

Nine schools representing a variety of environments in England were chosen in consultation with Local Education Authorities' science advisers who were asked to recommend what they considered to be ordinary mixed comprehensive schools typical of their locality. In some cases advisers directed us to schools which they felt would 'do a good job' for us, and in others to schools which they felt were in need of some help. The age range of most of the schools were 11–18 or 12–18 secondary high schools, but two were 9–14 middle schools. A total of 12 classes of pupils in these schools were selected in consultation with heads of science as being of about average ability and in each school a control class was selected that was as like the experimental class as could be judged. In this way there were matched experimental and control classes in each school. Some control classes were taught by the same teacher as the experimental classes and others were taught by different teachers. Four experimental classes (three from the middle schools) were of the 11+ age group (UK year 7, US grade 6) and eight of the 12+ age group (UK year 8, US grade 7). These separate cohorts will be referred to simply as the '11+' and '12+' groups.

All pupils, control and experimental, were given a pre-test of two Piagetian Reasoning Tasks, described in Chapter 2. There were no significant differences

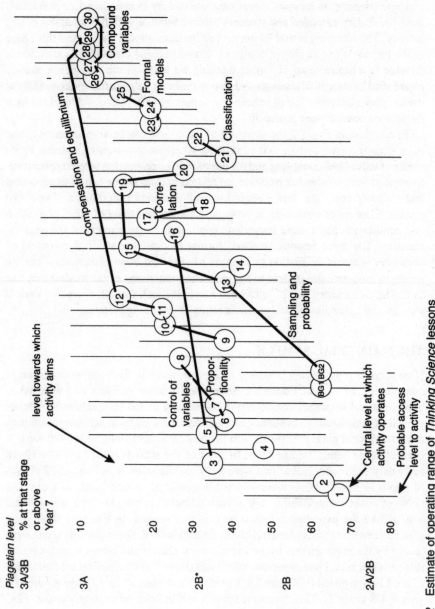

Fig. 5.2 Estimate of operating range of *Thinking Science* lessons

between experimental and control groups in mean levels of cognitive development before the intervention, but the 11+ group was somewhat more able than the 12+ group relative to their age.

## PREPARING THE TEACHERS

It was considered most unlikely that the *Thinking Science* activities would achieve the aim of raising levels of thinking if the teachers did not understand something of the underlying theory on which they were based and we did not expect these psychological foundations to become readily accessible through the printed material alone. Accordingly an inservice teacher education (INSET) programme was devised based on the 'inservice-onservice' model. The inservice element consisted of one day workshops held at the researchers' college base. One such day was held in each of the three terms of the two-year programme, except that one was substituted by a residential weekend. These inservice days consisted of a mixture of theory, practical introduction to the activities and, as the project progressed, feedback from the teachers on difficulties and successes with the activities as written.

The onservice element consisted of project staff visiting the schools. The purposes of these visits were to maintain the enthusiasm of the project teachers, to model some lessons, to participate in some, and on occasion simply to observe and then discuss with the teacher afterwards. In retrospect, the choice of this model of INSET was probably far more important to the subsequent success than we realised at the time. Chapter 9 will be devoted to discussing the implications for INSET generally.

## THE PROGRAMME

The two-year programme was based on the density/duration considerations discussed in Chapter 4. This did not mean that schools were expected to give up their entire science content curriculum for two years. In fact the programme was aimed as an 'intervention' not only in students' cognitive development, but also in the science curriculum. Our proposal was that once every two weeks a *Thinking Science* lesson should be substituted for a regular science lesson (usually a 70-minute period). Typically years 7 and 8 in British schools may have two such lessons per week. We were asking, then, for about 25 per cent of the regular science curriculum to be replaced by the special intervention activities.

Schools were visited and agreed to participate in the project in May and June of 1985. The 12 experimental classes were ready to start to follow the *Thinking Science* programme at the beginning of the new academic year, September 1985. The first INSET day was held early in September, and immediately after that the pre-tests were administered and then the *Thinking Science* teaching programme started.

One school (1 experimental and 1 control class) withdrew after two terms because the style of *Thinking Science* was too teacher-centred for their liking.

Another, working under especially difficult circumstances, failed to deliver the intervention even approximately as planned. The remainder continued with the programme as planned for two academic years, until July 1987. In some cases we had to do some special pleading to ensure that the experimental and control classes, with their teachers, continued as units from the first year to the second year. Nevertheless, there were some movements between classes at the end of the first year, and inevitably there were other changes of pupils over the two-year period.

After the two-year intervention programme, students were no longer maintained in identifiable 'experimental' and 'control' groups, but mixed together as they chose options for the subjects they would continue with. In the case of three of the 11+ classes the end of the intervention coincided with the end of their middle school period, and pupils moved to four different high schools. Wherever they went, we continued to monitor the progress of as many of the ex-experimental and ex-control pupils as we could find for two or three years after the end of the *Thinking Science* intervention programme, until they reached the end of their compulsory schooling period, aged 16 years. We have no reason to suppose that those who moved from the schools in which we were able to trace them for testing, or who missed particular tests, were in any way systematically related to whether they had been 'experimental' or 'control' pupils.

## TEACHING *THINKING SCIENCE*

Something of the flavour of a *Thinking Science* lesson and the ways in which the elements are built in by a good practitioner can be obtained from the following account observed by one of us during an actual lesson in an inner city comprehensive school with a class of 12 year-olds. The lesson is TS5, 'Roller ball', in which balls of various masses, materials, and sizes are used with a track. One ball – the 'target ball' – is placed at the lowest point on the track, and other balls – 'roller balls' – may be rolled on to it from varying heights. The distance that the target ball moves as a result can be measured.

This lesson had a very high density of the type of pupil activity which is most directly linked to the acceleration of their thinking. You could almost reach out and touch Vygotsky's Zone of Proximal Development, as so many pupils were contributing bits and aspects of insight which each could benefit from, each in his own way. This would not have happened without the teacher using skills of classroom management of a high order, different to many skills of good instruction. Apart from the hard intellectual work which the pupils were induced to take part in there was a remarkable social benefit amongst a very varied group of students who in other circumstances might have been difficult to handle. They were well motivated because the activity challenged them intellectually without leaving them floundering and, perhaps more importantly, they had been led to realise the value of learning co-operatively.

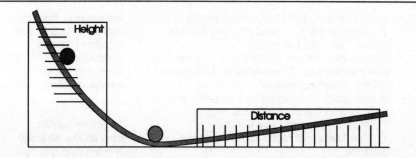

*Fig. 5.3*  Roller ball apparatus

| Time | Dialogue/action | Commentary |
|------|-----------------|------------|
| 0.00 | | Pupils in. Register taken. |
| 0.05 | T calls Ps to front. Apparatus is set up on demonstration bench, eight or nine varied balls on view. T asks Ps what they think they are about to investigate. | |
| | Ps: | 'Weight of balls' |
| | 'Time and distance balls go' | |
| | T intervenes with the more precise language of Roller Ball and Target Ball. She asks Ps what they meant. | So far this has been concrete preparation. Students are being familiarised with the apparatus and the vocabulary that will be used. |
| | Ps: 'Distance Roller Ball travels' | |
| | 'How far Target Balls go' | |
| | 'Distance Target Ball travels' | |
| | T cautions Ps to listen to each other. | |
| 0.10 | T takes glass marble as Target, and offers steel and brass as possible Rollers. Asks pupils 'which'. | |
| | Ps: 'Steel' | |
| 0.15 | T releases steel Roller from top position. Target Ball goes so far that it falls off end of the track. Changes to brass ball as Target and releases a glass marble from lower position. | |
| | Ps: '. . . you dropped them from different positions!' | There is some cognitive conflict here as pupils can |
| | 'not a fair test!' | see that the gross |
| | T: 'Can I make any conclusion from these two experiments?' | changes T is making cannot lead to a fair |
| | Ps: 'No, no!' | test, and yet most |
| | T sends Ps back to workplaces. They are in five working groups of between three and five pupils each. One in each group has the responsibility of reading the worksheet to some of the others and ensuring that meaning is understood. | cannot see clearly what experimental strategy is needed. |
| | The worksheet sets a series of Roller Ball problems concerning the best ball to use | This is construction zone activity. Pupils |

next, after one given test, to investigate the effect of height, mass, etc. The first one is about the effect of height.

Groups discuss well and actively, with very few 'passengers'. T circulates to each group asking probing questions.

In one group Ps have chosen two different balls to drop from two different heights.

T: 'What do you think you will observe?'

P: 'The Target will move about the same distance.'

(He is using a compensation strategy rather than controlling variables.)

T: 'What will that tell you about the effect of height.'

0.25    P: ??

Pupils have worked through the first exercise only. They continue to discuss, while T circulates keeping them on the task.

0.34    T: 'You can have six minutes more.'

0.45    T goes to side of lab and says 'Now we will have your feedback'. Asks group 1 to talk through exercise 1.

Ps: 'Use red marble in high position and yellow marble in the low position . . . only difference is colour, so it is a fair test.'

Group 2Ps: 'Use large steel ball in high and low positions to make fair test.'

Group 3Ps, talking about another problem, comparing the effect of brass and steel balls: 'You should release both from the same position.'

T: 'Why?'

P: Otherwise you don't know whether it's the height or the . . . whether its brass or steel that makes the difference.

T: Which is the input variable and which is the outcome variable?

T then continues the experiment with pupils helping and also with pupils constructing and completing a table for results on the board.

---

are working from the conflict situation and together trying to construct an adequate experimental strategy.

Cognitive conflict here as the strategy chosen by pupils fails to produce a satisfactory solution.

This is reflection of the amount of discussion that is going on about the problem.

They have the idea that they may not use the same ball twice, and assume that colour would make no difference.

Metacognition here as pupils have to think about their solution and justify it. A bridging question as it brings in an idea from an earlier TS lesson.

## BRIDGING OUT OF *THINKING SCIENCE*

The 30 published CASE lessons should be seen as exemplars of an intervention strategy. There is nothing 'magic' about the content of those particular activities and teachers who have used them and who have sufficient curriculum time can and do develop their own interventions based on the *Thinking Science* model. For example, the Glendale (Arizona) Union High School District adopted *Thinking Science* as their grade 9 introductory science course. Schools would typically use two lessons per week to cover one of the published activities and then invent new bridging activities to reinforce the use of the same reasoning pattern. Here is an example of such an activity which Glendale Union teachers developed:

> The reasoning pattern of *compensation* had been the subject of two special activities in the *Thinking Science* curriculum. Now the teachers wanted to invent a new activity which consolidated and built upon this reasoning pattern. They gave their students 100 ml beakers filled with glass balls. Different beakers contained balls of different sizes: small, medium, and large. The concrete preparation phase involves getting students to focus on the variables and notice that the balls have different sizes but the beakers are all the same size. Now the teacher conjures an image of water being thrown on dry earth and being absorbed (bridging from the real world), and asks 'which size balls will allow more water into the beaker?' Pupils try different answers and are asked to defend their ideas. 'Large balls have large spaces between them', say some pupils. Others think 'small balls have many more spaces between them' (construction zone activity). Once the parameters of the problem have been established, pupils measure the volume of water needed to fill the different beakers to the 50 ml mark. The results produce quite a lot of cognitive conflict. They share their findings, reflect on what they had believed before the experiment (metacognition), and are encouraged to provide new explanations in terms of compensation of size of spaces by numbers of spaces (bridging of the reasoning patterns from previous lessons).

We consider that the process of teachers themselves inventing bridging activities of this type is so important that it has been made a key feature of the inservice programmes run to introduce CASE methods to teachers.

In the next chapter, we must examine the evidence we have for the CASE method having any permanent effect on students' cognitive development and academic achievement.

# Chapter 6

# Evaluating the programme

## THE EFFECT OF INTERVENTIONS ON SCHOOL ACHIEVEMENT: A PROBLEM

It is a scandal of the intervention literature, from HeadStart onwards, that although evidence has shown that the interventions have had effect on tests closely related to the intervention methodologies, few appear to have been accompanied by increased general school achievement of more than very modest amounts. Often no difference at all is found in comparison with controls. For example, Barnett and Escobar in an extensive survey of the economic costs and benefits of early intervention (Meisels and Shonkoff 1990) were able to cite only one example of increased school achievement. The Perry preschool programme had resulted in 67 per cent of an ex-preschool group graduating from high school, compared with 49 per cent of a comparable control group. What is the point of so much investment of effort by teacher and student if it did not result in better learning?

In reporting their replication of Feuerstein's IE, Shayer and Beasley (1987) realised, too late, one obvious explanation of this. All interventions hitherto had featured immediate post-tests of achievement, and of varying forms of crystallised intelligence. They confessed sorrowfully:

If one considers both achievement tests and tests of crystallised intelligence, and asks the question 'When did the pupils develop the skills which show on the test-items?' the answer has to be 'Some of them before the intervention even began, and many during the period of the intervention itself'. If one postulates some kind of exponential learning curve still on the rise at the end of an intervention, then only towards the end of the intervention will its overall effect be sufficiently large substantially to modify the path and content of pupils' school learning. Its potential effect on a post-test of achievement given at the immediate end of the intervention will be heavily diluted by pupil experience unaffected by the intervention . . . . *The right way to test the effect of an intervention programme such as IE is on fresh learning experienced by the experimental and control groups after the intervention has finished rather than on standardised tests of achievement.* If this interpretation is correct, it makes one grieve for the studies which have in part been lost, including the one presented in this paper, for lack of understanding of this point.

In addition, for tests of crystallised intelligence, one needs to consider that in the process of item analysis in the original test construction, items which get thrown out are those which reflect idiosyncratic experience rather than general experience. Items which remain in the test will relate to very general skills and knowledge in the culture much of which is not learnt in school specifically. Even if the underlying competence of students has been affected by an intervention – as we argue the fluid intelligence results have shown for IE – it may very well be a couple of years before enough general experience has been re-processed with students' new higher powers to show up on crystallised intelligence test-items. There must *in principle* be a delay for effects to show on such tests. This delay does not apply to tests of school achievement, provided the knowledge and skills they test are specific to the learning which has taken place after the intervention.

## THE CASE PROJECT

In evaluating the effects of the CASE project the lesson of the Shayer and Beasley experience was learned and the test programme designed accordingly. The duration and timing of the treatments, the tests, and the inservice days as applied to experimental and control groups is summarised in Fig. 6.1.

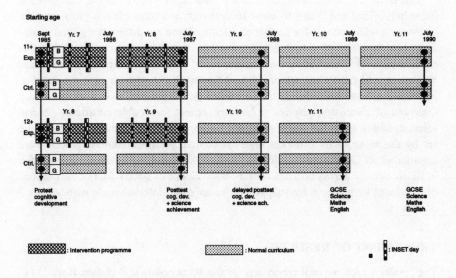

*Fig. 6.1*   Experimental design of the CASE project

**The testing programme**

Testing occasions were:

- *pre-test*, before the intervention began
- *post-test*, immediately after the two-year intervention
- *delayed post-test*, one year after the end of the intervention
- the *General Certificate of Secondary Education* (GCSE) taken two (for those who started at 12+) or three (for those who started at 11+) years after the end of the intervention

The tests of *cognitive development* used were the Piagetian Reasoning Tasks (PRTs) described in Chapter 2, which yield a decimal score on the scale 1 (early preoperational) to 10 (mature formal operational) with a standard error of about 0.4. The particular PRTs used in the trials were:

- **pre-test:**   volume and heaviness, pendulum
- **post-test:**   pendulum, probability
- **delayed post test:**   probability

Where two PRTs were used, the mean score was taken.

*Science achievement* was assessed at post-test by a common achievement test devised by the teachers to be a fair test of the objectives of their science curricula for the previous year. At the delayed test, each school's end of year science test or mean of module tests was used. These tests thus, by definition, covered the objectives of each school's curriculum. Scores were converted to percentages before further treatment.

The *General Certificate of Secondary Education* (GCSE) is the examination taken in England and Wales by most 16 year-olds as a school leaving examination and/or as a selection test for further education. There are different regional examining boards, and within each board a number of syllabus options. Note that this experiment took place before the introduction of a National Curriculum in Britain. Schools would choose the regional board they wished to use for each subject. For instance a school could decide to enter some pupils for one, two, or occasionally three out of chemistry, physics or biology, others for double certificate general science, others again for single general science, and these examinations might be set by the same or by different regional boards. Norm-referenced grades were awarded in all GCSE examinations on a scale A–G and unclassified, eight grades in all, moderated across boards to ensure equivalence of standards. For the purpose of treatment here they were mapped on to an equal-interval scale with values 7 down to 0.

## TREATMENT OF RESULTS

The results which we will report are for the 10 experimental classes (four '11+'

starting in year 7 and six '12+' starting in year 8) in seven schools that continued with the programme, more or less as intended, for a period of two years.

Post and delayed cognitive development scores could be reported simply as raw gains over pre-test scores, comparing control and experimental groups. The common science achievement test could be reported as a comparison between experimental and control means, although this would ignore any difference between starting ability levels as assessed by the pre-test. However, the variety of tests amongst different schools used for the delayed achievement measures and for the GCSE made it impossible to make such simple comparisons. For these measures, the method of *residualised gain scores* was used (Cronbach and Furby 1970).

The method depends on the fact that PRT scores are fair predictors of subsequent academic success. In each school separately (to lessen variation due to differences between examinations taken and differences in school ethos), the pre-PRT score of each pupil in the *control* group is plotted against their subsequent GCSE level. Such a plot is shown in Fig. 6.2. The regression line drawn through the points represents the best prediction one can make of the GCSE grade likely to be achieved by a pupil starting from any given level of cognitive development four or five years previously. If now the same prediction equation is applied to each of the pupils in the *experimental* group, a prediction can be made of the most likely GCSE grade each experimental pupil would obtain if there were *no* systematic difference between control and experimental groups. For example, in Fig. 6.2, the prediction for a student from one school whose Piagetian level was just at the early formal boundary (7.0) on entry in year 8, would be a 'D' grade in science at GCSE four years later.

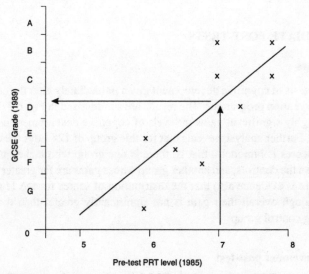

*Fig. 6.2* Example of regression of GCSE grade on a pre-PRT score. Control group from School 11

Finally, we compare each experimental subject's grade predicted on this assumption with the actual grade that they obtained. The difference is the residualised gain score (rg score). For any group of students the mean rg score is a measure of the extent to which their development or learning has been different from the initially matched control group.

For convenience of comparisons, all results will be reported in terms of rg scores. Note that rg scores build in comparison to controls and that by definition the mean rg score of a control group must be zero. A more extended discussion of how this approach relates to the raw data is given in the discussion of 'added value' in Appendix 1.

Results will be presented separately for the two groups, 11+ and 12+ (remember, these represent the ages at which pupils *started* the intervention programme) and separately for boys and girls. For each experimental group, the number of subjects (N), their mean residualised gain score (M), the standard deviation of the rg score ($\sigma$), and the probability that the mean score is significantly different from that of the corresponding control group (p<) will be shown. For significant differences, the effect size (e) is also shown in units of standard deviation of the control group ($\sigma_c$) – see Chapter 3 for a discussion of effect-sizes. The distribution of the rg scores for the experimental group is shown as a histogram.

In many of the distributions we claim evidence of bimodality, that is, that there are two distinct peaks in the distribution of scores. This is based on computing the cumulative chi-squared ($\chi^2$) values for the numbers occurring at each interval compared with those expected on the basis of normal distribution. A sharp rise in the significance of the $\chi^2$ value indicates that a second peak in the distribution is significant.

## 1987 IMMEDIATE POST-TESTS

### PRT post-tests

These are the tests of cognitive development given immediately after the end of the two-year intervention programme. The results are summarised in Fig. 6.3. The 12+ boys made highly significant gains in levels of cognitive development compared with controls. Further analysis reveals that for this group of 12+ boys the distribution of gain scores is bimodal – that is, there is one group who make little or no better gain than the controls, and another group whose gains are far greater than the controls. There is evidence also that the distribution of scores for the 11+ girls is bimodal, although overall their gain is not significantly greater than that of the corresponding control group.

### Science achievement post-test

This was the common science achievement test taken by many of the schools immediately after the intervention. At this point, no significant differences emerged between any of the experimental and control groups, although it should be noted that the experimental group lost about 25 per cent of its science curriculum time to the *Thinking Science* intervention lessons so it may be considered a virtue that their achievement remained at the same level as that of the controls. This result is in accordance with the argument at the beginning of this chapter that it is not reasonable to expect an intervention programme which addresses underlying cognitive functioning to show an immediate effect on academic achievement. It is only after the completion of the intervention that the subjects have the opportunity to apply their newly acquired cognitive skills to new learning.

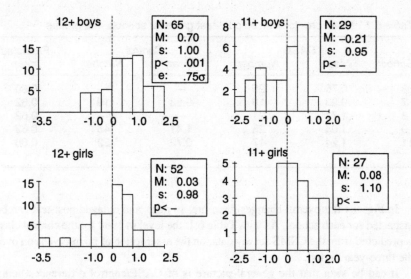

*Fig. 6.3* Post-PRT residualised grain scores for experimental groups: means, etc., and distribution

## 1988 DELAYED POST-TESTS

### PRT delayed post-test

This was the measure of cognitive development as assessed one year after the end of the intervention programme. Here we have to confess that we have left in the research literature a false view of this result. In Shayer and Adey (1992) and Adey and Shayer (1993) it was stated that in the year following the intervention the control students caught up with the ex-CASE students on Piagetian tests, so that the effect of the intervention had then disappeared. In Table 6.1 the mean gains on Piagetian test results from pre-test (1985) to delayed post-test (1988) are listed for each school. In the last column a prediction is added for the expected mean level in 1988, given the control pre-test level, by using the CSMS survey data presented in Fig. 2.7. The problem here is with missing data, since we had no delayed post-test data for the controls in schools 3 and 8. The two large control classes from school 9 swamped the data from the other two schools. But it can be seen that in all except school 3 the CASE class gains were well in excess of those predicted from the CSMS survey data, even in school 9 (1.04 compared with 0.62 predicted). In schools 7 and 11 the controls gains were in line with prediction, so that in general the effect of the CASE intervention was sustained until delayed post-test in 1988. The problem was that the control classes gains in school 9 were also in excess of prediction.

*Table 6.1*    Mean pre- to delayed post-test gains for schools and groups

| School | CASE | | Control | | Predicted |
| | Mean | Number | Mean | Number | mean |
| --- | --- | --- | --- | --- | --- |
| 3 | 0.76 | 25 | — | — | 0.60 |
| 7 | 0.93 | 19 | 0.63 | 19 | 0.62 |
| 8 | 1.71 | 21 | — | — | 0.62 |
| 9 | 1.04 | 25 | 1.41 | 45 | 0.62 |
| 11 | 1.24 | 17 | 0.72 | 22 | 0.66 |

In Fig. 6.4 the overall changes from pre- to post- and delayed post-test can be inspected for each school. As with Table 6.1, the level in 1988 for the control class is predicted from the CSMS survey data, on the assumption of no intervention over the three-year period.

It can be seen that the general picture is of CASE/control differences being maintained until delayed post-test. For school 9 there were in fact negligible gains from post- (1987) to delayed post-test (1988) for boys and girls in the CASE class, and also for the girls in the control classes. The control boys put on a large spurt of 0.9 levels during this period. We have no explanation for this anomalous result, except to note that the teacher of the CASE class did teach one of the control classes.

Further evidence is available from the laboratory school results where Philip Adey and Carolyn Yates trialed all the *Thinking Science* lessons. Here the classes were tested at the end of the first year of the intervention as well, so in Fig. 6.5 it is possible to make the comparison with the control class before and after the CASE intervention. This was a group where the intervention started at the beginning of year 7, with an 11+ group, a year earlier than the schools illustrated in Fig. 6.4.

It can be seen that the CASE group gained steadily on the control class during the period of the intervention. In terms of the CSMS survey shown in Fig. 2.7, the CASE group made a gain of 24 percentile points during this period, while the control followed up the same development curve on which they were at the outset.

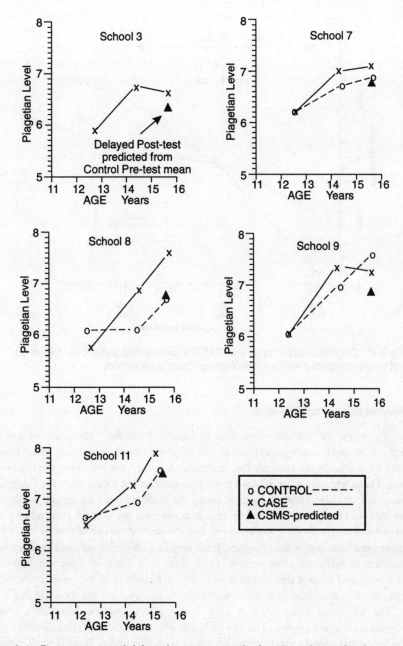

*Fig. 6.4*  Pre- , post- , and delayed post-test results for 12+ cohort schools

After the intervention both continued to develop in parallel along the trajectories that had been reached by 1986.

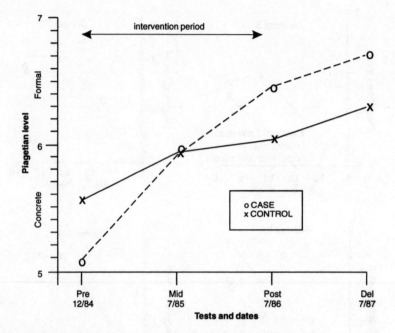

*Fig. 6.5* Cognitive development of CASE experimental group over two and a half years compared with a control group: laboratory school

## Delayed science achievement

At this point the authors were able to benefit from the experience of the IE replication and ask schools to provide end-of-year examination results which tested only what science the students had learned during the year following the intervention. These were the schools' own tests, very different in nature from the Piagetian measures already reported. In most cases the students were no longer in classes which could be identified with previous experimental and control groups but were mixed and taught by different teachers. In the case of three out of four of the '11+' groups students had actually moved from middle to high schools and so were in a completely different environment. Here then is a direct comparison between ex-CASE and control students of their ability to benefit from the same instruction. Results, with examination scores transformed to percentages, are shown in Fig. 6.6.

The 12+ boys again show a very strong effect, and the bimodality noted previously is again evident. The 11+ girls also show a significant effect, confirming the suspicion raised already about an effect with this group. Note that all groups

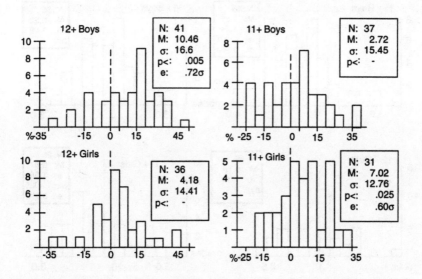

*Fig. 6.6*   Delayed post-science residualised gain scores (%) for experimental groups: means, etc., and distribution

show positive effects, although it does not reach statistical significance for 12+ girls or 11+ boys.

## 1989/90: GCSE EXAMINATIONS

The group of six 12+ classes completed their year 11 (US grade 10) at secondary school and took the GCSE examinations in June 1989 two years after the end of the CASE intervention programme. The 11+ group of three classes took their GCSE in 1990, three years after the end of the intervention programme. We analysed GCSE results for science (amalgamated results for whichever combination of chemistry, physics, biology, and integrated science papers an individual took), mathematics, and English. Results for science are shown in Fig. 6.7.

The effect on the 12+ boys' group is even stronger than in delayed science achievement results reported above. This group averages one grade higher than controls after individual pre-test differences are taken into account. This represents an effect-size of one standard deviation, achieved two years after the end of the CASE intervention programme. The 11+ boys and the 12+ girls show no significant effects but the girls who started the experiment aged 11+ do show a significant effect. Their science grades have been enhanced, compared with controls, by two-thirds of a standard deviation. Thus the hints from earlier data that there was some effect with the 11+ girls has now shown up strongly in externally set and marked national examinations of science achievement *three* years after the end of

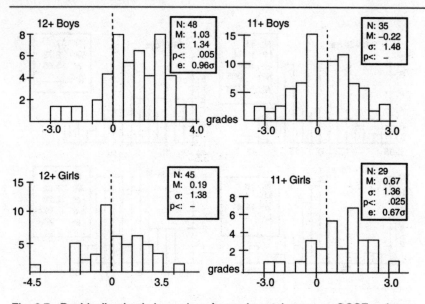

*Fig. 6.7* Residualised gain in grades of experimental group on GCSE: science

the intervention. By any standards this must be counted as a long-term effect. In both of the groups which showed significant effects, bimodality of distribution is again apparent, indicating that some benefited far more than others from the *Thinking Science* experience.

Results from the other subjects throw more light on the underlying psychological model. Fig. 6.8 shows the results for GCSE mathematics. Results follow a similar pattern to those in science, with significant effects achieved in the 12+ boys' and 11+ girls' groups. The former result is weaker than that for science and is consistent with a possible 'knock-on' effect of the mathematical nature of many of the *Thinking Science* activities on achievement in mathematics itself, although the longevity is again remarkable. For the 11+ girls the effect is stronger than for science (over $0.7\sigma$), as well as being longer lasting even than for the 12+ group. This could be taken as evidence for the effect of the intervention on general underlying cognition. For both groups there is again evidence of bimodality of distribution of gains.

For a completely different domain, we turn to the GCSE English data. Before presenting results, it is worth looking at some tasks typically required for GCSE English:

1. A tape recording of some dialogue is played twice and a transcript provided. Students are asked to write assessments of some of the characters portrayed, to describe the views of one of them on a particular issue discussed in the dialogue, and to write their own response to these views.

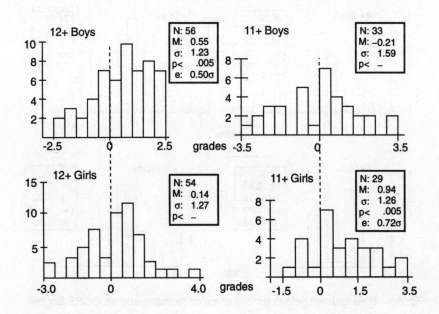

*Fig. 6.8*  Residualised gain in grades of experimental group on GCSE mathematics

2.  Three extracts from guide books describing the same place written in different styles are presented. The student is asked to write two pieces in different genres: one describing the place from an historical perspective, and one providing technical information useful for a group making a school visit to the place.
3.  A free composition of about 600 words for which one hour is allowed. A choice of one out of five topics is given and each is stimulated by a title, an opening sentence, a picture, or the topic of one of the earlier questions. Assessment includes a consideration of planning and drafting as well as of the finished product.

From this brief description, it will be seen that required skills include analysis and comprehension as well as imagination, creativity, and style. Enhanced achievement in English assessed in this way following an intervention set in a science context would look like far-transfer of an effect from one domain to another very different from it. The experimental groups' residualised gain in grades on GCSE English is shown in Fig. 6.9.

These results show significant effects in three out of the four groups. As before, there are effects in the 12+ boys and the 11+ girls although rather weak in the former. Additionally, there is an effect in the 12+ girls' group. Even the one group which shows no overall effect, the 11+ boys, shows very marked bimodality of

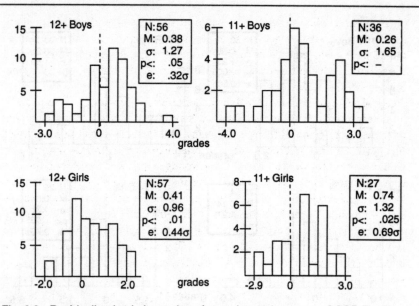

*Fig. 6.9*  Residualised gain in grades of experimental group on GCSE English

distribution and would have shown a significant effect if just one of two very low-scoring individuals had scored at the average for the group.

In concluding this section, there are a few general features of all of the results worth noting:

• Bimodality: It seems clear from the distributions of gain scores that some pupils from the 11+ and 12+ groups, boys and girls, have made great gains in achievement compared with controls, while others have made little or no gain. Even in those tests where the greatest mean gains have been achieved this can often be interpreted in terms of two subgroups: one, consisting of perhaps one-third of the group, making gains of two standard deviations or more while the remainder make little or no greater gain than the controls. Investigation of these high gainers reveals no systematic commonalities in their origins or other characteristics that can be accessed. One possibility is that the whole *Thinking Science* approach suited some students better than it did others and that within each class it was those who became cognitively engaged who gained the most benefit. Unfortunately, the design of the experiment and limitations of time and money did not allow us to carry out the in-depth classroom observations and interviews with pupils that might have elucidated this suggestion further.

• The effects observed were not restricted to one or two classes but were spread across all experimental classes. Thus the effects cannot be ascribed to one or two exceptional classes or teachers.

• Those who made the greatest gains in academic achievement were not confined either to those who started from a low level and might therefore be thought to have much to make up nor to those who were more able to start with and so might have been considered to be 'ready' for the development of formal operations. High gainers came from the full range of starting abilities (Adey and Shayer 1993).

- Age and gender differences: That the major effects were with 11+ girls and 12+ boys may tempt one to suggest that there is a critical period for the development of formal operations as there is for many other cognitive and psycho-motor functions. On this argument, the well established earlier maturation of girls would account for the fact that it is the younger girls and the older boys who show the most marked effects. However there are a number of confounding factors which undermine confidence in such an explanation. As well as their age difference our '11+' and '12+' groups differed from one another in their general ability (the younger ones being somewhat more able) and in the types of schools in which they received the intervention. The younger group were mostly in middle schools where there is a strong class-teacher structure. The 12+ group were all in high schools organised around subject teachers. Perhaps the former provides a social environment more conducive to girls' personal response. The critical period argument cannot be rejected out of hand but further work would be needed to give it credibility. We will return to this issue in Chapters 8 and 10.

## INTERPRETATION

On the face of it, the evidence presented of long-term far-transfer of the effect of the intervention, set in a science context, to enhanced achievement in English two and three years later supports the hypothesis of a general cognitive processor which can be positively influenced by appropriate intervention strategies set in the context of the ordinary curriculum.

We should, however, consider alternative explanations, starting with the idea of *confidence*. The suggestion is sometimes made that the intervention has boosted the confidence of students in their own abilities, and that this in turn improved learning across domains. There are empirical and theoretical objections to this 'explanation'. Empirically one would expect the strongest effect of confidence on test scores to be immediately after the intervention, when pupils felt most 'boosted' by being told how clever they were. In fact the most striking results do not occur until a year or more after the intervention during which time previously experimental pupils are not differentiated in any way from previously control students. The theoretical objection is that the notion of confidence is never operationalised and no mechanism is offered to link confidence with enhanced achievement. Without such a mechanism the global notion of 'confidence' remains vacuous as a causal explanation for improved learning. Any mechanism proposed would necessarily involve some sort of cognitive model which takes us back to where we started. So the confidence 'explanation' is not an explanation at all.

Another explanation proposed for the effect on language is that of independent language development. It is suggested that while the *Thinking Science* programme was set in a science context it encouraged reasoned discussion amongst pupils exploring the meaning of new vocabulary in the search for explanations of physical events. It is then supposed that such linguistic activity had a permanent effect on linguistic development and it is this which results in improved English scores. The argument here is the domain-specific one that the intervention programme affected scientific, mathematical, and linguistic capabilities at the same time in parallel with one another unlinked by any central processing mechanism. The evidence does not allow one to reject this explanation outright but to science teachers-turned-psychologists who in this project worked through science teachers and the science curriculum it seems unlikely that our intervention directly influenced language behaviour more effectively than language teachers and language curricula (which of course were common to experimental and control groups) did.

A more subtle variant of this argument (Shayer and Adey 1993) is that the CASE intervention affected more in the students than is revealed by their performance on Piagetian tests. This can be explored by considering the relationship between the gains in cognitive development during the intervention period and the subsequent gains to GCSE. Of the 11+ girls group 19 out of 29 CASE students attained an rg score of more than one standard deviation in one or more GCSE subjects. In Table 6.2 these students are divided into two columns according to whether their rg scores at the post-test PRT were greater or less than one standard deviation.

*Table 6.2*    Numbers of subjects gaining higher than expected GCSE grades (1990) related to Piagetian gains at post-test (1987): 11+ girls

| GCSE subjects with rg score > 1σ | CASE | | Control | |
|---|---|---|---|---|
| | Post-test PRT rg score > 1σ | Post-test PRT rg score < 1σ | Post-test PRT rg score > 1σ | Post-test PRT rg score < 1σ |
| Science + Maths + English | 5 | 0 | 0 | 1 |
| Science + English | 1 | 0 | 0 | 0 |
| Science + Maths | 1 | 2 | 0 | 2 |
| Science only | 2 | 3 | 0 | 0 |
| Maths + English | 0 | 2 | 1 | 0 |
| Maths only | 0 | 1 | 1 | 3 |
| English only | 0 | 2 | 0 | 1 |
| Totals | 9 | 10 | 2 | 7 |

Science appears in all of the nine entries in the first column, so increased Piagetian level is a *sufficient* condition for higher-than-expected performance in science. This was the evidence for a causal relation which had been looked for. However, high Piagetian gain was not a *necessary* condition: five girls in the second column had high science rg scores. There seems to be another pattern of effects for both English and mathematics, with probably equal numbers in the two alternative groups. For girls at least, high performance on mathematics (five results in right-hand column) and science may be related to the language skills which they share with English, as well as from the kind of thinking which is assessed by the Piagetian tests. Table 6.2 also shows light on the bimodality noted earlier. Although only about 40 per cent of the CASE girls had rg scores above one standard deviation in any one subject – compared to 16 per cent expected by chance (see Table 6.3) – 66 per cent of girls had rg scores above one standard deviation on at least one subject. Thus the bimodality of the results was not simply due to the CASE style suiting a minority of students.

*Table 6.3*  Comparison of percentages of CASE and control students attaining rg scores greater than 1σ at GCSE: 11+ girls

| Subject | % with > 1 σ rg score in GCSE subjects | | Difference | |
| --- | --- | --- | --- | --- |
| | *CASE* | *Control* | *t* | *p* |
| Science | 48 | 18 | 2.4 | <.01 |
| Maths | 38 | 19 | 1.9 | <.05 |
| English | 37 | 13 | 2.1 | <.025 |

Sample size for each group approximately 29

A comparable analysis for the 12+ boys shows a somewhat different pattern which is probably a true sex differential. In Tables 6.4 and 6.5 the CASE and control groups are compared side-by-side. Here high Piagetian gain is a sufficient condition for high performance on science *or* mathematics. Of the ex-CASE boys, 63 per cent achieved rg scores more than 1σ on at least one subject, compared with 19 per cent for the controls. Of the ex-CASE students, 53 per cent achieved rg scores more than 1σ on Science, compared with 17 per cent for the controls. Although the ex-CASE boys' results were significantly higher than the controls for English as well, the causative relation between increased achievement in science and mathematics and the previous effect on Piagetian post-test seems far clearer than was the case for the 11+ girls. It can be seen from Table 6.4 that there is no significant difference between CASE and controls for the 12+ boys who achieved less than one standard deviation rg score at post-test. Only if the ex-CASE boys had large effects at post-test on the Piagetian tests was their subsequent achievement greater than the controls.

In Tables 6.6 and 6.7 the corresponding pattern of results for the 12+ girls can be inspected. Here there were no significant differences between CASE and control students on the Piagetian post-test, and yet there are substantial differences between the groups in GCSE achievement. In Table 6.6 – in strong contrast to the boys'

*Table 6.4*   Numbers of subjects gaining higher than expected GCSE grades (1989) related to Piagetian gains at post-test (1987): 12+ boys

| GCSE subjects with rg score > 1σ | CASE | | Control | |
|---|---|---|---|---|
| | Post-test PRT rg score > 1σ | Post-test PRT rg score < 1σ | Post-test PRT rg score > 1σ | Post-test PRT rg score < 1σ |
| Science + Maths + English | 8 | 2 | 1 | 2 |
| Science + English | 1 | 2 | 0 | 0 |
| Science + Maths | 3 | 2 | 0 | 2 |
| Science only | 5 | 2 | 0 | 2 |
| Maths + English | 0 | 1 | 0 | 0 |
| Maths only | 5 | 1 | 2 | 2 |
| English only | 0 | 3 | 0 | 2 |
| Totals | 22 | 13 | 3 | 10 |

*Table 6.5*   Comparison of percentages of CASE and control students attaining rg scores greater than 1σ at GCSE: 12+ boys

| Subject | % with > 1σ rg score in GCSE subjects | | Difference | |
|---|---|---|---|---|
| | CASE | Control | t | p |
| Science | 53 | 17 | 3.9 | <.001 |
| Maths | 39 | 13 | 3.2 | <.01 |
| English | 36 | 15 | 2.6 | <.01 |

Sample size for each group approximately 58

results – there is no difference in achievement between ex-CASE and control students whose rg scores at Piagetian post-test were above one standard deviation. As with the 11+ girls' results shown in Table 6.2, there is a pattern of higher achievement in mathematics, English and science which is not correlated with Piagetian post-test results.

This suggests that as well as the intended intervention effect of increasing science (and other subjects) achievement through higher-level cognition, school achievement was affected for the girls through factors which do not show up on Piagetian tests. It may be that the Vygotskyan element of the CASE intervention, in addition to contributing to the Piagetian gains, assisted particularly the girls in using language as an active element of learning. The hypothesis is that the extra experience of collaborative discussion has born fruit not just in English itself, but also in increased confidence in approaching mathematics as a language. This in its turn suggests that a simple central processor model may not be enough, on its own, to account for the data. One could suggest, speculatively, that the Piagetian account

*Table 6.6*    Numbers of subjects gaining higher than expected GCSE grades
(1989) related to Piagetian gains at post-test (1987): 12+ girls

| GCSE subjects with rg score > 1σ | CASE | | Control | |
|---|---|---|---|---|
| | Post-test PRT rg score > 1σ | Post-test PRT rg score < 1σ | Post-test PRT rg score > 1σ | Post-test PRT rg score < 1σ |
| Science + Maths + English | 4 | 3 | 2 | 2 |
| Science + English | 0 | 3 | 0 | 1 |
| Science + Maths | 0 | 0 | 1 | 0 |
| Science only | 1 | 0 | 2 | 0 |
| Maths + English | 0 | 3 | 0 | 0 |
| Maths only | 0 | 2 | 1 | 1 |
| English only | 0 | 4 | 0 | 2 |
| Totals | 5 | 15 | 6 | 6 |

*Table 6.7*    Comparison of percentages of CASE and control students attaining
rg scores greater than 1σ at GCSE: 12+ girls

| Subject | % with > 1σ rg score in GCSE subjects | | Difference | |
|---|---|---|---|---|
| | CASE | Control | t | p |
| Science | 21 | 14 | 0.9 | n. s. |
| Maths | 23 | 12 | 1.45 | <.0.10 |
| English | 33 | 21 | 2.5 | <.01 |

Sample size for each group approximately 54

is sufficient for the right brain aspect of development and learning, but that to
account for the left brain aspect of thinking current models coming from
neuropsychology need also to be considered. Some evidence from brain-growth
data will be presented in Chapter 8 (p. 142).

## A lag-effect on girls' science achievement

One rather curious feature of the data is especially well illustrated by the 11+ girls.
In common with other groups, they showed no effect in science achievement at
post-test. No overall effects were observed in the post-intervention Piagetian
measure nor in the delayed science test, although some bimodality was noted in
each. Only three years after the intervention programme do significant overall
effects become apparent. Correlation studies show that the GCSE gains, at least for
science and mathematics, are linked to cognitive growth during the intervention
period. Why did the effect take so long to appear?

It is as though the intervention programme sowed a seed of success which took time and the influence of routine instruction to mature. This may be related to the often observed widening of the gap between the most able and the least able throughout the period of schooling and is the obverse of the tendency of the unsuccessful, least able, pupils to fall increasingly far behind their peers as the years pass. The cognitive acceleration programme seems to have lifted some pupils on to a cognitive developmental track of a steeper slope such that the distinction between them and their control group peers becomes increasingly apparent over the years.

## FURTHER EVIDENCE

The evidence presented and analysed above relates to what should properly be called the CASE II project since there had been a precursor, an exploratory CASE I project. There are two further sources of evidence related both to gender/age differences and to the bimodality found in CASE II. It has to be remembered that the CASE II research was closer to being a primary effect study than a replication study (see Shayer 1992). In order to find out whether the method worked at all it was essential to adopt an experimental/control group design within each school so that each school had only one class receiving the CASE treatment. This approach is not optimal in terms of how schools operate. It is far better if the whole of a department adopts a new approach so that each teacher benefits from the experience of all the others. With only one class there is a greater possibility that the effect of the method is confounded with idiosyncratic teacher effects. CASE III was a follow-up project (also funded by the ESRC, Grant No. R000 23 2223) conducted in a few schools in Cambridgeshire designed to investigate in much greater depth than in CASE II the workings of the CASE method. Evidence from CASE III points to effects that can be obtained when a whole science department adopts the methods. A completely different type of replication was carried out in two primary schools in Korea, from where evidence was obtained about the effectiveness of CASE methodology in a culture (Korean) and school arrangement (primary) very different from the original CASE II project. Some results of each of these investigations follow.

### Parkside School

One of the CASE III Cambridge schools, Parkside, adopted the CASE approach for all 105 of their year 7 (grade 6) entrants. Initially all students were given Piagetian pre-tests in order (a) to get a measure of the range of the intake and (b) to serve as a reference-point for the school to monitor the effects of using *Thinking Science* over a period of two years, and then subsequently. The distribution of the school intake (Table 6.8) shows that the mean level of Parkside pupils was just above the national average (about the 55th percentile), but that this was more

*Table 6.8*   Range in Piagetian levels in schools' 1989 intake (cumulative percentages)

| Stage | 11+ distributions | |
| --- | --- | --- |
| | National Survey (1975) | Parkside |
| 3A and above (formal) | 8.3 | 4.9 |
| 2B* Concrete generalisation | 34.1 | 28.4 |
| 2B Mature concrete | 64.3 | 71.6 |
| 2A/2B | 87.9 | 95.1 |
| 2A Early concrete | 95.8 | 99.0 |

because they were lacking in low-ability children, rather than having more high-ability children.

The science department had a policy of teaching a general science course for all in mixed-ability classes in the first three years through modules taught by subject-specialists. This meant that in each of years 7 and 8 each class changed teachers five times as they moved from module to module. Four introductory *Thinking Science* lessons were taught by all teachers initially, and thereafter the activities were distributed in relation to the subject matter being taught within the modules. Thus all students received the CASE approach from all five teachers. This is bound to equalise any differences which may depend upon each teacher's particular style.

It was then possible to make comparisons of the September 1989 intake at the end of their year 8 in July 1991 with (a) the CSMS national survey results, using the representative survey as an external control and (b) the results of the July 1990 year 8 who had had none of the CASE lessons and so acted as an internal control for the school.

Cumulative percentages are given in Table 6.9 for boys and girls separately. The 1990 year 8 figures indicate that in relation to the National Survey they were about at the 60th percentile – marginally more able than the 1991 year 8 at entry in 1989, but the difference is no larger than expected from normal year to year fluctuation.

The general intention of CASE-related intervention is to increase the proportion

*Table 6.9*   Range in Piagetian levels of students at the end of year 8 (age 13+) (cumulative percentages)

| Stage | National Survey (1975) | | Parkside 1990 | | Parkside 1991 | |
| --- | --- | --- | --- | --- | --- | --- |
| | Boys | Girls | Boys | Girls | Boys | Girls |
| 3B | 5.7 | 5.7 | 7.4 | 5.6 | 19.2 | 22.9 |
| 3A | 19.9 | 20.8 | 22.2 | 27.8 | 59.6 | 70.8 |
| 2B* | 42.4 | 41.6 | 44.4 | 63.9 | 82.7 | 89.6 |
| 2B | 64.2 | 63.8 | 88.9 | 91.7 | 100 | 100 |

of children with access to formal operational thinking by the beginning of year 9, to increase the probability of their next three years' learning leading to high achievement. Roughly speaking, Parkside appears to have increased the proportion of early formal (3A) thinkers from about 25 per cent to about 65 per cent. In the CASE II project gains like this were found to be strongly predictive of GCSE grades of C or above three years later.

The effect-size of the intervention on the Piagetian tests was $1.34\sigma$ by comparison with the norms of the national survey or $1.1\sigma$ by comparison with the previous year's students. In relation to the CASE II results for the 11+ cohort we see here that, yes, the girls also were affected more than the boys (an increase for the girls, relative to the CSMS survey, of 50 per cent showing early formal thinking or above compared with 40 per cent for the boys) but, unlike the CASE II results, the effect on the boys was large also.

**The Korean CASE replication**

The last year of primary school in Korea is grade 6 (UK year 7, when most students in Britain are in their first year of secondary school). The Korean education system shows a strong American influence since many of the trainers of teachers have themselves had periods of education in the USA. The Korean primary school teacher takes responsibility for all the lessons of a grade class for one year but subjects are taught formally with, for instance, one hour of Korean followed by one hour of mathematics, and so on through the day. They normally receive four science lessons per week.

The science professors at Inchon Teachers College wished to see whether the CASE approach might benefit children in the last two years of primary schools. They arranged for students in two schools to be given an accelerated one-year programme of 26 of the 30 *Thinking Science* lessons. This meant that one CASE lesson was given, instead of a regular science lesson, almost every week of the 34-week school year. In one school the experiment was tried in both grade 5 (mean age at entry 10/4) and grade 6 (mean age at entry 11/4), and in the other in grade 6 only. For each CASE class there was a control class of 50 children of equivalent range of ability who followed the normal science curriculum. Each pair of children sat at one table, well provided with the apparatus as described in *Thinking Science*. The teachers were well supported by inservice training, including weekly visits in their own school by Inchon staff. Both experimental and control classes received the same testing schedule.

Students were given pre- and post-tests consisting of:

- a group-administered Piagetian test *Volume and Heaviness* as used in CASE II
- a school-based test of science achievement which was largely of science knowledge
- Raven's matrices
- a widely used Korean test of science process skills.

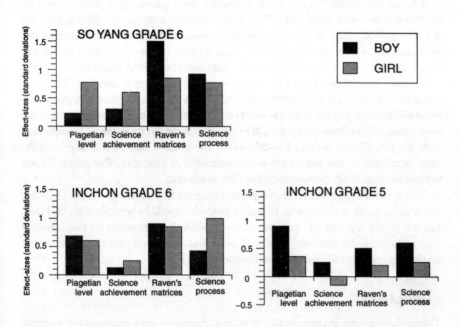

*Fig. 6.10* Residualised gain scores in standard deviation units from two Korean schools on four tests

Raven's matrices was added to the testing schedule as a measure of fluid intelligence which was independent of the Piagetian theory-base.

Figure 6.10 summarises the results in terms of effect-sizes. In the two grade 6 classes the gender variations from class to class can be seen. None of the effect-sizes for science achievement were statistically significant, with the exception of So Yang girls. Otherwise, the cut-off point for statistical significance was an effect-size of approximately $0.4\sigma$. The boy-girl *difference* for Piagetian level – $0.25\sigma$ – was just not statistically significant for grade 6, but a mean effect-size of $0.70\sigma$ for girls and $0.45\sigma$ for boys does support the differences shown for Parkside pupils of the same starting age.

The results for Raven's matrices for the grade 6 children are very striking and provide additional evidence for a general effect on the 'central processor'. For boys the mean effect-size was $1.2\sigma$, and for girls $0.85\sigma$. For reasons argued previously the effect on science process skills – a combined mean of $0.77\sigma$ for Grade 6, and $0.43\sigma$ for Grade 5 – would be expected as these are here-and-now capacity rather than knowledge which may have been gained before the intervention produced much effect on learning. Again, the results favour girls and in this case the difference between a mean for grade 6 of $0.91\sigma$ for girls, and $0.63\sigma$ for boys is statistically significant.

Effects for grade 5, except for Piagetian level gains, were smaller and all favoured boys rather than girls. This, taken together with the CASE II results for the 11+ cohort and the Parkside results, suggests the beneficial 'window' for intervention for girls may be just after grade 5 – that is from 11½ years on, but too much should not be read into the results from one class of 50 students.

Finally, inspection of the Piagetian test results shows that although there was some gain in the relative proportion of CASE students using formal operations, the main differences produced by the intervention were in the relative increase in the proportion of children moving to the concrete generalisation level. Comparison with the CSMS norms from Fig. 2.7 shows the grade 6 sample moving from the 46th percentile at pre-test to the 62nd percentile at post-test. The grade 5 class moved from the 56th percentile to the 79th percentile.

The evidence from the Korean replication seems to indicate that a use of CASE methods by grade teachers with 10 and 11 year-olds could be beneficial for children, but we would recommend that the more cognitively demanding of the *Thinking Science* lessons be removed and fresh activities generated more oriented to the concrete generalisation/early formal border (see Fig. 5.2).

## CONCLUSION

Taken together the evidence offered in this chapter is very encouraging to those who reject the idea of intelligence as a fixed potential and who believe that educational intervention rooted in well established theories of cognitive development can have long-term and replicable effects on young adolescents' academic achievement. Although the results do not present us with a perfectly clear-cut picture of what works, when it works, and how it works, they do provide a real indication of possibilities.

# Chapter 7

# Implications for models of the mind

In the last chapter we presented findings from a number of applications of one intervention project which has delivered good evidence of increased school achievement subsequent to its use. The results show that the delivery of an intervention programme based on notions of cognitive conflict, construction, and metacognition can produce long-term far-transfer effects in students' achievement and that the short-term effects, at least, are replicable. However, as soon as one starts to propose explanations for the results in terms of cognitive structure and modification one is starting the process of interpretation and, as all good constructivists acknowledge, interpretation must be made through a particular set of theoretical spectacles. No apology is due for this. The continued use of a pair of spectacles continually tests them. As long as they improve your vision and enable you to explain what you have seen and to plan action which is fruitful they remain useful and grow in validity as interpreters of reality. When your theoretical spectacles fail to interpret the world reliably and you start to bump into unexpected results then the time has come to seek modified lenses or, in extreme cases, to discard the spectacles altogether and try a completely new perspective from which to view reality.

## CAN THE PIAGETIAN MODEL STILL BE USED?

It will be clear from preceding chapters that our viewpoint is significantly influenced by a Piagetian perspective. The Piagetian model has been found satisfactory in predicting students' ability to learn science and, more importantly, in planning a teaching approach which has long-term beneficial effects by substantially raising students' academic achievement. Nevertheless, one must accept that difficulties with Piaget's theory have been raised by several authors during the 1970s to the point where some believe that Piaget's work has been finally discredited. We believe this view to be wrong, as wrong as to say that Galileo was discredited because Newton later dealt with difficulties which he had failed to address. We will deal with the main difficulties in a similar spirit: that is, some of them are genuine difficulties requiring further clarification of theory, and others arise from misunderstanding, inadvertent or wilful as the case may be.

Following publication of the CSMS data there was a spate of criticisms which may be exemplified by the following, from White (1988):

> While these insights of Piaget are powerful, it is unfortunately easy to convert them to a rigid system in which people are thought to belong to particular stages at particular ages, and in which no concern need be given to supplying them with experiences that may help them form advanced ways of thinking. It can be interpreted as a prescription against exposing young children to abstractions, and so can lead to an impoverished curriculum.
>
> (p. 82)

Such criticisms were perhaps understandable at the time, although we believe them to have been misguided even then. We hope now that our concentration on interventionist strategies in the present account will have reassured such critics of our credentials in the business of intellectual stimulation.

There were also some criticisms of the form 'stages = labelling, I don't like labelling, ergo stages must be wrong', which are unhappy mixtures of misunderstanding of the theory and prejudice arising from a particular social belief system. Such a position cannot be dealt with rationally and we will not attempt to do so. Of considerably more import are psychologically based questionings of the Piagetian paradigm, and these we will address in more detail.

### Wason and Johnson-Laird and Piaget's logical model

In 1972, in a book called *Psychology and Reasoning*, Wason and Johnson-Laird put into circulation what purported to be a proof that Piaget's theory was untenable. Their evidence came from results obtained by giving what has come to be known as the selection task (AD47) to psychology undergraduates, graduates, and professors. Subjects are shown four cards (Fig. 7.1). They are told that the cards have letters on one side and numbers on the other. They are then given the rule: 'If there is a vowel on one side of the card, then there is an even number on the other side' and are told to test whether the rule applies to the set of cards they have been shown. They are asked to identify only those cards they need to turn over to test the rule.

Most subjects, even the logic professors, fail to supply the correct answer which is card A and card 7. The reason card 4 does not need inspection is that the rule does not forbid there being a consonant on the other side. Likewise the D could be

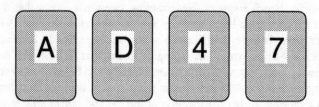

*Fig. 7.1*   The four-card test

backed either by an odd or even number, and the rule could still apply, but if either A is backed by an odd number or the 7 is backed by a vowel the rule is wrong in this set. It is particularly rare for subjects to spot that the card 7 is essential to the test.

The relation between the cards and the rule can be modelled exactly by the symbolic logic of propositions and the correct strategy deduced. Since even professors of logic, so Wason argued, have been known to fail the test, then any model of thinking of adolescents based on symbolic logic must be wrong. Piaget based his interpretation of adolescents' thinking on symbolic logic. Ergo, Piaget was wrong. The problem with this argument is that although Piaget described formal operations in terms of logical operations the variables which were to be operated upon always had some reference to the real world. In AD47 there is no semantic information on the relation between the letters and the numbers, other than being placed on opposite sides of the cards. They are just arbitrary symbols. Thus it is impossible for the subject to conceptualise what reality conditions might need specifying for the rule to be true or false and the type of thinking required is both formal operational and totally abstracted from reality.

Part of Wason and Johnson-Laird's argument depends on the use of a mistranslation. They claim that Piaget identified thinking with the propositional calculus as did Boole (1854) with his Laws of Thought. But Piaget did not write 'reasoning is nothing more than the propositional calculus itself' (Inhelder and Piaget 1958:305). He wrote 'le raisonnement n'est que le calcul comme tel que comportent les opérations propositionelles' (Inhelder and Piaget 1955:270). Smith (1987) translates this as, 'reasoning is nothing more than the calculus *comprised by/embodied in* the propositional operations'. A fine distinction, but on such fine distinctions do valid or invalid interpretations depend. It is the difference between using propositional logic as a convenient algebraic model of thinking, and identifying thinking with the model itself in a Boolean way. '$L_1/L_2 = W_2/W_1$' is an algebraic model, but needs to be 'read back' into the specifics of the balance beam to have meaning. Likewise with Piaget. Inhelder and Piaget (1958) make this quite clear:

> the discipline which deals with constructing a theory of mental operations by means of symbolic calculus . . . would use the algebra of symbolic logic as an analytic instrument in the same way that mathematical physics now makes use of the techniques and notations of mathematics. It would remain a branch of psychology, as mathematical physics is a branch not of mathematics but of physics.
>
> (p. 271)

More important is Wason and Johnson-Laird's misinterpretation of Piaget's description of formal operational thinking in itself. Unlike the AD47 test, Piaget's theory was never context-independent. Not only were all the investigations conducted within specific contexts, varied according to the underlying reasoning patterns, but Wason and Johnson-Laird's apparently clinching objection (1972: 193), that 'formal operational thought is . . . specific to a wide variety of tasks in which a causal and a logical analysis coincide', is merely an acceptable description. Each of these contexts were intended to allow the child to gather sufficient information within which to reason:

> Il ne faut pas perdre de vue, en effet, que même au stade III le sujet commence par classer les données, par les mettre en relation, etc., avant de traduire cette structuration concrète préalable (et toujours indispensable) en une structuration propositionelle.
>
> (Inhelder and Piaget 1955:263)

> Moreover, it is important to remember that even at stage III the subject begins by classifying the data, by relating them, etc. ; in other words, one must keep in mind that a concrete structuring of the data is an indispensable prerequisite of the propositional structure.
>
> (Inhelder and Piaget 1958:298)

That is, formal operations only operate on a situation that has first been described by the subject in terms of concrete models of seriation, classification, the number scale and so on. For example, the operation of implication is described by Piaget in his *Traité de Logique* (1949) where he prepared the model which later would be used to interpret Inhelder's experiments, as:

> Implication: $(p \supset q)$. If the conjunctions $(p.q)$, $(-p.q)$ and $(-p.-q)$ are true while $p.-q$ is false, we therefore have implication in the asymmetric sense 'p implies q':
>
> $$(p \supset q) = (p.q) \lor (-p.q) \lor (-p.-q)$$
>
> In classification terms implication corresponds to the inclusion P>Q, given that the class (P–Q) is empty.
> *example*: If p = 'x is a Mammal (P)' and q = 'x is a Vertebrate (Q)', then there are three cases which are true: PQ (mammals which are vertebrates), –PQ (vertebrates which are not mammals), and -P-Q (those which are neither mammals nor vertebrates). But the class P–Q is null because there are no mammals which are not vertebrates: the class P is thus included in Q, whence $p \supset q$ by exclusion of p.-q.
>
> (Piaget 1949:233, our translation)

Thus for Piaget, while the propositional calculus can be handled as a calculus in non-contextual form, his use of it as an explanatory model is invariably contextualised. It can be seen at once that AD47 is not an expression of this.

Lawson (1989) gave AD47 to groups of students who he had previously assessed as being either concrete or formal operational. As usual, all found it very difficult. He then gave a very small amount of instruction explaining the correct answer to this particular problem and thus provided the concrete experience upon which a formal operation could be performed. Some of the students benefited from this instruction and were subsequently able to solve parallel problems with ease while others made no sense of the instruction and continued to find the problems difficult. What distinguished these two groups? Those who understood the problem after minimal instruction were those who had previously been assessed as showing formal operational thinking capability. The solution of a formal operational problem requires both the intellectual capability of formal operations and some contextualising experience. Neither alone is sufficient.

Bond (1980, 1990) has expressed this context-related interpretation of the 16 binary operations in paper-and-pencil test form, each item supplying the relevant information and asking that the subject identify the relation which applies. Two examples of such items were given in Chapter 2 (p. 24). Note that these items are structurally equivalent to AD47, but that the semantic information has been given which enables the subject to identify the logical relation which applies. The items correlate highly (r = 0.73) with three Piagetian reasoning tasks based directly on growth of logical thinking (GLT) tasks and scale just where Piaget said they should, at the early formal border, with none of the paradoxes of the AD47 test.

All context-explanatory models of levels of thinking face the question of establishing whether subjects' prior experience of the field is adequate to permit their highest level of processing. Much of the confusion in the literature between pro- and anti-Genevans can be attributed to this. Even in GLT some of the tasks such as pendulum, flexible rods and equilibrium in the balance, allow the subject more readily to describe the data in relevant concrete schemata than others such as motion in the horizontal plane. A substantial aspect of Piaget's genius (and that of his co-workers) has been the ability to select such a high proportion of experimental tasks evoking optimal performance from children.

## Donaldson and task context

Margaret Donaldson and her co-workers are often quoted as having shown that young children can really succeed at tasks which Piaget had claimed should have been beyond them. In the early chapters of her book *Children's Minds* (1978), Donaldson seems to set out with the express intention of toppling some sacred cows of developmental psychology and her attacks on Piaget and Chomsky are remarkable for the almost desperate manner in which the evidence of new work with children is bent to the task at hand. The procedure is to take an established Piagetian task the results of which are not in dispute, change the task, obtain different results, and then to claim that had Piaget used the new task he would have found that children could succeed with it very well and that therefore they are far more capable than he had given them credit for. One example given this treatment is the 'points of view' task in which a child is seated at a table which contains a model mountain on which are certain features – a house, a tree, and so on. A doll is placed at another position around the table, and the child is asked 'what will the doll see?', and shown pictures of possible orientations of tree, house, and so on on a mountain from which to choose the doll's perspective. Children under the age of eight find this difficult and often choose the picture which represents their own point of view of the mountain. As a result of tasks of this sort Piaget claimed that young children were egocentric and were literally incapable of imagining the points of views of others. In the modification of this task which Donaldson describes a set of screens is placed on the table, a 'policeman' is placed at one point, and the subject is asked to place a doll such that the doll is hidden from the policeman. Children as young as 5 years old can generally complete this successfully. Donaldson explains the difference in terms of the familiarity of the latter situation in the lives of children compared with the mountain task and thus argues that what is difficult about the mountain task is not its requirement for decentration but its unrealistic context. Well, it may or may not be the case that the Donaldson subjects were quite accustomed to hiding from policemen but it is certainly likely that Piaget's Swiss subjects would have been quite familiar with points of view around a mountain. So the contextual familiarity argument is questionable. What is easy about the hiding from a policeman task is that the only imaginative demand on the child is the drawing of one imaginary straight line from the policeman to the doll and then seeing whether this line is intersected by a partition. This task is intrinsically far easier than arranging and re-arranging the elements of tree, house, and mountain in at least a two-dimensional array in the mind.

In dealing with the famous class-inclusion task in which Piaget found that, given six roses and four daffodils a child was inclined to say that there were 'more roses than flowers', Donaldson quotes McGarrigle's modification. Here 10 toy cows, six of which are black, are laid on their sides and said to be 'sleeping'. The question is modified: 'Are there more black cows or more sleeping cows?' Now children prove to be far more successful than in the original task. The claim here is not that cows are more familiar than flowers (indeed one must assume that the subjects were city children who were unfamiliar with the sleeping position of cows) but that 'the introduction of the word sleeping increased the emphasis on the total class'. Precisely. The nature of the task has been changed from seeking children's ability to see a subclass as included in the total class – quite a difficult idea for 6 year-olds – to counting separately two classes each of which has been clearly identified. No class inclusion is required. The child counts six black cows, and then counts 10 sleeping cows. Different task, different result, no comparison possible and certainly no threat to Piagetian hypotheses concerning the development of children's thinking.

## VYGOTSKY AND SOCIAL MEDIATION

'You can't get an ought from an is' runs Hume's principle. Satisfactory though Piaget's account of cognitive development is as a descriptive model, it does not follow that it tells us all we need to know about *how* children grow in their power to think. The Genevan account of cognitive development is by itself insufficient as a guide to educational practice for the maximisation of each student's potential. Both modifications and additions are needed.

In Chapter 1 we described Vygotsky's notion of a Zone of Proximal Development (ZPD) as the extra-intellectual power that is available to a child when her thinking is mediated through social interaction with adults or peers. It is important to note that on Vygotsky's account it is a mistake to think of the ZPD as wholly internal to the adolescent in the form of nascent or part-achieved strategies. It exists just as much in the social space which the child shares with his age peers. The extra half-skill the child may need to knit to his own to create a completed skill may just as well come from what another child says and does as from her own behaviour. Vygtosky (1981) argues

> Any function in the child's cultural development appears twice, or on two planes. First it appears on the social plane, and then on the psychological plane. First it appears between people as an interpersonal category, and then within the child as an intrapsychological category. This is equally true with regard to voluntary attention, logical memory, the formation of concepts, and the development of volition.
>
> (p. 163)

In Vygotsky's account the ZPD lies as much outside the individual in the skills, ideas, concepts and strategies located in the social space which he and his peers inhabit or create as it does in his own mind. The child internalises as a personal skill what he has approved, contributed to, and observed in his peers' practice. 'instruction is good only when it proceeds ahead of development, when it awakens and rouses to life those functions that are in the process of maturing or in the zone of proximal development' (quoted in Wertsch 1985: 165).

In a short life this remained only as a piece of advice and Vygotsky never had the chance properly to distinguish intervention from instruction. It is unclear how much of his account is descriptive, and how much prescriptive. Feuerstein took it prescriptively as a general aim for his Instrumental Enrichment procedures and in CASE we took it prescriptively, as indicating the probable value of peer collaboration in the learning process. Translating it into practice, the mediating role of the teacher lies in developing the skill of first framing the tasks for the pupils in such a way as to direct their attention to the problems they will meet and should discuss with each other. Then the whole class is encouraged to share the different insights and difficulties which the working groups have encountered. The ZPD is thus established collaboratively, and all pupils benefit.

## PIAGET AND VYGOTSKY: A MARRIAGE OF CONVENIENCE?

> A man enters into a dream alone, but when he comes to speak of it must use the Word, which is common to all.
>
> (Epigraph to Eliot's *Four Quartets*)

In Chapter 2, Fig. 2.7, development survey evidence was shown which substantially contradicts the simple age/stage model of development which features in books such as GLT. Our interpretation of the apparent contradiction is that Piaget and co-workers, by working with biologically 'good subjects' had described not the average child, but what the child under favourable circumstances of birth, upbringing and environment can achieve. In biological terms, they had described the genotype, whereas the phenotype is as shown in Fig. 2.7. This interpretation is possible only retrospectively following the success of the intervention strategy used in the CASE project reported in Chapter 6.

Indeed, one of the impulses toward the CASE work was a challenge thrown out to one of the authors in 1980 by Alan Clarke (Clarke and Clarke 1976). At this time the CSMS survey appeared to be one of the negative pieces of evidence against the Genevan account. 'If you want to go on using the Piagetian model', he said, quoting from Hull, 'bear in mind that one of the best ways of studying a phenomenon is to try and change it.' If an intervention model is incoherent, no successful change can issue from it. The Piagetian aspect of the CASE project provided at least the linkage by which the reasoning patterns of the students were addressed within the context of science learning. Given the success of the CASE intervention strategy – but only after its demonstrated success – one can now infer the genotype and identify it with the top 30 per cent of the percentile curves shown in Fig. 2.7, as described by Piaget. One can also assert that the Piagetian model has withstood one of the most stringent possible Popperian attempts to falsify it.

However, Piaget's account will not suffice to explain why the phenotype is as it is. Feuerstein's Vygotsky-derived model of cultural deprivation as caused by inadequate mediated learning experience needs to be imported to explain why 70 per cent of adolescents do not achieve the final formal operational stage of development. On this interpretation the driver of the CASE intervention would be the Vygotskyan aspect, responsible for allowing many of the students to realise their genetic potential.

Neat as this distinction may appear to be, we do not believe it to be the whole story. We have argued that prior knowledge is only the first necessary condition for learning in a given context, but it is not a sufficient one. A second necessary condition is a sufficiently high level of processing capacity in the student for the learning context to add to their conceptual or procedural knowledge. It will be remembered that substantial use was made of cognitive conflict in the *Thinking Science* activities described in Chapter 5. This notion is Genevan in origin, and features in two distinguished intervention studies: Inhelder *et al.* (1974) and Perret-Clermont (1980) with children in the 4–7 year age range. Perret-Clermont in particular engineered cognitive conflict on conservation and spatial tasks for children in groups of two or three and found that 'social interaction is beneficial to cognitive development even if the partner in the interaction is cognitively less advanced' (p. 162). She identified cognitive conflict in social situations as the essential engine of her interventions, and concluded: 'Social-cognitive conflict may be figuratively likened to the catalyst in a chemical reaction: it is not present at all in the final product, but it is nevertheless indispensable if the reaction is to take place.' This is a very Vygotskyan statement, although neither Vygotsky nor Feuerstein feature in her literature references.

How does it come about that this approach to intervention originated in Geneva? In a series of articles and a book Les Smith (1987, 1992b) has rendered the Anglo-Saxon world a considerable service first by going back to the original French in Piaget's writings and pin-pointing some serious errors of translation, but more importantly from a philosophical background he has described in detail how the philosophical aspect of Piaget's 'genetic epistemology' is an essential part of the description of developmental psychology, rather than a psychological irrelevance as Wason and Johnson-Laird appear to argue. This is because

> We *all* make deductions (i. e. the *valid* ones) in the *same* way, using content which is individually specific and context-relative. The epistemic subject is the intra-individual processor responsible for the making of valid deductions and analogous logical performances.
>
> (Smith 1992b)

If this were not the case argument, resulting either in agreement or disagreement, would be impossible. Piaget chose in his life's work to describe how it comes about that 'The Word is common to all' – that is, how that which is the same underlying reasoning develops from its earliest manifestation in the breast-seeking activities of the new-born child. Since reasoning is the essential subject-matter of philosophy, philosophical language is an essential part of the *tertium quid* in which the growth of that which has to be described by philosophy is observed by the psychologist in empirical studies of children.

Creating a learning situation based on the Genevan descriptions of successive powers of processing amounts to a deliberate challenge to students to make steps which might take years if left to chance. The use of the Piagetian schemata or reasoning patterns in the design of activities – in Feuerstein IE and the CASE project – leads directly to cognitive conflict, whether deliberately planned or arising naturally from the investigation. If children find that their attempts to *assimilate* the task to their existing repertoire of ideas is less than successful, then they may make the next step of *accommodation*, increasing the power of their ideas to the situation which demands the increase. Thus this cognitive conflict aspect of the CASE model contributes to the engine as well as to the linkage which connects it to the learning subject-matter of science. The Vygotsky aspect adds to this by showing the teacher how different mediation is from her usual teaching role, and also serves to describe the type of social interaction which is likely to be useful to the students.

## INSTRUCTION, INTERVENTION, AND SCIENCE EDUCATION

Two stories in particular have emerged from science education research in the last 15 years and it will be worth considering what light, if any, is thrown on these stories by the evidence presented in Chapter 6.

One of the lines concerns the alternative conceptions that children hold about scientific phenomena, and attempts to change these into conceptions more acceptable to the scientific community (see, for example, Driver *et al*. 1985, Champagne *et al*. 1985, Osborne and Freyberg 1985). The other story was about the complexity of scientific concepts and the limits imposed on understanding by pupils' levels of cognitive development (see, for example, Karplus 1979, Shayer and Adey 1981, Lawson 1989). Protagonists of both schools are concerned about the ineffectiveness of much current science teaching, whether it be by traditional chalk and talk methods or by activity led 'discovery' methods. The former minimises activity by the student which is seen as essential for effective learning while the latter too often degenerates into practical activity for its own sake without the cognitive activity which is the necessary basis of all learning.

Both 'alternative conceivers' and 'cognitive developmentalists' focus on what goes on in children's minds when faced with the scientists' view of phenomena. Describing the phenomena is one thing, explaining them in terms which are scientifically useful is something else entirely. It is a matter of observation that when a rubber sucker is pressed against a smooth surface it requires some force to pull it off again but it requires considerable mental activity to comprehend, let alone to construct, an explanation for this observation in terms of the greater bombardment of particles of gases in the atmosphere on the outer surface of the rubber compared with the inner surface.

Both groups agree that our perceptions are influenced by our current beliefs. How you describe what you observe depends upon the theories you hold about that particular topic. It is a common observation in court-rooms that what a witness reports he has 'seen' (and what he sincerely believes that he has seen) will depend on his relationship to the accused. It is not so readily accepted that what a scientist 'sees' is also influenced by the theory she holds and that two scientists with different theories will 'see' different things in the same event. Just how far this principle can be taken depends on one's stance *vis-à-vis* the existence of an objective reality but to pursue this here would be to digress too far.

Most importantly, both approaches rest on the belief that pupils must construct knowledge from their own experiences and that knowledge cannot be transferred from teacher to pupil in a pre-digested form which requires no re-interpretation on the part of the learner.

Differences between the approaches rest in the relative emphasis placed on a developing central cognitive processor, or on previous experience. For example, a cognitive developmentalist would point to the 10 year-old's inability adequately to explain why the sucker sticks as evidence of the immaturity of his cognitive processing mechanism, while an alternative conceiver might emphasise rather the child's inexperience and the need to link new experiences to existing conceptions.

Alternative conceptions theory makes important use of Ausubel's distinction between rote learning of isolated facts and meaningful learning in which new knowledge is linked to a framework of existing knowledge. Meaningful knowledge is seen as growing from and on existing knowledge, the alternative conceiver's favourite quote being that of Ausubel's (1968): 'The most important single factor influencing learning is what the learner already knows. Ascertain this and teach him accordingly.' One consequence of this position is that the movement has focused on the child's development of knowledge and understanding within particular topics and subject domains. On this basis, they have produced an impressive catalogue of the types of misconceptions held by pupils in many and diverse topics: electric current flow, the shape of the earth, nutrition in plants, and many more.

Concentration on particular topics and discounting the role of the central processor does not allow links to be made between a child's understanding in one area and her likely level of understanding in another. The fact that a child has difficulty explaining the stuck rubber sucker in terms of atmospheric pressure tells the alternative conceiver nothing about the same child's likely comprehension of activities about photosynthesis. In contrast, if a central processing mechanism is at least partly responsible for difficulties in learning, this allows one to make good predictions of an individual's performance over a wide range of problems from a sampling of their performance on one or two.

Monk (1990, 1991) has re-analysed some key alternative conceptions through cognitive-developmentalist spectacles. He showed that it is possible to map the quality of pupils' conceptualisations as reported by Shipstone (1984), Ramadas and Driver (1989) and others directly on to the ages at which pupils attain the stages of cognitive development reported from the CSMS survey (Fig. 2.7). While the alternative conceptions workers have provided a rich and useful set of descriptions of typical alternative frameworks, Monk's work offers an *explanation* of how these alternative conceptions arise, in terms of the children's cognitive processing capability at different ages. It also provides an explanation, which has predictive power, for the difficulty of changing preconceptions.

The alternative conceptions movement themselves have produced some striking evidence of the resistance of children's misconceptions to change (see Gauld 1986 for a remarkable example), and others (Kuhn *et al.* 1988) have shown that children, and even adults, do not readily correlate the evidence of experiment with their hypotheses in order to change permanently their concepts. It is difficult to account for these difficulties without recourse to some maturing general cognitive function. In the limit, the alternative conceptions approach suggests that anything can be taught to any child provided one structures the learning experience well enough, a view which takes too literally the famous quotation from Bruner: 'Any idea or problem or body of knowledge can be presented in a form simple enough so that any particular learner can understand it in a recognisable form' (1968:44). This is an optimistic stance, well actualised in the Children's Learning in Science Project (CLISP 1987) and a stance from which one may look down on cognitive developmentalists who may seem to have little to offer the teacher except strictures about what can *not* be taught. We have argued elsewhere (Shayer and Adey 1981:146) that Bruner did not mean by this that cognitive developmental levels were of no importance but others have also interpreted him as suggesting that if you only structure the learning materials well enough, there is no intrinsic limit to what a child of any age can comprehend. Even those familiar with the literature in this area may be surprised by the source of this quotation:

it undoubtedly overstates the case to claim that any subject can be taught to children in the preoperational stage or in the stage of concrete operations provided the material is presented in an informal, intuitive fashion with the aid of overt manipulation or concrete-empirical props . . . some ideas simply cannot be expressed without the use of certain higher-order abstractions. These latter kinds of concepts would be intrinsically too difficult for pre-school and primary school children irrespective of their method of presentation.

This and more, explicitly attacking the perceived Brunerian position from a cognitive developmentalist, implicitly matching, perspective, was written by David Ausubel (1965:260).

We hope that the interventionist stance of this book has moved the cognitive developmentalist position on from that of imposing limits to learning, to the provision of a method for radically improving the psychological conditions of learning.

## TRANSFER AND THE 'CENTRAL PROCESSOR'

The rather parochial debate of the last section has a more global implication. In Chapter 2 we outlined the debate between those who concentrate on learning within domains and those who attempt to influence cognitive processing common across all domains. At that point the hopes of the latter group might have been dismissed as wishful thinking since the evidence seemed to balance somewhat heavier on the side of domain-specific learning as the practicable route to improved education. The results of the CASE project have thrown some weight on the other side. An intervention delivered within the context of science has indeed produced significant effects in English, a distant domain, and at the end of Chapter 6 we reasoned that the existence of a central processor which was amenable to educational influence was the best explanation for this far-transfer effect.

Is this notion of a central processor adequately described by the schemata of formal operational thinking? No – no more than a description of a cat flattening itself to the ground in preparation to leaping at a bird tells us what a cat is. In the work of Case (1985) and Pascual-Leone (1969, 1984) use is made of a measure of short-term memory (M-demand) in terms of the number of chunks of information a child can handle while on a thinking task, on a scale from 3 to 7. Giving an information-processing slant to Piaget's account of concrete and formal operations, some of the Piagetian concrete tasks are described in terms of M-demands of 3 or 4. This is closer to our meaning; underlying the Genevan descriptions of concrete and then formal operational thinking are successively more and more complex levels of processing each of which determine – in fields of spatial, numerical, verbo-logico, causal reasoning, etc. – the difficulty of tasks the child can succeed on.

Our own implicit model is one in which Piaget's concrete operational schemata are over-learned procedures for structuring incoming information from the senses.

Putting a set of objects into some perceived order (seriation) or classifying them according to one or more salient variables (classification) are programmes that run so fast (say 100 to 200 milliseconds) that a mature individual has the illusion that he has just seen the objects that way *ab initio*. Bearing in mind the very short window in time which is available for thinking as described in the working memory literature there is no way in which Miller's (1956) magic number 7 for the maximum number of chunks of information which can be handled in a thinking act could do the work of problem solving unless there were peripheral processing capacity which the moving, conscious part of the brain can access. Such peripheral capacity would consist of programmes which run very much faster than working memory itself and would be accessed from working memory, given data from the temporarily stored chunks which are there. Such programmes might be 'search all combinations'; 'look at proportional relations between four chunks'; 'relate variables to a search strategy which will find the dependency relation between the variables', etc. Obviously these hypothesised 'programmes' are Piaget's formal operational schemata: combinatorial thinking, ratio/proportion, control of variables, etc. Only if the schemata can be utilised unconsciously can they be used constructively by the conscious mind, as Piaget was at pains to point out.

Baddeley (1990:71) describes a 'central executive' with two fast-running 'slave systems', a 'visuo-spatial sketch-pad' and a 'phonological loop', which provide very short-term stores of information for the central executive to use. Norman and Shallice (1986) provide a neuro-psychological control of action model, which again has a 'supervisory attentional system' which regulates the relation between input and output. It seems likely that the automatised reasoning patterns which we suggest do the work of higher-level thinking must be analogous to Baddeley's 'slave systems' of visuo-spatial sketch-pad and phonological loop, or there simply would not be the time in the fading coal of working memory to test and accept, or test and reject possible relationships to fit the observations.

The most detailed account of the possible relationship between models of working memory and Piaget's account of concrete and formal operations is given in Pascual-Leone (1988). He argues a rather rigid distinction between what he calls the 'silent operators' of M-power (M) and interrupt function (I), and executive schemes and mental operations (E). M and I are said to be analogous to computer hardware, and E analogous to software. In order to run, a high-level mental operation (say, early formal) may require an M-capacity of six chunks. However, it will not have time to run if the mental field is confused by alternative representations and conflicting executive schemes. Thus the subject has to suppress the task-irrelevant structures through the I-operator to give the appropriate executive scheme clear space in time to run. Given these conditions, there will just be time in working memory for a subject to run a mental operation on the temporarily stored information, such as 'control variables appropriately'. Pascual-Leone (1988) gives Table 7.1. In this account 'e' is a constant representing the mental capacity available at the end of the second year of life. Pascual-Leone also gives due weight to Vygotskian notions of mediation when he discusses cognitive development. One

*Table 7.1*   Predicted maximum M-power values as a function of age, and their
correspondence to the Piagetian substage sequence

| M-power (e + k) | Piagetian substage | Normative age |
|---|---|---|
| e + 1 | Low preoperations | 3,4 |
| e + 2 | High preoperations | 5,6 |
| e + 3 | Low concrete operations | 7,8 |
| e + 4 | High concrete operations | 9,10 |
| e + 5 | Substage introductory to formal operations* | 11,12 |
| e + 6 | Low formal operations | 13,14 |
| e + 7 | High formal operations | 15-adults |

* Note: this is equivalent to our Concrete generalisation level

interpretation of our own intervention data which we have presented in Chapter 6, and others' in Chapter 3, is that our 12 and 13 year-olds, for various experiential reasons, have failed to utilise their growth in M-power to produce more powerful executive schemes and all that is being added is structured opportunities to do this. On this interpretation, the growth in M-power would be a genetically determined and age-related development, as Pascual-Leone argues, present in all children.

In view of the developmental data presented in Fig. 2.7 we think this interpretation is unlikely. It is probable that Pascual-Leone, like Piaget before him, has based his measurements of M-power on rather small numbers of 'good' (i.e. unrepresentative) subjects. Thus while not questioning the detail of Pascual Leone's description of mental functioning, we doubt whether the 'hardware/ software' distinction is completely valid. It seems to us as though the pupils we have described as engaging in construction zone activity and metacognition in Chapter 4 were doing more than developing algorithms (executive schemes and mental operations). The 'central processor' we have been trying to argue for would indeed be the M, I and E interaction which Pascual-Leone describes, but in which the 'silent operators' and the executive schemes are developmentally interdependent. It is far more likely that our 13 year-olds really were 'e + 4' and 'e + 5' in terms of M-power, rather than the 'e + 6' which would be the genetic programme, and that through varied opportunities of cognitive conflict, metacognition, and so on the small steps of grasping more powerful schemes of thinking slowly expanded their mental working space as well.

## CONCLUSION

IQ testing could have been said to 'work' in the sense that IQ tests are in fact pretty good predictors of academic achievement and so can be used, if one is so inclined, to select and stream pupils. But it is, justifiably in our view, a most unattractive idea to educators because of its implication of fixed potential and the lack of opportunity it affords educators to do more than feed instruction matched to the supposed intellectual capacity of different groups of pupils.

The personal construction of knowledge by children is a very attractive idea because it builds in the notion of individual empowerment and a very strong role for the educator in structuring learning material such as to lead each child from what she knows and understands already to greater understanding still. However, the idea is as yet under-theorised and teaching schemes based on it alone have not shown long-term effects in terms of more elaborate conceptualisation by students.

The marriage of Piaget and Vygotsky and the addition of the elaborations and interpretations of Feuerstein and of our own earlier work produces a model of cognition which is both attractive to educators and which works. It emphasises the maximisation of every child's potential intellectual power through social interaction in the classroom under the management of the teacher, and promises significant gains in academic achievement arising from the realisation of the sort of thinking which Piaget always believed every adolescent should be capable of. We have responded to Alan Clarke's challenge. An intervention heavily dependent on Piaget's account of operational thinking has produced large effects on theory-independent national school examinations.

# Chapter 8

# Other domains, other ages

We have shown that an intervention delivered within the context of science to 11–14 year-old students can have long-term effects on their academic achievement in a range of other subjects. In this chapter we will explore the potentialities for cognitive intervention through the 'doors' of other domains and at other ages. First, we will consider generally the possibility of context-independent cognitive intervention. Then we will look at the generalisation of the intervention methodology from a particular set of activities to science teaching in general and to other subjects in the secondary school curriculum. Finally, we will consider the age issue, including the possibilities of work with younger pupils and what of the intervention methodology could be relevant to vocational, pre-college, or managerial training. As a preface it will be necessary to expose certain assumptions about the nature and purpose of the curriculum which underlie our arguments.

The curriculum is viewed as everything that takes place in the space defined by the teacher, the students, and the materials (print and other) which is intended to bring about learning. This explicitly proposes that the curriculum cannot be defined simply by sets of objectives, or attainment targets, nor by sets of textbooks and worksheets, but must include the way that teachers and students interpret and use the materials. The curricula in two classes using the same set of materials and working to the same set of objectives may thus be rather different from one another since each teacher will interpret the materials according to their own experience and predilections, and each set of students will react to them in different ways according to their background and interests. Both or neither may accord closely with the intentions and theories, written or implied, of the curriculum developer or textbook authors. The curriculum as delivered may represent a useful elaboration or a sensible local adaptation or it may so pervert the original intentions of the materials that it is unlikely that their objectives will be achieved. More generally it will represent each teacher's takeover of the materials in the necessary process of making it her/his own.

This view of the curriculum means that guidelines given for possible types of activities cannot address more than half of the story. The other half is the process of working with teachers to achieve enough commonality of models and of purpose so that the delivered curriculum approximates closely to the intervention principles outlined already. The matter of changing practice in the classroom is dealt with in the next chapter.

## CONTEXT-FREE INTERVENTION?

We have seen in Chapter 3 that at least one context-independent intervention – that of Feuerstein's IE with 12 to 14 year-olds – has been shown able to deliver large effects on psychological tests of here-and-now thinking ability, on Piagetian tests, on cognitive functions, and on various tests of fluid intelligence. In terms of the development survey presented in Chapter 2 for the purpose of assessing the effects of interventions, gains of the order of 25 percentile points or more were achievable over a two-year period. Yet no evidence exists in the literature of an accompanying subsequent increase in school achievement by students who have experienced this or other context-independent interventions and this tends to cast doubt on the psychological models used. On the other hand, the mistake in experimental design described at the start of Chapter 6 of using immediate post-tests for school achievement suggests that this is what statisticians call a 'type 2' error, failing to find an effect which was really there. Since none of the authors who reported earlier interventions used subsequent fresh learning as their test of school achievement we just do not know that the effect was not there for them to find. The delayed post-test effect-sizes from the CASE II project on science achievement coupled with the non-effect at immediate post-test is strong evidence for this view. Note also that in the Korean replication of CASE, although the immediate post-test results on science knowledge achievement were non-significant, highly significant results were found on science process skills which are arguably addressed directly by the intervention.

The evidence given in Chapter 3 that when some of Feuerstein's IE principles were applied directly to instruction in first-year university physics (Mehl) or year 9 high school chemistry (Strang) large effects on science learning were achieved suggests the likely success of such a strategy. If it works directly on students, how much better might its results might be if previously the students had had two years' IE? This issue – that of the relation of interventional to instructional practice – we propose to defer until Chapter 10, and here to focus on the possibilities for intervention.

We certainly do not mean to rule out the use of context-independent interventions. We are sure they have an important place when properly used but both from our own direct experience and also feedback from schools using special thinking skills lessons such as Feuerstein IE, de Bono's CoRT, or the Somerset Thinking Skills materials, we know there is a major problem. Unless teachers from all subject areas take an active part in teaching these courses the dynamic is not created by which the way in which they teach their own subject can be transformed to mesh with the gradual changes in the students. Worse, if they do not have direct experience of the vocabulary and strategies which the students are using, an extra communication barrier is created between them and their students. At this date, 1993, we do not have a single described case-study showing how a school can make the needed quantum-leap in their teaching practice and administration so at best can only speculate.

It appears to us that good applied research is needed by which schools are assisted by researchers with the time and resources to provide the ideas, monitoring, feedback and critical testing required. Two major sources of ideas would be (a) the specifics of bridging already offered in the teachers' guides to Feuerstein's IE – a very rich source, but under-described in terms of underlying principle, and (b) the collaborative published work of Perkins and Salomon (1989) on the Low and High roads to Transfer, discussed in detail in Chapter 4.

## CONTEXT-DELIVERED INTERVENTION: SCIENCE

CASE II was a context-delivered intervention. The intervention principles were expressed through the domain of science by a team of researchers all of whom were experienced science teachers and who were well versed in the nature of science and in the practicalities of its delivery in high schools. Our hypothesis to explain the generalisation of its results from science to mathematics and English learning was that, since the students improved their reasoning patterns in a science context, already much of the work of abstraction required for transfer may have been done by them in the process of bridging what they had learnt in the *Thinking Science* lessons to their other science lessons.

It follows from our view of the curriculum that we cannot claim that the set of activities published as Thinking Science could, by themselves, constitute an effect-ive cognitive intervention programme which will dramatically raise students' data-processing capabilities and hence their academic achievement. The interven-tion that achieves these goals is a product of the materials and their use by teachers. The question now arises, whether the teacher could not produce a similar interven-tion using other materials? The answer must be 'yes', but it will require a significant act of invention based on thorough understandings both of interventionist aims and the nature of the subject matter through which these aims are to be achieved.

We will look first at some alternative possibilities still within the domain of science, starting with the direct application of *Thinking Science* principles to existing science curriculum material and progressing to more distant interventions based on other psychological constructs and models.

### Adapting existing material

The adaptability of materials for interventionist purposes varies widely. Unsurpris-ingly, traditional instructional materials which emphasise the acquisition of knowledge do not generally lend themselves to teaching for the promotion of higher-level thinking. Less obviously, nor do 'activity-based' materials where the activity is an end in itself. Such curriculum materials are based uncritically on the belief that practical work is necessarily a good thing. The questioning of this assumption (Hodson 1990, Woolnough and Toh 1990) has coincided with the realisation amongst many teachers that simply following a recipe to complete a practical exercise serves little useful purpose. It is the use that is made of the data obtained that is important. Data may come variously from laboratory experiments, from field observations, from reading or from pictures or other AV sources. What matters in the development of scientific (and we would claim general) thinking is the interrogation of this data that takes place.

Many modern science curriculum materials do provide opportunities for introducing features of a successful intervention programme: cognitive conflict, metacognition, and bridging. Within the current generation of science curriculum materials in the United Kingdom there is a distinct trend to make better use of practical activity through class and group discussions both on the evidence for particular points of view and on the social issues concerned with the application of science. This technique of encouraging reasoned discussion amongst pupils is borrowed from successful practice in social studies and recognises the constructivist principle that learning is not just a matter of absorbing information, nor even of discovering information, but involves a paradigm shift in belief by learners which is most likely to be brought about by open discussion.

Although the approaches advocated in such materials do not by themselves constitute the sort of intervention which promotes the general development of cognitive processing they do lend themselves fairly readily to adaptation. With interventionist principles and the reasoning patterns of formal operations in mind, it becomes possible for a teacher to create something of an interventionist curriculum using existing materials. Dignon (1993) has shown how this can be done for one junior secondary science programme, *Science in Process* (SIP) (ILEA 1988). Each activity in some SIP books was studied in the light of the *Thinking Science* principles, in particular looking for opportunities to develop formal reasoning patterns. Where, as was frequently the case, the textbook simply gave information, Dignon re-arranged the material to provide more cognitive challenge in line with the principles outlined in Chapter 4.

> Regrettably (SIP spread 6.13) 'Up and Down' already gives away an effective control of variables strategy via a given diagram (a frequent weakness of SIP). It was decided to learn from Rollerball (a TS activity). After discussing what might affect how far a car would roll after coming down a slope . . . a few examples of variables not being controlled were shown. Class comments were invited with regard to the faults in the experimental method before the open-ended investigation from the second half of the SIP spread was set.
>
> (Dignon 1993:116)

The whole of a year 8 (12+) in a school was pre-tested with PRT II Volume and Heaviness and then taught this enhanced SIP for two terms. The total programme consisted of 20 'Thinking-SIP' lessons – 10 per term. Post-tests showed that this group had gained in cognitive development significantly faster than would be expected on the basis of national norms with effect-sizes of $0.2\sigma$ and $0.25\sigma$ for boys and girls respectively. Although small, these are statistically significant effects and are remarkable for having been achieved over a relatively short time period. Even allowing for the possible effect of pre-testing as training for the post-tests, they suggest possibilities where a teacher internalises the principles of cognitive acceleration and applies them to whatever science curriculum they normally teach. It is interesting to note also that the gender differences found in the CASE II results were entirely absent in this experiment.

An example contrasting even further with *Thinking Science* is provided by Phelps' (1993) use of CASE principles for the promotion of students' process skills. Here there is a parallel with Mehl's use of Feuerstein's IE principles to facilitate better learning strategies in undergraduate physics, described in Chapter 3. Phelps chose not to lay emphasis on the reasoning patterns of proportion, correlation, control of variables, etc. in a metacognitive way from activity to activity. Rather, he structured the lessons in biology and physics for mixed-ability year 8 (age 12+) classes to direct attention, in context, to the independent variables which might need to be controlled, the independent variables which needed to be altered, the process of measuring change of the dependent variable, the establishment of relations (functional or correlational) between the variables, and also inverse or compensatory relationships. To do this he made use of much of the technical vocabulary such as input, outcome, values, variables embodied in *Thinking Science* activities. In this he can be seen to be using the parameters of concrete preparation and, to a lesser extent, cognitive conflict but discarding some of the Piagetian and Vygotskian elements of the CASE method. As expected, over the course of one year there was no difference at all between experimental and control classes on Piagetian tests, but in terms of two parallel forms of process skill tests, given as pre- and post-test, there was an overall effect-size of $0.91\sigma$ in favour of the experimental classes by the end of one year. Moreover, although there was no difference between the groups on science achievement tests given in term 1 and term 2, there was a mean effect-size of $0.52\sigma$ between the groups in their learning of the content of term 3. This differential was maintained over the next year, so that in the end of year 9 science examinations the classes who had had the CASE modified process skill approach the previous year still showed a $0.42\sigma$ differential over the controls in their next year's learning.

A very different approach is exemplified by the work of Collings (Collings 1987, Shayer 1987, 1988) who used a different psychological model – that of field-dependence/independence – and applied it with an interventionist intention within the context of science. Field-independence is the aspect of thinking which allows a person to distinguish between the salient features of an object of thought or perception and the immediate field of relevant or irrelevant experience in which it is embedded. Previous research by Lynn and Kyllonen (1981) had showed that the cognitive restructuring element of field-independence overlapped substantially with measures of formal operation thinking. Collings designed a one-year intervention for 12 to 13 year-olds in which the training was delivered within a science lesson context. He produced materials designed for individual learning, mainly computer delivered, which the students could be given in periods of about 20 minutes during science lessons. These included:

- disembedding the simple from the complex
- reorganising information to produce new patterns
- looking for information systematically
- making comparisons
- ignoring irrelevant and confusing information
- ignoring the gestalt of organising the visual field into a coherent whole

The overlap between this list and the cognitive functions shown in Table 3.2 was not accidental. Following a careful reading of Feuerstein, a metacognitive approach was built into the project and students were encouraged to analyse their own thinking strategies and to 'bridge' between the field-independence (FI) activities and the content of their other science lessons.

Pre- and post-tests were given to three experimental classes, one taken by Collings and two others by an inexperienced teacher. With one of these the teacher used only the FI activities on their own and with the other class the metacognitive and bridging aspect were added as with Collings' own class. There were two control classes. About 20 per cent of the students' science time in the experimental classes was devoted to the FI activities. In the pre-post-test comparisons comparing experimental and control classes all the effects were statistically significant. On the Group Embedded Figures Test (GEFT), directly testing gains on the psychological model used, Colling's class showed an effect-size of $1.34\sigma$. On the Piagetian Reasoning Task Volume and Heaviness the same class showed an effect-size of $0.92\sigma$, showing a more general effect of the intervention on students' thinking ability not obviously related to the specifics of anything trained. The inexperienced teacher's class with FI training showed an effect-size of $1.09\sigma$ on GEFT but only $0.36\sigma$ on Piagetian operations, whereas his class with metacognition added showed an effect-size of $1.13\sigma$ on GEFT and $0.68\sigma$ on Piagetian operations. The difference between $0.36$ and $0.68\sigma$ was statistically significant so that it appears that the metacognitive aspect assisted the transfer to formal operations. By now it will not be surprising that on ordinary tests of school science achievement during the year the experimental classes did neither better nor worse than the control classes. Collings did not have the time available to test the classes' fresh science learning in the year following.

## OTHER SUBJECT AREAS

We have maintained throughout that there is nothing special about science in relation to the promotion of cognitive development. Formal operational thinking is not restricted to higher-level thinking in science and science as a school subject is by no means the only door through which higher-level thinking may be promoted. We worked through science, because we were trained as scientists and science teachers and have some understanding of the structure of scientific thinking. We believe that it is feasible in principle to develop programmes for the development of formal operations in other subject domains but no one should be under the illusion that this will be a simple or straightforward procedure. In Chapter 2 we described in some detail expressions of the schemata of formal operational thinking set in science contexts and the development of a (science) curriculum analysis taxonomy (CAT) from a wide reading of Piaget's accounts of responses characteristic of different levels of thinking. The principle here was that to make a success of this Piagetian approach to science, it was necessary first to be able to formulate the main abstract descriptors for the underlying teaching aims of science. To design an intervention in a domain other than science will necessitate doing for that domain what has been described for science. An analogous application to the domains, say, of mathematics, history or English is very likely to require a different set of descriptors as a starting point and only after these have been developed can the principles of concrete preparation, cognitive conflict, metacognition, and bridging be applied in the design of activities for the promotion of higher-level thinking in that domain.

The essential steps, described in detail in Shayer (1981), are:

1.  Restate your curriculum as objectives. In Britain an easy ostensive definition of this can be given: simply use, for your subject, the National Curriculum objectives as published by Her Majesty's Government. Essentially the list should be long enough to permit abstraction from it in step 2. Maybe 40 or 50 objectives are needed to cover all major levels of learning.

2.  By abstraction from the list in 1, arrive at the list of the main abstract descriptors necessary to define your subject. The suggestion is that Miller's magic number 7 (±3) is a good guide. You need no more than your working memory can easily deal with. In the British National Curriculum for science (DES 1988) 17 'Attainment Targets' were initially chosen. This was found too many for Education Ministers to handle, so was then reduced to four for the 1991 version. This was actually a bit of a fudge for they then needed to be subdivided again to 16 'strands'. But the 'abstract descriptors' we talk about are not just topic headings, as in the National Curriculum. They need to describe the main underlying kinds of performance and understanding teachers are looking for in distinguishing between good and not-so-good students, whatever the topic. Only an experienced subject teaching specialist can do this – a psychologist's good guess would never be good enough.

3.  Import an interpretative model to help make your theory falsifiable. In the case of a Piagetian model, this would involve writing down specific learning objectives at four different levels (2A, 2B, 3A, 3B) in your own subject based on a reading of the Genevan literature, with some help from Shayer and Adey's (1981) taxonomy. But other models are conceivable: what is required is that they allow, for example in the case of history, a hypothesis to be made (and tested) of the factors which are responsible for the increasing difficulty of different aspects of the subject.

4. Test (attempt to falsify) your model. Here several steps are collapsed:
   (a) get an independent estimate of your students' level of development;
   (b) translate your step 1 objectives (grouped by step 2) into test items;
   (c) define competence levels you will accept (for success on the items);
   (d) trial the test (and refine the items to improve their communication with the students);
   (e) test your model. Administer the validated test to the students for whom you have the independent estimate of level; and lastly,
   (f) respond to feedback.

If steps 2 and 3 have not been wholly valid then the results of 4b–c will not be consistent with 4a. At this point the steps are re-cycled until the model is either satisfactory or falsified and rejected.

Now it is necessary to use the validated taxonomy from steps 2 and 4 to pinpoint a series of activities which would address as many as possible of the subject-specific reasoning patterns. Each activity would need to be designed to include learning tasks in which appropriate concrete preparation and cognitive conflict could be included and initially should cover the range mature concrete to early formal in cognitive demand-level. Later in the course the activities in the same strand of reasoning pattern type could be designed to go deeper in understanding. The course as a whole would have a spiral structure in which most of the spectrum of reasoning patterns were addressed at a lower level and then all revisited at higher levels.

For CASE the whole process took one year (1982/3) for an initial feasibility study and three years (1984–7) for three people for the full CASE II project – and this was starting from the base of having steps 1–3 virtually completed already by the CSMS project.

Next we comment on some of the problems and possibilities – and in some cases of work done already – for intervention within domains other than science. John Biggs and Kevin Collis started to map out some of this territory 10 years ago, and their SOLO taxonomy (Biggs and Collis 1982) remains a useful source of examples of different levels of thinking within some school subject domains.

### English

Significant progress in the development of a curriculum analysis taxonomy for English (steps 1–4 outlined above) has been achieved by Esther Fusco (1983) who took four descriptors – classification, correlations, proportional reasoning and causality – from Shayer and Adey's (1981) taxonomy and translated their definition and instances into the context of English comprehension. In addition, four more descriptors – seriation, frames of reference, spatial/temporal relationships, and formal logic – were defined from Fusco's experience as an English teacher and reading of Piaget as more particularly relevant to English. These descriptors formed the rows of a taxonomy (Table 8.1) with Piagetian sub-levels as column headings. In each cell of the taxonomy Fusco provided literature-specific descriptions of expected performance. For example, proportional reasoning is interpreted as different levels of analogical reasoning and one of the six descriptors for late concrete is 'Analyses simple comparative propositional relationships, instanced by good/evil in *The Lion, the Witch and the Wardrobe*'. At the early formal level comes 'Compares relationships that are implicitly stated, and explains reciprocal events in a story' (instanced from Tom Sawyer and Anne Frank's *Diary of a Young Girl*). Fusco showed that it was possible to use this taxonomy so that experienced English teachers could (a) produce satisfactory agreement in assessments of the level of demand of specific texts, and (b) produce reliable assessments of the levels of understanding of the texts shown by different students.

*Table 8.1*　Teachers' analysis form used for books in Fusco (1983)

| Schemata | Cognitive level | | | | |
| | Preoper-ational | Early concrete | Late concrete | Early formal | Mature formal |
| --- | --- | --- | --- | --- | --- |
| Classification | | | | | |
| Seriation | | | | | |
| Spatial/temporal relationships | | | | | |
| Correlations | | | | | |
| Proportional reasoning | | | | | |
| Frames of reference | | | | | |
| Causality | | | | | |
| Formal logic | | | | | |

The important principle shown here is that although the developmental model drawn from Piaget is general, it requires to be 'read in' to the context of the school subject and its reliable use in literature depends in addition on the subject specialist's expertise. The 'general' model offers an interpretation of expertise the specialist already possesses so that its use depends on her intelligence and imagination.

The task of designing a cognitive intervenionist programme in an English context remains to be done. As with development of the analysis tool it will require someone with subject expertise and the ability to identify the nature of cognitive conflict within the literary domain.

**Mathematics**

In mathematics there is a generalisation comparable to that described for English when we are asked to analyse the structure of a system as a group, a ring, etc., depending on its properties of associativity, commutativity, and so on. In this way the properties of the system 'addition in the set of positive and negative whole numbers' can be compared with the properties of a self-correcting steering system for a boat, but this is seen only if the analyst knows enough about both numbers and servo-systems.

For secondary education this domain presents a double problem in that much scientific learning involves the application of mathematics, and many children also leave primary school with blocks and deficiencies of various kinds which give them trouble both in their mathematics and their science lessons. In one school which featured in the CASE III research the whole of the first-year entry of one high school was given the PRT Volume and Heaviness as a measure of the range and quality of their intake. It was noticed in the analysis of their test results that a substantial number of students – particularly but not exclusively the girls – were offering strategies for the formal items involving calculation at a Piagetian level well below their level as assessed by their performance on the test as a whole. The school asked for further information so the whole of the year 7 entry (age 11+) were given a sample of the CSMS maths tests (Hart *et al.* 1985). Around a quarter of the entry were showing performance in place value and ratio/proportion well below expectation from their Piagetian test results. By contrast, their competence on use of the four operations of addition, subtraction, multiplication and division was above-average. The distinction is between mathematics as a descriptive language (concrete operational), for which their primary schools had prepared the children well, and the process of reflecting on the rules of that language, or reflecting on which mathematical model might be an appropriate one to use. Ask the children how to find out how many apples you need to give 20 children three apples each, and they readily supply 'three times twenty'. Ask them how much bigger 60 is than 20, and they answer either '60 minus 20' – a wrong model – or more often 'I was never any good at that kind of maths'. Here it is necessary to step outside the possible relations between the two numbers, and select the multiplicative relation as the more useful way of looking at it. The children can certainly divide 60 by 20, but they are much less likely to see that the answer 'three times as big' is a better way of looking at the relation. Yet unless they can make this qualitative change in their secondary school students can neither make progress within mathematics itself in, for example, algebra as a language with self-consistent rules or in those aspects of science which require mathematical models.

Thus although some aspects of mathematics such as ratio, proportion, and compensation can be and have been addressed with some success within the *Thinking Science* course, much of mathematics requires a different approach. Whereas the rules of the game of science are whether a model works in prediction and explanation, in mathematics the criteria are consistency of the language used and fruitfulness in saying new things with the new symbols. The cliché 'mathematics is a language' has to be read with the corollary, 'but language as described by a grammarian'. It was easier to use a Piagetian model to describe degrees of comprehension in English because, as in science, the focus is on looking through the data presented to find meanings and connections. The content of mathematics is hierarchical in its structure and learners' misconceptions and errors are often due to their failure to utilise an appropriate level of abstraction in relation to the language of mathematics. Development of the intervention art for secondary mathematics may require a judicious blend of the construction and metacognition parameters described in Chapter 4.

**History**

It is tempting for scientists to view history as a rather inexact scientific enterprise: the collection of evidence, attribution of cause and effect, and the building of general models of the way that events occur. If we were to do this it would be easy enough to apply our scientific versions of formal thinking to the historical domain but the reality is that history has its own characteristic qualities quite distinct from scientific thinking. In particular, historians are more inclined to see their job as one of interpretation of events in the light of the conditions obtaining at the time, rather than trying to draw general conclusions about what might happen at another time and another place. The 'evidence' for history is not given, it is selected by the researcher. It will not speak for itself but must be interpreted in the light of the historian's understanding of the conditions of the past that produced it. History must employ a range of interpretations and explanations, and historical events cannot be understood without reference to the motives and beliefs of the participants:

> historians cannot therefore describe the past with the objectivity of natural scientists. They have to make a selection from the mass of evidence available and offer an interpretation of why and how events occurred as they did. Their viewpoints will at times differ and their perceptions will change over time. Contemporary events continually change historians' perceptions of what went before.
>
> (National Curriculum History Working Group 1989: Final report, p. 7)

The burden here is on interpretation, and historians recognise the impossibility of arriving at 'truth' (except in quite concrete instances such as the date of the battle of Bannockburn) since every historical situation can only be interpreted through the filter of an individual's knowledge and beliefs. (There are some who say the same of science, but we are not amongst them.)

In interpreting history, some characteristics of formal operations are the ability to form hypotheses, to see more than one point of view, to interpret a behaviour in the light of the conditions obtaining at the time (rather than apply today's values to medieval government), and to accept lack of closure. Ultimately it is to recognise the prejudice of one's own interpretation. Significant work has already been done in the analysis of historical understanding, from the pioneering work of Peel (1967) and Hallam (1967), through to more recent work by Dickinson and Lee (1978), and Ashby and Lee (1987). The last-named have demonstrated stage-like development in historical understanding, although they are not yet prepared to grant that their 'stages' relate to Piagetian stages.

The extent of work already completed in this field makes it a promising candidate for further studies in cognitive acceleration and it is not difficult to imagine the form that an intervention programme might take. Conflict may be provided by challenging the interpretation given by a student: 'is there not another way you could look at it?' 'But what did you make of . . .?' 'Put yourself in the shoes of . . .'. This last, in particular, is the basis of empathy which has become such an important element in modern history courses. Also, history taught as interpretation rather than as the learning of facts is a fertile field for the sort of inter-pupil discussion which gives many opportunities for metacognitive reflection on students' own thought processes and thus meets one of the requirements of cognitive intervention.

## Foreign language learning

We have more difficulty applying the cognitive-developmental model to the skills required to learn a foreign language than to the subjects discussed so far. Biggs and Collis (1982) attempt to apply their SOLO taxonomy, isomorphous with Piaget's developmental stages, to the translation of phrases from French to English but their cognitive structural analyses of examples are not convincing. It is notable that unlike other sections of their subject-by-subject analysis, there are no literature references to the psychology of foreign language learning.

Traditional methods of learning a second language involve the learning of rules of grammar and structure and the memorisation of vocabulary. The analytical aspect of such an approach might well be enhanced by the availability of formal operations with their associated ability to abstract generalisations from specific examples and so consciously to build rules of production. This is the meta-linguistic approach requiring consciousness of language structures. It is a hard road to second language acquisition but one which is commonly taken by many who find themselves, as adults, living in a country whose native language is not their own. But there is another route to second language learning which is far more closely related to the method by which we learn our first language: the activation of an innate language processing mechanism in the context of a particular new language. This is the basis of the communicative approach to second language learning. Its relationship to first language learning has been demonstrated by Newport (1991) and her co-workers who showed the long-term quality of English as an acquired second language of Koreans working in a university environment in the United States dropped off sharply as a function of the age at which the subjects started to learn English, flattening out at a minimum from about 17 years onwards. It appears that second language learning, far from being assisted by the development of higher order thinking as the meta-linguistic method might require, actually requires certain elementary structures to be active and not to have been overtaken by more complex methods of processing. Added to the probable requirement for a psycho-motor skill of encoding a series of sounds and reproducing them accurately, it appears that the teaching of foreign languages is not an area of the school curriculum which lends itself easily to cognitive interventionist methodology.

It is, however, an area which lends itself to experimentation with efficient instruction. Programmes such as 'Accelerated Learning' (Rose 1985) make much of the fact that their methods are based on latest research 'on the brain and human development', but inspection of their materials shows that they have made excellent use of what we know about instruction but none at all of interventionist methodology. It is noteworthy that it is in the area of modern language learning that Accelerated Learning has made its most obvious commercial impact.

## Arts

The aesthetic and the intellectual are not readily teased apart. It is certainly the case that mature and able students produce work which is qualitatively distinct from younger and less able students although it is difficult, almost by definition, to characterise the nature of this quality using words or to be certain how much of the difference is attributable to cognitive development and how much to experience and acculturation. The Gulbenkian Foundation report (1982) adhered to the doctrine that there are a variety of intelligences of which the aesthetic-creative is one, and distinct from (their view of) science as logico-deductive. It has been a message of this book that such distinctions between subject domains, while important, are not so deep-rooted as to warrant being described as different intelligences. Indeed, in their championing of the development of creativity through arts education there is an assumption that creativity, as an aspect of intelligence, will be transferable from the contexts of the arts, in which they are introduced, to 'real-life' uses in quite different domains. Examiners of student art look for qualities such as form, use of colour, design, and composition. Any student can be instructed in the production of each of these qualities and yet the judge may look at a painting or other work and see that although certain criteria have been achieved on each dimension, the whole is not satisfactory. As in all other domains, formal operations means abstracting from the particular, rising above sets of rules of production to make something which is not simply original but which integrates aesthetic qualities in a new whole.

> one of the key features of the aesthetic mode of discourse and awareness (is) the breaking apart and/or bringing together in new ways what have previously been concepts and even categories of a strictly conventional kind.

> The arts promote a very real integration in our sense and appreciation of the range of meanings that are present in one organic whole. This characteristic of synthesis is to be found in no other mode of discourse.
>
> (Gulbenkian Foundation 1982:22, 23 respectively)

Cognitive conflict in the arts may involve both analysis of work – the students' own and others' – and offering the challenge of alternative analyses, and also the continuing challenge of new syntheses within given constraints. Knowing what an individual can produce enables the teacher to question and to suggest better integration. The role of metacognition in art is even clearer. Indeed, the metacognitive process of explaining why and how a work was produced is so much a part of the art world that art is sometimes endangered as a method of expression by talking about itself too much.

## OTHER AGES

Two important studies shed light on aspects of the age/stage issue. Lovell and Shields (1967) and Webb (1974) selected children between the ages of 8 and 11 years of very high ability as assessed by the Wechsler test. The first took a cut-off of three standard deviations, and the latter four standard deviations above the mean. We know from the CSMS survey (Fig. 2.7) that about 5 per cent of 11 year-olds show early formal operational thinking (cut-off $1.65\sigma$ above the mean) so if 'mental age' alone is the criterion for the development of formal operational thinking, a child of 8 who is four standard deviations above the mean should be well in advance of an 11 year-old only $1.65\sigma$ above the mean. Lovell and Shields used the equilibrium in the balance, pendulum and chemical combinations tasks as individual interviews in the orthodox Genevan manner and Webb used equilibrium in the balance, and floating and sinking likewise. Neither of the studies found any of the children showing even early formal operational behaviour on the tasks before the age of 10. This seemed at the time strong evidence for the original Genevan age/stage model, with formal operational thinking age-limited to appearing initially at about 10 or 11 years.

However, there is another interpretation. In a series of papers Herman Epstein both proposed (1980) and later successfully defended against earlier criticism (1986, 1990) the thesis that there were spurts and plateaux in brain growth on a separate genetic time schedule than the adolescent growth spurt. Two of his sources of evidence are given in Figs 8.1 and 8.2. The proportion of total brain energy in the rest condition has shown to be strongly correlated with IQ as assessed by the Wechsler test.

It appears that there is a major brain-growth spurt around 11 years of age, and its magnitude seems about three times greater for girls. There is another around 14, and here the relative proportions are reversed. Subsequently, Epstein asked Shayer to see if there were spurts in the CSMS survey data parallel to these, and these are shown in Fig. 8.3 (Shayer and Williams 1984). The data represented in these figures can be interpreted if we make the hypothesis that the brain-growth spurts are specifically related to Piagetian stage. The brain-growth spurt at 5/6 is genetically time-tabled for the development of concrete operations, and that at 10/11 (possibly some 6–9 months later in boys) is the genetic programme for the onset of formal operations. Neurologically, what occurs is not an increase in the actual number of cells in the cerebral cortex but an increase in inter-neuronal dendritic growth, presumably in preparation for a more complex 'wiring-up' in relation to relevant

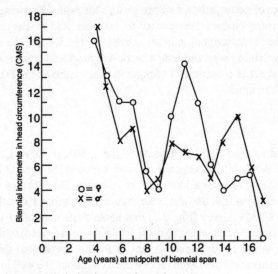

*Fig. 8.1* Increments in brain growth against age

experience to come. These preparatory brain-growth phases are well described in mammals in relation, for example, to use of the eyes and Epstein's interest was in the question: what do they anticipate in the human? Presumably if the child does not receive the appropriate experience to utilise the new nerve-fibre growth, no new and useful neuronal connections will be made. Conversely, the period following a brain-growth spurt should be the period at which intervention experiences should be most effective, and this is a possible explanation of the larger effect for the younger girls and older boys found in the CASE results reported in Chapter 6.

Our view of this evidence is that the Webb and Lovell and Shields studies definitely establish that age sets a lower limit of about 10 years on the appearance of formal operations (at least if we limit ourselves to four standard deviations above the average; Ruth Lawrence, a mathematical prodigy who, intensively coached by her father, obtained a scholarship to Oxford University to read mathematics at the age of 12 years is presumably much higher than this). The parallelism between the age of the brain-growth spurts and the population growth spurts on Piagetian tests is very suggestive and needs to be born in mind as a possible explanation of the data, and also some of the features of the intervention evidence reported in Chapters 3 and 5. No competing explanatory model has been offered for the Webb and Lovell and Shields data.

### The primary age group

Following publication of the CASE II results, many primary school teachers and parents asked 'Can we use the same methods for promoting higher-level thinking

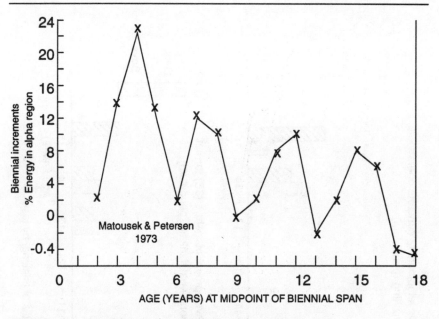

*Fig. 8.2*    Age-dependence of resting brain alpha energy

with younger pupils?' We should look at what the evidence available suggests could be answers to this question.

First, there are some relatively trivial ways in which the CASE method might be used with 9 or 10 year-olds. One might, for instance, convert the mechanics (apparatus and examples) of the existing *Thinking Science* activities to make them more suitable for the primary environment, seek applications of the reasoning patterns in more everyday and qualitative forms, and be prepared to accept a smaller proportion of the pupils benefiting from the experiences. It would also be possible to see year 6 (grade 5) as a preparatory phase for a more intense intervention programme in year 7. This preparatory phase might concentrate on concrete preparation activities, establishing and generalising the terminology of variables and relationships in concrete contexts. Such approaches could be tried by any teacher who has some understanding of the principles of cognitive intervention which we have described. But note that the replication of CASE in Korea suggested that while the programme could be started in a modified form for children as young as 10/6, the effects were not generalised until the children were a year older.

The evidence from Lovell and Shields, from Webb, and from Epstein discussed above must cast serious doubt on the practicability of a programme aimed at the promotion of formal operations in children much younger than 10 years. There is, however, a way suggested by the brain-growth spurt data in which one could imagine some key features of the CASE approach being translated for use by 6 and

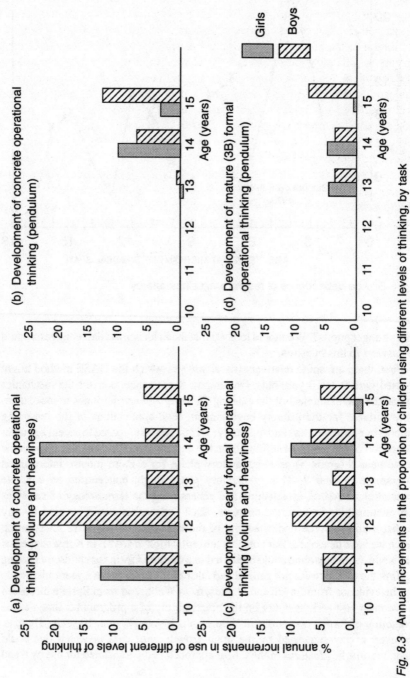

Fig. 8.3 Annual increments in the proportion of children using different levels of thinking, by task

7 year-olds. This would be an intervention where the goal was the promotion of mature concrete operations. Here it is important to refer back to Fig. 2.7 in light of our criticism of the original Genevan age/stage model. There we argued (a) that Piaget had only described the genetic programme, and (b) that the phenotypic realisation of the programme was limited to only the top 30 per cent for formal operations and only about 20 per cent actually approach the time schedule given in the growth of logical thinking (GLT) for the last stage of development. An analogous differential exists for the concrete operations stage. Although the 'average' child does not achieve mature concrete operations until about 11, various studies in the literature show children in the top 20th percentile range getting to this level by 8, so again it is probably these who are realising the genetic programme. In fact, we think that one of the major causes for children not making the transition to formal operations at 12 or 13 is that the prerequisite for making this step would be the completion of the concrete operations stage in all parts of the psychological spectrum before 10 or 11. The children in the top 20 percentile range have the last three years of their primary experience to apply their concrete operations to a range of new learning material and so achieve concrete generalisation.

In this principle lies the seed of a major project waiting to be undertaken by people well versed in the nature of concrete operations, in the principles of intervention in the cognitive developmental process, and in the practical realities of primary schools. Shayer *et al.*'s (1988) multicultural study of the emergence of concrete operations from 6 to 11 years could provide an invaluable foundation for such a project. As described in Chapter 2, this monograph uses data from Australian, English, Greek, and Pakistani children's responses to a wide range of concrete tasks to test Piagetian, neo-Piagetian, and intelligence-factor models of the mind. From this work and from the original Genevan work could be developed activities at an appropriate level to provide cognitive conflict to 6 and 7 year-olds in the process of their developing the quantitative-relational (conservation, measurement, and number tasks), qualitative analytic (classification and ordering) and imaginal-spatial (imagery, mental rotation, and perspective tasks) components of concrete operational thinking. As with the CASE project, such a research and development project could almost certainly benefit from some of the methodology of the Feuerstein Instrumental Enrichment (IE) project since that project also has the first major objective of completing the concrete operations stage.

An important pointer to the form that such a project would take is offered by the work of Resnick *et al.* (1992). In view of our earlier distinction between context-delivered and context-independent intervention, it is significant that in designing an intervention for socially disadvantaged first grade (6/7 years of age) children, Resnick and co-workers set it in the context of mathematics. They state:

> We are trying, in this project, to create an apprenticeship environment for
> mathematical thinking in which children can participate daily, thus acquiring
> not only the skills and knowledge that expert mathematical reasoners possess,

but also a social identity as a person who is able to and expected to engage in such reasoning.

(p. 228)

It is clear that they are overtly rejecting the notion that they were in the game of decontextualising knowledge and competence. They also overtly reject the notion that it is necessary for children to master simpler components before they try to learn complex skills (the Gagné learning hierarchy approach). Their programme, in which an important feature was to bring the parents into the process of their children's mathematical learning, was guided by six principles:

1. Draw children's informal knowledge, developed outside school, into the classroom.
2. Develop children's trust in their own knowledge.
3. Use formal notations (identify sentences and equations) as a public record of discussions and conclusions.
4. Introduce key mathematical structures as quickly as possible.
5. Encourage everyday problem finding.
6. Talk about mathematics, don't just do arithmetic.

For the 'talk' referred to in 6, 'our programme uses a combination of whole-class, teacher-led discussion and structured small-group activity by the children'. The reader is referred to Resnick *et al.* (1992) for further detail, but it can be seen that there is considerable overlap between this description of class-management of 6/7 year-olds, and the Vygotskian element of the CASE intervention for 12/13 year-olds described in Chapter 5. The effects achieved from this admirable primary effect study (Shayer 1992) were a staggering $1.9\sigma$ in terms of pre- and post-tests using the California Achievement Test for mathematics in relation to the previous Grade 1 class. At the end of the year the *lowest* achieving child was at the 66th percentile. The *highest*-scoring child from the preceding year was at the 51st percentile. Although no evidence was offered, it would be surprising if there were not a more general effect on the children's thinking, as well as the increased mathematics achievement.

In Britain at least there has been a long tradition of early primary education methods based implicitly on Piagetian notions of the active learner. It may be that the theoretical origins of the method are sometimes lost and with it the sharp cognitive demand which it should incorporate. A project such as that suggested in this section could assume a great deal of goodwill and 'good practice' amongst primary teachers, build in a rediscovery of the theoretical foundation and, with it, practice more focused on the purpose of promoting cognitive growth.

## Further education

In the UK 'further education' is a technical term meaning education after the legal school leaving age of 16 but not including higher education. Higher education is, broadly, education leading to a university degree or its equivalent. This technical distinction is actually quite convenient for it roughly defines two post-secondary populations which have somewhat different requirements for cognitive acceleration. We will consider each separately.

Students who in the UK follow sixth form courses to 'A' level examinations and then enter university, and who in the US complete high school graduation and enter academic programmes in college are generally in the more able half of the population (although the smaller proportion of the population who go into higher education in the UK compared with either the USA or Australia mean that the ability of this group is higher than that of its American or Australian counterparts). In all countries the aim of this group is achievement within an academic field which will almost certainly assume formal operational thinking as a prerequisite. It is the obvious failure of many members of this supposedly intellectual group, especially in mathematics and the science, which has been the spur to a number of important cognitive acceleration programmes referred to in Chapter 3 under the heading 'Can formal operations be taught?' Does the limited success of these programmes indicate that 17+ is too late to repair damage caused by inadequate cognitive stimulation in early adolescence or younger? The answer depends on what one might hope to get out of an acceleration programme. It almost certainly is too late to capitalise fully on the growth in the neural network which took place at 11. However, Mehl's work described in Chapter 3 shows what possibilities there are if the focus of the programme is narrowed somewhat and trained upon cognitive strategies within a particular context. The identification of deficient strategies and design of programmes to remedy these deficiencies can have substantial effects on achievement.

Note that the reason that such programmes which focus on 'thinking skills' (a term we have studiously avoided in connection with cognitive intervention programmes) can succeed with this population is that fundamentally they have the processing capability to make use of them. This is the same argument that was used in our discussion of de Bono's work, and it applies to all academic 'study skill' programmes: to understand the heuristics being offered itself requires a certain level of processing power, or working memory space. College students, even those using only concrete generalisation, have the ability to understand a rule to 'Consider all factors', and given adequate examples and practice *within a given context* the rule may well be useful to them in designing experiments or evaluating competing arguments. Mehl's results show both the strength and weakness of the approach: very large effects in the domain in which the cognitive strategy programme was set, but no transfer to other domains.

For the other half of the population who pursue some sort of education after school, there has been a recent upsurge of interest in Britain in designing National Vocational Qualifications (NVQs) which have a common foundation across all trades and skills. A central theme in these discussions is the need for a 'common core' shared by NVQs and the academic qualification routes (Jessup 1991). There have been many attempts to define such a common core, but one element that recurs is 'problem solving skills'. This brings us back to the problem with problem solving, discussed in Chapter 3: everyone agrees that problem solving a good thing, but no one can agree what it looks like, how general it might be, nor how it can be assessed as part of a core common to plumbers and to literary critics.

In spite of these theoretical problems, recent empirical evidence suggests that there can be some mileage in an intervention programme designed to enhance cognitive strategies of students in vocational training and pre-vocational training. Blagg *et al.* (1993) has reported significant effects in schemes for trainees including students with special educational needs, technical students, and British Aerospace apprentices. The Thinking Skills at Work (TSAW) materials use many of the same foundations as Somerset Thinking Skills, based originally on Feuerstein's Instrumental Enrichment programme, but the subject matter of modules is tailored for particular vocational courses. A commerce course, for instance, might ask students to order stockroom items but require first an assessment of the problem and a plan for how it might be solved before a final order is made.

A newspaper report of the TSAW project says 'One advantage was that the course made the students work in teams – a technique which would be useful to the engineers in their working lives' (*Times Educational Supplement*, 5 March 1993:13). We suspect that the reporter has slightly missed the point here. The purpose of 'working in teams' is not so much practice for later life as an essential Vygotskyan element of the programme: the social construction of cognitive strategies.

In summarising this section on post-secondary education, we must conclude that no evidence has been found for a genuine intervention effect – in terms of long-term far-transfer – with older students, but there does seem to be real promise of enhancing achievement through cognitive skill programmes. These may be aimed either at structuring the learning situations in such a way that deficient learning strategies are avoided explicitly and more efficient ones promoted (Mehl 1985) *as if* the students had the ability to produce them spontaneously, (rather than as the fast-running programmes 'hard wired' into the brain which we aim for with younger students), or at providing concrete thinking skills set in very specific contexts. The field of post-secondary education is wide open for someone to prove us wrong in our pessimistic assessment of the possibilities for cognitive intervention with this age group.

# Chapter 9

# Changing practice

In the last chapter we expressed the Stenhousian view of the curriculum as all of the transactions which actually take place in the classroom and emphasised the inadequacy of any printed material, whether it be a science worksheet or a National Curriculum, to define the curriculum (Stenhouse 1975). At best such material can provide a framework within which the teacher can create the sort of learning she wishes. This is why school departments tend to choose books and other curriculum material which seem to accord well with their current policy rather than material which might bring about radical change. It follows that if one is interested in introducing a new sort of learning the provision of print and other audio-visual material alone, however sophisticated, is unlikely to have a radical effect on teaching practice. For real change some process of teacher induction is required.

In this chapter we first look at the general problem of evaluating inservice education for teachers (INSET), then consider some successful and less successful models of INSET and the research evidence on what does work in terms of student achievement. Features of INSET in the original CASE II project are described, some consideration given to its strengths and weaknesses, and then a new model for INSET is developed and its current expression outlined. Although our INSET is focused on the specific task of helping teachers change their practice towards a more interventionist mode, much of our experience will be of quite general use to INSET providers.

## EVALUATION OF INSET

The ultimate question to be asked of an inservice teacher education programme intended to change teaching practice is: can its effects be observed in pupils? Answering this question turns out to be rather difficult and the INSET establishment (see for instance Bolam 1987, Eraut *et al.* 1988, and Bridges 1989) consequently prefers to enumerate the methodological and financial problems associated with evaluating INSET in terms of pupil outcomes and then turns, perhaps a little too quickly, to 'formative' evaluation processes as the only workable form of evaluation available.

Some of the difficulties of evaluating an INSET programme in terms of whether or not it has had any measurable effect on pupils are:

*Interaction effects.* Twenty years ago Gardner (1974) presented an elegant study showing how the use made by different pupils of a given teacher behaviour was mediated by personality, such that the application of a simple process-product model could easily lead to erroneous conclusions. Where a particular teacher characteristic at first sight appeared unrelated to pupil performance, deeper analysis showed that it positively affected pupils of one personality type, and negatively affected pupils of a different personality type.

*The dilution effect.* A teacher, like anyone else, is subjected to a great variety of stimuli every day. An INSET event, however impactful it may appear to be, has to compete with all of the other stimuli in shaping the teacher's behaviour. The ascription of a particular behaviour to a particular INSET experience is not necessarily straightforward. Exactly the same is true of the pupils' experiences. It is difficult to ascribe a particular pupil outcome to a particular stimulus provided by the teacher. Multiply these effects together, and the link between an INSET input and a pupil outcome becomes very tenuous indeed.

*Uncertainty over best possible effect of an input.* So much of what we do in INSET courses is based on unsupported assumptions about what constitutes effective teaching and learning. 'Process skills' in science, 'the communicative method' in language teaching, and 'new mathematics' have all had their dawns and middays of fashion amongst practitioners and teacher educators. The measurability of outcomes associated with such assumed good practice remains problematical. The problem is that if you are not sure whether or not teaching system X works, in any sense, then an evaluation of INSET in system X which shows no gain in pupil learning may either be because the INSET was poorly delivered, or because system X does not work. There is no way of telling which.

From this brief list of difficulties, we can draw up criteria for possible types of INSET for which process-product evaluation might be useful. We will start with the last, since this where we have a new advantage.

*Uncertainty.* We have shown that the CASE intervention method does lead to long-term gains in secondary students' ability to learn. Given a system that has been shown to work under the conditions of its development, it becomes possible to assess the effect of INSET with more certainty. If we run INSET programmes to introduce CASE (our System X) to a new group of teachers and there is no effect on their pupils, then we can be fairly certain that the INSET has not been good enough. Knowing that CASE teaching, when thoroughly taken on board by teachers, does have an effect on pupil learning allows us to isolate the INSET as the weak link if we do not get a similar result after a new and modified programme of training.

*Dilution.* We propose a gin-and-tonic model here. Both gin and tonic have fairly distinctive flavours. If you cannot taste the gin (or cannot detect it by the effect that it has on you) then you need to increase the concentration. It is unrealistic to think that a one-day INSET session is going to have much lasting effect on teachers' practice, let alone on students' learning. Just how much exposure is required to produce a permanent effect on students is a matter of empirical investigation, and later we will present some evidence about the concentration required.

*Interaction* remains a problem. In the CASE II project we did find that amongst each group of pupils some (between 20 per cent and 40 per cent) achieved gains of two standard deviations or more, while the remainder showed little difference from controls. Whilst this allowed us to report overall significant gains, it left us wondering what were the pupil characteristics of the high-gain group that differentiated them from the low-gain group. Since we had used no personality or learning-style measurements we have no way of answering this. This story is salutary, and emphasises the value of some sort of personality inventory even in relatively hard-nosed process-product research designs ostensibly looking only for cognitive gains.

## INSET MODELS

### Inservice-onservice in Indonesia

The 'inservice-onservice' model that was used in CASE II had its origins in Indonesia where the government was trying to upgrade the work of science and mathematics teachers in secondary schools throughout the country. Indonesia has the fourth largest population in the world spread over a 3000 mile archipelago containing many cultures, religions, and languages. The secondary school population is growing rapidly as the general population growth rate is compounded by the government's determination to make secondary education available to an ever increasing proportion of the population. Previous large scale INSET projects had been based on the 'cascade' model. Activity methods had been introduced by expert practitioners to provincial super-trainers, who transmitted the methods to regional trainers, and so on. After the first one or two steps of the cascade the grasp of the methods by the trainers became so tenuous that the only method of transmission with which they felt comfortable was formal lectures and the crystallisation of activity methods in sets of rules. Little or no effect was observed in schools.

The directors of the PKG (*Pemantapan Kerja Guru*: Improving the work of the teachers) project were determined not to repeat this mistake. The INSET model they devised involved selecting instructors from amongst the best secondary school teaching practitioners in each province, training them in both the content and methods of modern science and mathematics teaching, and then sending them back to their provinces. There they had initially to go back to their schools to practice the new methods. After one semester, they started to run INSET courses for teachers in their locality. The important features of these courses which we borrowed for CASE INSET were:

- they were relatively long-term courses, spread over one semester or one year, and
- they involved a mixture of
  - inservice workshops where the teachers met to learn about new materials, practice new methods and feedback on their experiences so far, and
  - work by the instructors in the teachers' own schools

The great strength of this approach was immediately obvious to an observer: teachers could first practice new techniques in the relative safety of the inservice workshop, and then be helped to put them into practice in the 'real' world of their own school. Whatever the particular conditions of their school they could not say 'this will never work in my school' and they could not, as so many of us do, keep finding excuses to put off the day when we will start something new. They had to start the new methods immediately because an instructor was coming to visit, but at the same time could feel confident in making new starts because of the support which the instructor provided. At the next inservice day they had the chance to discuss their experiences with instructors and other teachers.

Adey's experience of working with the PKG project and Eggleston's (1984) evaluation of the project convinced us that if there was to be change in teaching practice towards an interventionist methodology it would need the support of work in schools by the trainers/researchers and accordingly this element was built into the project proposal.

### Joyce's findings: empirical support

After CASE had been running for some years it was gratifying, although not especially surprising, to find good empirical evidence for our dedication to work in schools. Bruce Joyce and his co-workers (Joyce and Showers 1980, 1988) noted that an INSET programme designed to introduce a new method may include the following features:

- the provision of *information* and theory about the method
- *demonstration* of the method by the trainers
- an opportunity for participants to *practice* the new method during the workshop
- provision of *feedback* to participants on their practice
- *coaching* of participants in the method in their own school setting

They noted further that the following outcomes were possible from an inservice programme:

- teachers' *knowledge* about the method is increased
- their *skill* in using the method is increased. In other words, they are better able to use the methods
- their *classroom practice* is changed. This is distinguished from skill development in that not only can they do it, but in fact they do do it as a matter of course in their teaching.

Joyce and Showers undertook a meta-analysis of nearly 200 studies of the effect of INSET. They state their conclusions strongly, summarised in Table 9.1. Note that these are cumulative effects. We do not, for instance, have information on the relative effect of coaching in school which does not include a theory element in the training, and so would be wise not to assume that 'practice is all'. In fact experience suggests just the opposite: if teachers are not given a chance to understand why they are being asked to change their practice they are far less likely to do so. Nevertheless, the message from Joyce's work is clear. Work in schools is necessary, if not sufficient. If you do not get into schools, you are not going to have any effect on what happens in them.

Table 9.1   Mean effect-sizes in standard deviation units of different INSET procedures on possible INSET outcomes

| INSET feature | Outcome: development of teachers'... | | |
| | knowledge | skill | practice |
| --- | --- | --- | --- |
| give information | 0.63 | 0.35 | 0.00 |
| + demonstrate | 1.65 | 0.26 | 0.00 |
| + opportunity to practice | | 0.72 | 0.00 |
| + feedback | 1.31 | 1.18 | 0.39 |
| + coaching in school | 2.71 | 1.25 | 1.68 |

Source: after Joyce and Showers 1988:71

**Evaluation of IE in Somerset**

An insight into the importance of onservice work in schools is gained by comparing the Shayer and Beasley (1987) evaluation of Feuerstein's Instrumental Enrichment (FIE) described in Chapter 3 with the government-funded Lower Attaining Pupil Programme (LAPP 1983–1988) which focused on pilot studies to help underachieving students in their last two years of compulsory education.

A meticulous evaluation of the IE element of LAPP was conducted by the Chief Educational Psychologist of Somerset, Nigel Blagg, who received training in IE with the first cohort of teachers. Pupils received pre- and post-tests of mental abilities (British Abilities Scale), cognitive development with a Piagetian battery, tests of achievement in reading, mathematics and work study skills, and various tests of behaviour, self-esteem and attitudes to school work. The net conclusion of the evaluation was that there were no differences whatsoever between IE and control classes on any of the product or ability measures used. The best that can be said is that on a few of the behavioural and attitudinal measures the IE pupils deteriorated less than the controls over the period of five terms before they left school. This is the most thorough report of a non-effect that we have seen.

Can we put Blagg's (1991) conclusion together with the Weller and Craft (1983)

report of the Schools Council IE project and conclude that IE is useless? We do not believe so, and believe that in Chapter 3 we have fairly selected those studies which have established its potential. Indeed one of the prime motives for Shayer and Beasley's replication of IE was unease at the way in which the Schools Council IE project and the IE element of LAPP were being implemented. At the time it appeared as if the error of the infamous 1947 British government groundnuts scheme was being repeated: going to full-scale production without learning from pilot-studies. If hurried and under-supported use of IE was going to be reported, it was important to find out what IE could deliver under optimal conditions. A review of the respective conditions for implementation will make this clear.

The factors making for possible success of the Shayer and Beasley (1987) study were (a) unstinting support from the Head of the Special School, himself a psychologist, creating a school atmosphere favourable to teaching the students concerned; (b) the age range chosen, starting at 12+, which much of the evidence in this book has shown to be a good 'window' for intervention; (c) very substantial inservice support for the teacher involved; and (d) substantial onservice support. Shayer was present at between one and two hours a week for the IE lessons conducted for the first two terms of the replication, and there was always time for discussion with the teacher after the lessons.

By contrast, the LAPP programme was used with years 10 and 11 (15+ to 16+). The students were already disaffected, and although their mean IQ was only on average $0.65\sigma$ below average (91.7) their scores on tests of school achievement averaged over a standard deviation below normal. Nearly all the students left the four schools of the Somerset LAPP study at Easter in year 11, so already at the outset of the project would know they had only five terms of schooling to go. Blagg (1991) reports that 'the project did not arise out of local enthusiasm for FIE', but was hastily organised by the Chief Education Officer only a term before the project was due to begin.

> The attitude of senior management toward Instrumental Enrichment at the outset of the project in each of the four schools would be best described as neutral and relatively uninformed.

> Both staff and pupils, in some schools, were hostile and cynical about being withdrawn from chosen options to participate in an unknown course... and... the unfortunate initial implementation period left a legacy of discontent in some schools.

The inservice provision was relatively generous. All 12 teachers received a full week of FIE training and the five who joined from the outset received three further one-week training courses in the second and third year of the project. The others had one further week. However, three of the 10 classes involved in the project did not have continuity of the same teacher in both years and only three classes were taught throughout by a teacher with one year's previous experience of teaching IE. So this was an *inservice*, but not an *onservice* model of training. No support staff with previous experience of teaching IE and with understanding of its principles and theory visited the IE lessons in the schools to assist the teachers with the specifics of the methodology.

Table 9.2   Implementation factors in two IE replications

| Factor | Somerset | Shayer/Beasley |
|---|---|---|
| Heads supporting initiative as within-school policy | No | Yes |
| Onservice training provided | No | Yes |
| Inservice training provided | Yes | Yes |
| Age range of students | 15+ to 16+ | 12+ to 13+ |

It is the case that students in the Shayer and Beasley study received on average over twice as much exposure to IE: 3 hours per week over six terms compared with an average of 1.6 hours a week over five terms in LAPP. However, close inspection of the Blagg data reveals no difference between the classes which had received an above average number of hours compared with those who had received below average and we are therefore inclined to put more weight on the factors described by Joyce as affecting the outcome of school change. In Table 9.2 these factors are compared.

To some degree these factors are interactive. The age of the Somerset students, the fact that they were already labelled – by themselves or others – as relative school failures, and were already looking to early school leaving, is part of the cause of their poor attitude to IE. By contrast, at the special school of the Shayer/Beasley study the 12 year-olds were in a supportive atmosphere which made them relatively willing to be challenged to more demanding thinking and learning behaviour. But the Joyce research cited above supports the view that two of these factors might have been crucially causative. Lack of an internal school policy, identified with the headteacher, actively promoting the curriculum change is one, and absence of the onservice element of the teacher training is the other. It is significant that both of the other studies cited in Chapter 3, Feuerstein and co-workers (1980) and the Vanderbilt study in North America (Shayer and Beasley 1987), featured onservice participatory and coaching visits by experienced IE trainers.

## FIE and MACOS: a cautionary tale

The IE training referred to above for the LAPP project in Somerset was bought in from Curriculum Development Associates (CDA), Inc. of Washington DC, a commercial agency. The model used is one of withdrawal of the teacher for one-week intensive courses in which they are told about and shown the specifics of the teaching methodology and also introduced to the theory underlying it. In the case of IE each week covers one year's average school coverage of IE instruments.

CDA were also responsible for the INSET in relation to *Man, a Course of Study* (MACOS). MACOS was a most interesting piece of curriculum for 10 to 12 year-olds designed in the early 1960s with the close involvement of Jerome Bruner. It undertook to introduce children, at their level, to the processes and findings of the social sciences and social biology and pioneered new and appropriate methods of class management. The class discussion style had some overlap with that used in Lipman's philosophy. Yet who, in Britain or North America, knows what is being talked about in this paragraph? The cautionary tale is to do, not with the training methods CDA use, but with the way in which both MACOS and IE at the time of the Somerset study had legally tied the publication of the course materials to the purchase of CDA training. It was only possible to buy or even inspect the course materials and teachers' guides after the training had been paid for. Reflecting on CDA's publication strategy, Shayer and Beasley (1987) concluded that:

> It can therefore be predicted that IE will suffer the same fate as *Man, a Course of Study*, and for the same reason. This fate is of (a) being fossilised in its present form, and (b) of only reaching a tiny proportion of those whose professional skills might be affected by it. The contrast between the effect of MACOS on British school practice, compared with that of the Nuffield science courses, openly published and plagiarised on all sides like all good curricula, is instructive. The experience, theory and fruitfulness of the Feuerstein team is too valuable to remain locked up in a commercial agreement.
>
> (p. 117)

The lesson for those involved in INSET for school innovation, and in particular those involved in the promulgation and development of intervention skills which are the subject matter of this book, is that a teaching strategy which is standing still is a strategy that is dying. Those who successfully offer onservice training, in whatever method, had better go as prepared to learn from the experience as to teach. Only by being part of the process by which new teaching skills are developed, recorded, and made publicly available for other teachers likewise to develop them further, can the trainer of teachers find ground to stand on which is defensible. And they will still find buyers for what they offer, never fear.

## CASE-INSET

In introducing the CASE intervention methods to teachers we have taken a strong line on the role of theory, especially psychological theory, in changing practice. We concluded above that although the provision of theory alone has no effect on practice it remains reasonable to suppose that an understanding of some underlying learning theory is necessary for teachers to understand why they are making the changes that they are making. If one were not to do so, it would be to cast teachers in the role of technicians who could be instructed to follow set procedures to produce a certain result. Clearly this would be an absurd position which would be incompatible with the view of the curriculum as the complete matrix of teacher–pupil–material interactions in which the teacher is a responsive and responsible professional who can react to his or her students flexibly in the light of their responses and of the objectives of the curriculum or intervention.

Accordingly, the provision of some theoretical understanding of the nature of concrete and formal operations, of possible mechanisms for cognitive development and what may be done to encourage them, and of the role of cognitive conflict and metacognition became a strand which ran right through the CASE-INSET programme. This theory-base was delivered through short lectures, critical readings and discussion, and the application of theoretical principles to practical activity design and analysis of classroom scenarios.

Building some theory into an INSET (or for that matter pre-service) programme recognises the teacher as a professional but it also does far more than that. It is an essential step in the transfer of ownership of the methodology from the researcher to the teacher. This is constructivism for teachers. We understand that pupils must construct knowledge for themselves and, in CASE, must construct also their own reasoning patterns from the material that we give them. So also must teachers construct the methods of cognitive intervention for themselves.

While it is generally true that some understanding of the learning process is essential for successful teacher development, it is especially important in interventionist teaching which requires a combination of analytical and inventive teaching strategies. Analysis is required to 'read' an individual response or the progress of a whole lesson in terms of the levels of understanding exhibited and challenge provided. Invention is required to provide the right type and level of stimulus in the context of the lesson and of the cognitive objectives of the programme. No specific rules can be given for this invention, and the teacher must rely on his or her growing understanding of the principles of intervention on top of their normal professional competencies. The building for themselves of intervention strategies is related to the sense of ownership that teachers build in taking on a new methodology. Until one has made a method one's own, with one's own idiosyncratic interpretation and colouring by personality and the particular school environment, it will remain an 'add-on' skill which is easily lost when the external stimulus of the INSET programme or research project is removed. This may be especially true with Feuerstein IE where the teachers do not have the support of having the intervention lessons placed within the context of subject teaching with which they are already familiar. The curriculum in the classroom is created and managed by the teacher. Ownership of a methodology enables it to be built in naturally to this classroom curriculum to achieve the desired effects.

This is not to say that psychological theory is the only, or even the most important, element in the sharing of ownership. Of at least equal importance is the opportunity to reflect on practice. We sometimes talk of the provision of feedback by teachers at INSET workshops as if its only purpose is to allow the programme devisers to learn what works and what does not and so to alter their programme.

This certainly is one function of feedback, and one that might be seen as a new ownership right of teachers as they take a curriculum method on board, but of more direct relevance to teacher development is the opportunity that the giving of feedback provides for the teachers' own reflection on what has happened. Here we have the metacognitive process at work again. The process of sharing experiences with other teachers and with researchers means putting into words both accounts of what has occurred, for good or ill, in lessons and also an evaluation of those events in the light of the overall aims of the cognitive intervention programme. Participants at INSET workshops often report that the most valuable experience has been a chance to talk with other teachers. This is partly because teaching is an isolated profession, both in the daily work in closed classrooms and in the sense that we are never quite sure if other schools are like ours, and there is some reassurance either in finding that other schools and teachers are having the same trouble as you are, or that your conditions are genuinely much worse than those of others. But it is also because the process of de-briefing a series of lessons in a professional environment gives one a safe opportunity to re-live experiences and bring to consciousness, perhaps for the first time, the extent to which the intended structure of the lesson (concrete preparation, cognitive conflict, pupils' metacognition, and bridging) was managed. The re-discovery of Dewey's (1933) recognition of the role of teacher reflection (Zeichner and Tabachnick 1991) is encouraging to the enterprise of those concerned with change in classroom practice.

The CASE-INSET programme followed the long-term inservice-onservice model of PKG, gradually sharing ownership with teachers and allowing them to practice new skills and to feedback on them in a supportive atmosphere. After a couple of cycles of:

- this what to do
- this is why you do it
- do it
- tell us about it
- this is what you do next

and so on, the INSET group of teachers and researchers became comfortable with one another and participants began to internalise much of the principle of cognitive intervention: cognitive conflict and metacognition. The action became thought (Butler 1992); now the thought must become action.

This is the point at which participants start to invent bridging lessons in which some of the intervention parameters are used to design opportunities for students to recognise reasoning patterns in the context of their ordinary science learning. The development by teachers of their own interventionist activities in the INSET workshop environment is a critical part of the transfer of ownership of the core message and methods into teachers' own contexts. We have emphasised from the start that the curriculum materials called *Thinking Science* simply offer an exemplar set of activities which provide opportunities for cognitive conflict and metacognition. Used by someone who has no familiarity with those ideas, either intuitive or instructed, they are unlikely to assist students significantly in terms of cognitive development. On the other hand, a teacher who has come to understand the principles well through instruction, practice with the examples, and reflection should be able to build them into new contexts without recourse to the particular exemplars of *Thinking Science*. Teachers start to write their own activities in our INSET workshops so that they can externalise and bring to the front of their consciousness the features which assist cognitive development and at the same time place these in curriculum content contexts which are important to them. In the case of IE this last step has up to now seemed so formidably difficult that no published example can be cited of it having occurred – but see the different strategy of Mehl and Strang described in Chapter 3.

There is some danger in this process since it is not initially easy to focus on the intervention purpose and prevent content objectives from dominating the cognitive features. In states which have a prescribed National Curriculum teachers sometimes are so concerned about the achievement of externally set attainment targets that when they are asked to write their own intervention activities in the context of content which is relevant to them they lose sight of the interventionist objectives. Awareness of this danger helps to forestall it. Activities developed by teachers during the workshop are shared with other participants and the discussion which follows helps to shape ideas.

Some readers may object that, in spite of the talk of ownership, we are presenting a distinct message of transfer of methodology from the 'experts' (researchers, instructors, INSET providers) to the 'novices' (teachers), rather than a democratically explored discovery together of the way forward. We make no apologies for this. We have had the good fortune to be able to explore the process of cognitive acceleration both theoretically and practically for a number of years and it seems perfectly proper that we behave as guides for others exploring the same territory. Of course, during each exploration we all discover something new and move our thinking forward.

## CASE II: GOOD RESEARCH BUT POOR SCHOOL DEVELOPMENT?

In the last section we tried to show how effective INSET uses learning theory, feedback mechanisms, and mini-curriculum development activity to transfer ownership of a methodology to teachers as reflective professionals. Now we must consider how work with individual teachers must be seen within the context of whole departments.

In the original CASE project INSET was not the prime purpose but a necessary means by which the teachers could be introduced to the experimental methods. The school visits also played a major role in monitoring progress and the collection of feedback in order to meet the research agenda of investigating effects on achievement of the CASE intervention and the curriculum agenda of producing a set of trialed exemplar curriculum materials. In CASE II one or two teachers from each school were involved in the project. They were teachers who had, at least, shown some interest in the project from early on and who with continued support from the research team were able to maintain and develop the CASE methods in the classes designated as 'experimental'. In some cases they used the same methods and some of the same activities with other years (but not with other classes in the same years). Their sense of ownership was heightened by the knowledge that they were participating in a research project the outcome of which was an open question. Their feedback on the progress of the activities was genuinely sought by the researchers anxious to know how the draft activities worked out in practice. Nevertheless, at the end of the project period very few of them continued to use the CASE programme as a regular component of their curriculum. Why was this?

It is true that some of the CASE teachers were promoted and moved to other schools but for others it was almost certainly the case that, with the withdrawal of support by the researchers, the individual teachers felt isolated within their departments. In only one of the schools did *Thinking Science* become departmental policy during the project and in that school every science teacher was inducted into the methods within the school and the materials were made part of the standard year 8 curriculum. The key to implanting a new methodology lies at departmental level.

## CASE-INSET now

In the INSET programmes we ran after the full impact of the cognitive intervention methodology had become clear we insisted that we work not with individual teachers but with whole departments. Only in this way can individual teacher development, shared within a department, both spread the word by example and also provide a supportive environment for the individual as common experience develops. A communication strategy needs to be established within the department such that the intervention methods are enriched through the sharing of its various applications. This also serves the important function of making the methods public, unattached to any individual, such that it remains alive as members of staff leave and are replaced. Furthermore, an implementation and management strategy which is public can more easily be transferred to other departments and become part of a whole-school policy.

Establishing such a strategy requires careful attention to intra- and extra-departmental management mechanisms and sensitivities and the mapping of these on to the INSET features we described in the last section in a way which is both practical and cost-effective. Clearly it is not practical to expect all teachers in a science department to attend the same INSET workshop; the cost in supply cover and disruption in the school would be prohibitive. Accordingly, we recommended a pattern in which one member of the science department would be designated CASE co-ordinator, and she or he would attend each INSET workshop. A second teacher would accompany the co-ordinator, usually a different person on each occasion.

## Coaching in CASE

We have made much of the importance of work in schools by inservice tutors if a new method is to become part of the school's normal practice. Joyce and Showers' (1988) view on this in-school process, which they call coaching and we have called the onservice element, is that demonstration and action are far more powerful than verbal direction. One responds to a teacher's incomplete mastery of a technique not by talking about it but by demonstrating the technique in the teacher's class. Apart from the practical problems of such a view, there is a suggestion in this approach that there is a 'right' way of teaching which suits both coach and trainee. This is in contrast to the established experience of teacher educators that students cannot be given general rules or methods but that each must be helped to find their own style. Furthermore, the 'demonstrator' view seems to de-emphasise the role of reflection by teachers in changing their practice.

We have adopted a more traditional view of the role of the tutor in school. As described already we would normally discuss with a teacher the lesson he/she was about to teach. We would then participate in the lesson, sharing the teaching, discussing afterwards successes and areas for potential modification. This is of course a very expensive process in terms of paying for the trainers' time, especially if one is aiming to train whole departments rather than introduce a new method to one or two teachers. The solution is to maintain the rate of school visits at the same level as it was for individual teacher INSET – two days per term in the first year and one day per term in the second year – but to develop procedures within the department designed to share expertise. These include regular departmental meetings to discuss progress, difficulties encountered, and solutions found, and peer coaching.

In Joyce's view peer coaching should follow the idea of teaching by demonstration. The coach is always the one who is teaching. The observer is learning. If the observer wants to convey to the teacher an alternative way of doing something she or he will demonstrate it when the roles are reversed. We have taken a more relaxed view of the mechanism of peer coaching. The only common essential is that teachers should learn to feel comfortable about walking into others' classes and about others walking into theirs. This alone can be a major innovation in some departments but once the plunge has been taken people soon become accustomed to the opportunity it provides for sharing experiences. Naturally providing the right kind of non-judgmental atmosphere in which all members of a department can help and learn from one another is a key role for the head of department and the INSET co-ordinator.

## Schools as units for policy

To this concentration on the department as a unit may must be added recognition of the role of a school's senior management in the introduction of a new method. It is obvious that tacit support must be provided, but what is the nature and level of action required of heads (principals), deputy heads, and heads of department for an innovation to be successful? At the bottom end, a belief that the innovation is a 'A Good Thing' is not enough. We have had experience of heads who have read of our results and determined that their schools should take on the CASE project, without either looking into the commitment that is required of the school or discussing these commitments with the head of the science department who will be charged with implementing the new work. This is not to say that every headteacher must concern her/himself with the detailed theory and practice of the intervention methods but one firm conclusion of the INSET research reported by Joyce is that without active involvement of the headteacher innovations in schools deliver no effect of value to the students. It is essential that a head, or a delegated deputy, should spend some initial time looking into the costs in terms of staff time required and acceptability of outside visitors, and readiness of the science department to make some commitment to the innovation. Now one cannot simply expect this commitment to spring ready-armed within senior management and the science department. There will be a degree of persuasion and negotiation required before some minimum level of commitment is achieved. Key people will need to be convinced of the long-term potential of the innovation and this will inevitably involve some form of 'selling'. It could be that an education authority will need to 'sell' to a headteacher, or headteacher to a head of science, or a head of science to her or his department, or any of those processes in reverse. We have found that in this process of persuasion evidence of success can be a powerful method of getting attention but is seldom sufficient by itself in persuading teachers of the importance of the innovation within their own school environment. Only by trying it out and discovering for themselves the benefits (and the associated but satisfying hard work) do teachers become convinced of the value of interventionist methods for their students.

### Encapsulating the INSET

We have taken a strong line on the need for school-based coaching, a theoretical foundation, and adequate time for effective INSET to introduce an intervention programme. However, not only is the inservice-onservice programme we offer at King's College London rather expensive, but we are limited geographically in the schools we can sensibly reach for onservice work. Accordingly we have also instituted programmes for trainers. At the time of writing the first cohort of trainers are completing their two-year programme and are already running CASE-INSET programmes in many parts of Britain, while the second cohort have started to develop their programmes for implementation in the 1993/94 academic year not only in Britain but also in continental Europe. Clearly this is a far more cost-effective way of providing interventionist training to many schools.

Finally, as disbelievers with respect to the efficiency of print or other media by itself to deliver change, we find ourselves in a difficult position when faced by schools which find the inservice-onservice programme expensive but ask for materials to help them introduce CASE methods. In order to help to meet such requests we have developed, with financial assistance from British Petroleum, an 'INSET pack' (Adey 1993). This consists of a programme of INSET activities which a head of department or other INSET provider can run in her or his school over a two-year period, following the model of our own 'live' inservice-onservice. It includes the necessary theory base and practice with activities linked to the principles of cognitive conflict, metacognition, and so on. Most importantly it includes examples on videotape of good practice in each of these principles which can form the basis of discussion within a department or other group of teachers who have decided to introduce CASE-type teaching. It is very likely that for this to be useful and successful one member of the department – not necessarily the head – would need to teach at least half a term ahead of the others and also take on the responsibility, for the department, of internalising much of the theory so as to organise the INSET effectively. It is part of our programme for the future to conduct a long-term evaluation of the use and effectiveness of this INSET pack.

# Chapter 10

# Really raising standards

Whether or not educational standards have actually fallen in any general way remains an open question the answer to which depends on sub-questions such as, 'What measures do you use for your standards?' and 'Does the claim refer to the whole population or just to an educated elite?' We do not propose to pursue these questions here because (a) there is a clear public perception that standards have fallen and this perception has been assiduously fostered and then capitalised upon by politicians and then by those sections of the media who serve the politicians. The perception is a reality which needs to be addressed; and (b) what does it matter whether standards have fallen or not? There can be nothing wrong in striving for higher standards anyway.

We are claiming in this book that we have a way of raising educational standards. The method we propose is based on a psychological model of development and of learning and if the reader is inclined to sympathise with a recent British Minister of Education (Kenneth Clarke) who dismissed such models as 'barmy theories' then we would draw their attention to the hard data of actual results in terms of higher grades in nationally recognised and publicly set examinations (Chapter 6) and suggest that such effects cannot be obtained by idle dinner-table speculation about 'what the education system needs'. To make real changes in a system one needs to understand its inner workings. No psychologist could claim that they have a full and complete understanding of the processes of development and learning, but we do claim that the theoretical model we have been using for 20 years continues to provide a basis for fruitful experiment and has now yielded sufficient detail of the mechanics of development to allow us to tweak up its power output significantly.

In this chapter we will see first what happens when we explore some popular recipes for raising standards in the light of the developmental model, then we will review the potential of interventionist methods for substantial long-term gains in academic achievement and show how this has been worked out in some particular schools. Finally, we will propose developmental plans for individual schools and see what are the implications for National Curriculum and research policies.

## SELECTION, ELECTION, OR 'LOWERING STANDARDS'?

Universal secondary education is a relatively recent phenomenon, even in the Western world. In the period between The First World War and The Second World War education beyond 14 was provided only for a small minority of the population selected on general ability and on the ability to pay, yet it was during this period that the basic pattern was evolved of what is still considered to be the feasible and accepted content of secondary education.

The relation between school teachers and students can be looked on as a process of mutual adaptation and the evolution of syllabuses of major public examinations taken at 16+ such as the French Baccalaureat or the British School Certificate as an accommodation by successive generations of teachers to their students. Thus what can be attained by 12 years, what is a reasonable further goal for 14 years, and what finally is content that it is reasonable to examine when the students are 16 will be delimited, by various processes of trial-and-error, by the intellectual development rate of the students. For that selected population which was drawn from the upper 25 per cent of the general ability range (even allowing for less bright middle-class children) this meant, in Piagetian terms, 'concrete generalisation for all and early formal for some from 12 to 13; early formal by 14; and early formal for all and mature formal for some by 16'. It is hardly surprising that the first applied research using a Piagetian model (Shayer 1972) found that traditional British science courses required early formal operational thinking from 14 years of age. This merely showed that several generations of teachers had adapted the structure of their science courses to the intellectual development of the bulk of their pupils. Teachers will have been quite unconscious of this but will simply have taught to their pupils as much as they could each year. The system will have evolved with very similar results in each country.

Naturally the introduction of secondary education for all enormously increased the range of ability in secondary schools. Curricula developed for the selected top 20 per cent were no longer appropriate and in different countries different experiments were tried to cope with this dilemma. In Britain in 1945 the problem was solved by providing completely different schools for the new intake of a less able majority, retaining a traditional academic curriculum in the grammar schools. Psychometric tests were used at 11 years of age to determine which type of school a child would go to. Widespread popular discontent with being 'selected out' of opportunities for higher level education and the associated job opportunities led to the selective system being abandoned in most parts of Britain by 1970.

In many of the German states the problem of a wide ability range continues to be administered out of existence by a tripartite secondary education system: *Gymnasia* corresponding to the British grammar school, *Realschule* providing technical education with some opportunity for transfer to *Gymnasia* at 16, and *Hauptschule* offering a basic secondary education, apparently to everyone's satisfaction ('How glad I am to be a gamma', Huxley 1932). However, even where everyone seems happy with the system, there are some important reasons why it cannot, in principle, make the most effective use of a nation's intellectual potential:

1.  We now know that all selection systems used are unreliable and fail to reveal potential in far too many students. Once labelled as a 'failure' an enormous psychological burden is hung on the child, ensuring that he lives down to the (unreliable) prediction made about him.
2.  Research has shown (Clarke and Clarke 1976) that almost all the factors responsible for deficits in children's development can be remediated by one form of intervention or another. To categorise children arbitrarily at 11 or at any other age is unduly deterministic.
3.  Finally there is a rather general biological objection to selection. This is essentially the situation facing the breeder of race-horses or the agriculture researcher selecting grains to give better yields. In the short term the policy works and the selected strains do better than chance but in the long term another strategy is also needed: that of bringing back into the breeding chain other stocks to supply other, as yet unknown, factors which relate to performance. This is necessary because it is never possible exhaustively to describe the gene-pool that relates to desired combinations of performance. In the case of children the performance of selected students is gained at the greater expense of the lack of potential performance of those students who were rejected by selection.

In North America an empirical solution to the problem of intellectually demanding subjects such as physics, applied maths and calculus has been simply (a) to postpone them until the students are 16+, and (b) to make them elective, self-contained, one-year courses. Figure 2.7 shows that within the normal school age range this policy maximises the proportion of students able to benefit from the intellectually demanding courses at about 30 per cent of the whole. European experience suggests that this is far too late to begin serious learning in these subjects, and this may account for the apparently poor showing of the USA in international comparisons for both science and mathematics and the nationwide average drop-out rate of 30 per cent before high school graduation (Blank *et al.* 1993).

Although there are those in Britain who would favour a return to selective education, they have only just started publicly to come out of the closet. In the United States the option is never even considered, so anti-democratic is it.

None of this is to say that by keeping students in wide-band mixed ability groups all will automatically benefit. In such a class where all are provided with the same fare, just the opposite is likely to be true: the more able will be under-stimulated and the less able will be continually resorting to low-level early concrete strategies such as note-taking or copying diagrams in order to appear busy. The potential virtues of the American high school and the British comprehensive school as places of effective intellectual development are only realised where there is an understanding of cognitive stimulation geared to the varied needs of its population.

## NATIONAL CURRICULA?

In Britain since the 1970s, recognition of the inherent difficulty of older curriculum materials and a liberal-democratic desire to ensure that education was not restricted to an elite led to something of a backlash. One expression of the reaction in science was a spate of 'Noddy' (Americans read 'Micky Mouse') science courses which provided lots of activity, mostly recipe following, but no cognitive demand. Such courses kept children busy and therefore teachers happy but did little either to provide opportunities for cognitive engagement or even, since they were based on an 'activity for its own sake' principle, to provide scientific information. Such programmes are thankfully receding in popularity, but 'busywork' remains the fall-back position of the teacher faced with a class disruptive through lack of appropriate (for each child) cognitive stimulation.

But if none of selection, election, or the provision of undemanding curricula provide realistic solutions for educating a wide ability range of students, where does the answer lie? From both sides of the Atlantic envious eyes have been cast at Japan, and an educational answer that strikes like a light bulb is: a National Curriculum!

We would urge our American friends – for example those involved in establishing AAAS (American Association for the Advancement of Science) 'benchmarks' for grade achievements in science (Ahlgren *et al.* 1993) – to consider the British Government's legislation on the National Curriculum (DES 1988) as a most blatant example of erroneous thinking about the possibility of raising standards in schools. For each of the major subjects in the school curriculum it features detailed descriptions of desired standards of achievement at 10 levels of attainment intended to cover the compulsory school age range of 5 to 16 years. The error in thinking, of course, is the implicit assumption that the mere publishing of desired standards of achievement will lead to their improvement just by improving *instruction*. All you have to do as a politician is to say some rude things about inefficient teachers, put in a few sanctions to keep the teachers up to the mark, and, Hey Presto!, the improvement will happen. The analysis of the first full Key Stage 3 test results in science described in Chapter 2 reveals the fallacy of such reasoning. Only 14 per cent achieved level 6, rather than the 50 per cent 'expected'. The shortfall represents both the atheoretical foundation for the expectation, and the wishful thinking that an 'ought' must perforce become an 'is'.

Our view is that some improvement is attainable merely by teachers 'teaching-to-the-test', but that this will (a) be minor – maybe some 5 or 6 per cent more students achieving level 6 by 14 years, and (b) will be very short-lived, confined to the first year after the first full yearly use of national testing, after which no further change will occur. In science, and probably in other subjects, the learning outcomes described at level 6 and above in the National Curriculum require as a necessary condition at least early formal operations and this sets a natural limit to the extent to which standards can be improved merely by improving instruction.

Worse than this, misguided attempts to 'teach to the test' for Key Stage 3 assessed at 14 years may actually have an adverse effect on achievement at Key

Stage 4, assessed at 16 years. It was part of the 'self-regulating' process of curriculum evolution described above to take a long-term view of the best way to maximise achievement of secondary school graduates. This involved using the primary school phase for developing basic skills required for learning, these skills including not only reading, writing, and computation but in the best examples the general development of thinking. In the junior secondary phase it meant spending time on the vocabulary and methods of each discipline in the curriculum so that by the senior secondary phase – in England the last two years of compulsory schooling – students were as well prepared as could be expected within an instructional view of teaching to absorb information for the 16+ examinations. If, lower down in the school system, we narrow the goals to immediate instructional objectives which define particular content we revert to the simplistic and discredited view of the development of knowledge represented by Gagné's hierarchies of learning and Skinner's behaviourism. The overall five-year (or more) spiral curriculum planning becomes distorted and no distinction is made in the kinds of learning which can most effectively take place at different ages.

The great curriculum boom of the 1970s was enthusiastically driven by liberal ideals of child-centredness but, with some very honourable exceptions (SAPA, Science 5–13, SCISP, MACOS), took little account of the psychology of learning. Thus when such approaches came under attack in the business-like late 1980s they lacked the theoretical foundations to withstand the cold blast of the Back to Basics movement. As it became a popular sport amongst politicians of all tendencies to decry the state of schools and to call for improved standards, educators found themselves increasingly exposed with inadequate rational justifications for their sincerely held convictions. Their justificactory armour had been hung up and allowed to rust. Now we need it again and must oil and repair it and add the latest defence systems, some of which have been developed in this book. We use 'defence systems' in the usual euphemistic manner, since we intend to attack with them.

## DEVELOPMENT AND WHAT CAN BE DONE ABOUT IT

Mendel, some 40 years before Piaget, had to justify his existence while doing his pioneering work on genetics by teaching physics to grammar school pupils. He was the first to make notes on the differential intellectual development of his students in relation to their ability to understand his lessons (Olby 1967: 178). It is at present the received opinion amongst psychologists that schooling can make very little difference to achievement which is related to developmental differences (Coleman 1966, Weinert 1987, Meisels and Shonkoff 1990) but our attack on the issue of academic achievement requires us to challenge this opinion.

The overall model of development sustaining the argument of this book was shown in Fig. 2.7 (repeated here as Fig. 10.1). Two important aspects of this picture are (a) that the average pupil does not progress through the stages of cognitive development nearly as fast as is normally quoted in the Piagetian literature, and (b) that there is a far wider spread of cognitive ability than had been thought. One possible explanation for these discrepancies is simply that what Piaget and his co-workers described was in fact an accurate representation of the genetic programme of human development, but that the current population profile represents a shortfall from this programme caused by deficits in the cognitive stimulation of a considerable proportion of the population.

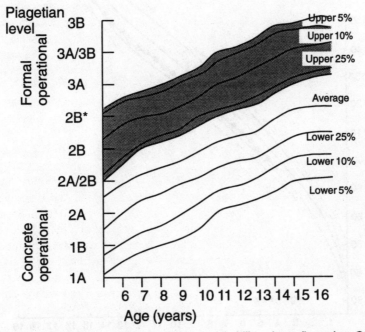

Fig. 10.1    Cognitive development by age and ability – boys (based on CSMS survey data, 1975–8)

On Tanner's curves showing boys' height against age, shown here as Fig. 10.2, note that the range of height of 12 year-olds does not overlap that of 6 year-olds. The shortest 12 year-old is taller than the tallest 6 year-old, at least within the middle 90 per cent of the population. In contrast, the CSMS cognitive development curves show a far wider range such that there is considerable overlap even between 6 year-olds and 16 year-olds. In the course of a demonstration that Jensen's (1973) interpretation of psychometric test data in terms of racial differences must be fallacious, Tizard (1975) cited data on the heights of London schoolboys taken from surveys conducted between 1909 and 1959. The mean difference between the heights of the boys at 12 years is 1.6 standard deviations, and the 7 year-old boys at the 90th percentile of the 1959 survey have the same height as the 12 year-olds at the 17th percentile of the 1909 survey, so there is a considerable overlap between

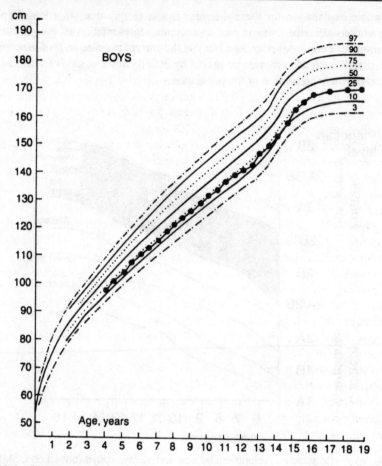

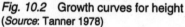

*Fig. 10.2* Growth curves for height
(*Source*: Tanner 1978)

the two sets of survey data – as indeed there is in Fig. 10.1. The usual interpretation of Fig. 10.2 is that as a result of substantial equalling out of nutritional opportunities between the 1910s and the 1950s in Europe, nearly the whole population of children can be said now to be realising the genetic programme for physical growth within, of course, the limits of variation dictated by real differences between families and between children.

While we cannot be certain that the pattern for cognitive development must necessarily be the same as that for physical, it is a real possibility that the CSMS curves in fact represent a deficit in cognitive stimulation. Were the overall environment as favourable to mental development of children as it has been to physical development in Europe since the Second World War then one would expect closer resemblance between the range of Tanner curves for height and the range of CSMS curves for cognitive development. On this argument, only the top 30 per cent of the current cognitive developmental range (shaded in the Fig. 10.1) represents the human genetic programme, the remaining 70 per cent representing deficits in the social and intellectual environment. It is not a coincidence that this top 30 per cent broadly conforms to the developmental pattern originally reported in Geneva.

We are now in a position where it may be possible to achieve a change in the process of mental development of the whole population of children equivalent to that obtained between the 1920s and 1960s for physical development, and over a similar period. What is required is an educational programme designed as an intervention in children's cognitive developmental progress.

In this book we have instanced one intervention programme – the CASE project – which based on principles of concrete preparation, cognitive conflict, construction zone activity, metacognition, and bridging has delivered striking increases in long-term school achievement as well as on psychological tests. We have given a relatively large amount of space to this (Chapters 5 and 6) because we needed to convince the reader that the notion of intervention was viable. It was essential to show specific evidence that schooling can make a difference, that the general raising of standards was possible. This established, it becomes possible to reflect on the relative scope both of other approaches to intervention, and of alternative approaches to improving instruction as well. By combining programmes of intervention with improvements in instruction itself the aim would be to bring the mental development of all children within the top 30 per cent range in Fig. 10.1. This would put students within reach of the attainment thought desirable – for example, that specified in the British *Science in the National Curriculum*.

In summary, it is not simply the case that teachers need to present the information required more efficiently, or that they need to get children involved in more active learning, or even that teachers need to know their subjects better – although all these may help when dealing with the instruction of the top 25 per cent. If the learning tasks involve too complex a processing of information the limiting factor to achievement will not be prior knowledge, but will be the inability of most students to process at that level. Repeating the work a year later – more of the same – will not help. For over 50 per cent of the students time and energy may be better spent, say in the first two or three years of secondary education, in activities which will accelerate their intellectual development to the point where they are able to cope with the demands of the curriculum. We have described and exemplified how this can be done and what results are possible from intervention methods. Now we should look at the implication of this model for curriculum planning.

## AGES FOR INTERVENTION: WINDOWS OF OPPORTUNITY

From what we now understand about the nature of intervention, a new curriculum model emerges. It has its own 'key stages' but these key stages are derived from understandings of brain growth and the critical opportunities for the development of higher stages of thinking, while the 'content' of the curriculum within these key stages are intervention activities designed to maximally promote the next stage of cognitive development. In Chapter 8 (p. 141), ages of brain-growth spurts were described and those at 5/6 years and 10/11 years were related to the development of concrete and formal operations respectively. Our concern has been with the latter of these two periods, although we did speculate in Chapter 8 about possibilities at the earlier age range.

In describing the nature of cognitive intervention immediately following the 10/11 spurt, maximising the opportunity to promote formal operational thinking, it is important to have a clear model of what is possible and what is cost-effective. It could be argued that the top 15 per cent of the population who appear to achieve early formal operations by 13 years of age and mature formal operations by 15 are in no need of intervention at all, but only good instruction. Furthermore, the next 15 per cent may require only a modification of the timing of the instructional sequence, since all will have at least early formal thinking by 15 years of age. The essential aim of intervention between the ages, say, of 11 years 6 months and 14 years would be at least to raise as many as possible to the early formal level of thinking by 14 years, making the strategies of good instruction accessible to them in the most content-rich years of schooling – years 9, 10 and 11 in the British system, and grades 9 to 12 in North America. In fact, the CASE II evidence has suggested that even for students lying in the top 15 to 30 per cent of the ability range the intervention was beneficial in hastening their move toward mature formal operations (3A/3B).

If we accept the evidence of Webb (1974) and Lovell and Shields (1967) that even the brightest of children show no formal operational thinking before the age of 10, then it would appear that the brain-growth spurt at 11 is programmed for this qualitative change. What is special about the top 15 per cent of children that they develop formal operations so soon after this brain-growth spurt? Here we can invoke a general biological feature of animal development, whether it be metamorphic changes or just stage-like developments, that an organism only passes through a developmental phase when it has completed all aspects of the preceding one. The top 5 per cent of children (Shayer *et al.* 1988) show already all the major features of mature concrete operational thinking before age 8. The top 15 per cent of children will already have had two to three years preceding the 11 year brain-growth spurt when they have integrated all aspects of concrete operations into the level of concrete generalisation. Given this, they then utilise the next developmental phase after 11 for its proper genetic purpose. For the other 70 per cent without an intervention programme to take them further the brain-growth phase at 11 (and the subsequent one at 14/15) will serve only to allow completion of the development of concrete operations, incomplete by 11.

### Girls in particular

We have so far presented the CSMS developmental survey data, on which much of our argument depends, only for boys. The equivalent data for girls shows that although they are marginally ahead of boys up to the age of 14, after this they show no further increase in formal operational thinking. On the other hand, less able girls keep pace with the boys up to 16 in the development of concrete operations (2B*) (Shayer 1989). Correspondingly, the pre-adolescent brain-growth spurts at ages 10/11 are more substantial in girls while the later brain-growth spurt at about 15 is more substantial in boys. It seems that unless girls have completed the transition to formal operations before 14 they will have missed the opportunity to complete the last stage of their cognitive development. More than seems to be the case for boys, for girls the 10/11 brain-growth spurt appears specifically to be timetabled for the development of formal operations. We have seen in the evidence from CASE II, CASE III, and in the Korean replication of CASE for 11 year-olds, that girls seem to benefit more than boys from intervention at this age. There seems to be a 'window' at 11/12 particularly favourable to the development of girls, and unless advantage is taken of this some girls will lose out later relative to boys.

The implication of this is that those with a concern for gender-fairness need to plan intervention strategies in schools so that in years 7 and 8 (grades 6 and 7) girls get the maximum opportunity to complete their cognitive development. This is quite in contrast to the practice which used to be followed when selective education for only the top 20 per cent was the rule in England. Then the scoring rules for the psychometric tests used for selection at 11+ were deliberately biased in favour of boys, since girls were already scoring higher on average.

## FORMAL OPERATIONS IN CONTEXT

In Chapter 8 the issue of context-independent and context-delivered intervention models was reviewed and a sketch made of the steps which would be needed if context-delivered intervention programmes were to be designed in the context of school subjects other than science. It was argued that there was no barrier in principle to this although it would require a major applied research effort. This is because of the specialised nature of formal models. Remember that the top 15 per cent of 14 year-olds already have early formal (3A) capacity, and that the 'traditional' school curriculum in terms of academic subjects evolved through specialist teachers adapting unconsciously to the development of the selected sample of the adolescent population they were charged to teach. As soon as evidence has to be weighed and judged – whether it be qualitative in history or literature, or quantitative in science, mathematics, or some aspects of geography – and conflicting interpretations are possible, then formal operational schemata such as control of variables, or proportion appear. But they are contextualised, doing their proper work within specialised domains with the well-known names of academic school subjects and the trades and professions of adult work-life. Lack of appreciation of this fact led to the misguided criticisms of the Piagetian model dealt with in Chapter 7. Anyone can make simple comparative judgements, whatever the field of application, for they require only concrete operations which are common to all, but it takes some specialised experience before someone perfectly capable of controlling variables in a scientific investigation can show an equivalent level of competence in weighing possible causes in history.

## REMEDIAL TEACHING: COME IN FROM THE COLD

One of the motives for initiating work on the CASE project was that when we replicated Feuerstein's Instrument Enrichment in a Special school in the early 1980s (Shayer and Beasley 1987) it seemed that this left the middle range of secondary students uncatered-for in intervention terms. If as a first approximation it can be said that IE caters for the bottom 25 per cent of the ability range, then it would be necessary as well to design an intervention explicitly for those between the 30th and the 70th percentiles. This may mean that whereas context-delivered intervention programmes are more suitable for the middle range of students, context-independent interventions are more appropriate for those more usually recognised as needing some form of remedial teaching. Is there any basis for this distinction in terms of psychological theory?

Concrete models are an essential part of most everyday activity and discourse. People need to be able to use language or concrete forms of representation swiftly to communicate information and ideas. Unless such communication is readily shared and understood ordinary trading and work would be impossible. Designers of television programmes are careful to use forms of graphical representation which can be processed using simple concrete models of comparison only. Concrete operational schemata of classification, seriation, conservation, of spatial relations and of the basic properties of numbers are very general. They do not depend on people's specialised knowledge of any craft or discipline in particular. In addition swift and productive perception and communication depends on the schemata acting in integration with each other. One can think of the qualitative difference between the average 7 year-old and the average 10/11 year-old primary school child largely in terms of the amount of integration of the use of concrete models which has occurred in the typical junior school practice. But we know that there are secondary school entrants at 11/12 lying in the range early to middle concrete (2A to 2A/2B). This means that they have some but not all of the concrete operational schemata and have hardly begun the process of integrating them for transactions in their daily life. This is usually perceived in terms of such students being slow or inadequate in their learning.

We argued above that if the intervention goal is the further development of formal operations then one only has the choice of a context-delivered programme. Does it follow from this that if one is considering the bottom 25 per cent of 11/12 year-olds that the choice *must* be a context-independent intervention? Not necessarily. There is the evidence from the Korean replication of CASE in the last two years of primary school that most of the effect was in terms of moving the students to the 2B and 2B* (concrete generalisation) level of thinking. However, since fluent use of concrete operations in any context whatever is a pre-requisite for adult competence it would seem better to concentrate effort for students in this part of the development range on a context-independent intervention, so that the integration of concrete thinking is promoted throughout the school day.

## SOME CASE STUDIES

At this point it may be helpful to describe from examples of three different schools some of the administrative issues which may face a headteacher and his/her staff in introducing an intervention programme.

A, B and C are all comprehensive schools in East Anglia. Each school has administered one of the Piagetian Reasoning Tasks (PRT II, Volume and Heaviness) to the whole of their year 7 entry at 11+. The interquartile range (the spread between the upper 25 per cent and the lower 25 per cent of the school intake) for each school is shown superimposed upon Fig. 10.1 for the national CSMS survey

*Table 10.1*    Statistics of year 7 intake in three schools

|                                                   | A    | B   | C    |
|---------------------------------------------------|------|-----|------|
| School mean percentile by national survey         | 63   | 53  | 32   |
| % of pupils below national 25th percentile level  | 10.4 | 22  | 36.5 |
| % of pupils at 2A level or below                  | 8.7  | 4.9 | 24.9 |

data on cognitive development. It can be seen that there are considerable differences and in taking an 'added-value' approach to administration decisions about introducing various forms of intervention in these schools, it is necessary to unpack the detail of the comparison, given in Table 10.1.

School A is a Community College serving several villages in its area, but it would be misleading to class it as a rural school: the intake is more like that in a relatively affluent city suburb. During the 1970s this area experienced a high-tech industry expansion so that over half of the village housing is new and serves that working community. In 1990 the school achieved the best GCSE results in the county, and this is at least in part attributable to the high level of its intake. The school average is at the 63rd percentile of the CSMS survey, 13 per cent have early formal capacity at entry, and 52 per cent are at the concrete generalisation (2B*) level or above, compared with only 34 per cent for the national average. Although School A has a relatively long 'tail' there are still only 12 pupils out of an entry of 115 who are in the bottom 25 per cent range of the national average, so that it is able to operate a mixed-ability policy for the whole entry, although they stream later on.

School B is in Cambridge City. Although the average of the intake at the 53rd percentile is a little above the national average, it is in fact 'creamed' by a number of independent schools in the city. Only 4.9 per cent – 5 pupils from an intake of

102 – show early formal thinking at entry, compared with 8.3 per cent for the national survey. School B is above average because of a relatively smaller proportion of lower ability pupils, compared with what might be found in a metropolitan area like London or Birmingham. Because there are only five pupils below the middle concrete (2A/2B) level, and the school intake is relatively homogenous, School B is also able to use a complete mixed-ability policy for their four-form entry. Staff concerned with remedial teaching come in to assist the one or two pupils in each class who need specialised assistance in their learning.

Both schools A and B have chosen to use the CASE *Thinking Science* as an intervention programme in years 7 and 8. Bearing in mind that CASE was designed for children between the 30th and the 70th percentile this seems to be the right decision, and the weekly feedback which teachers receive from students doing CASE activities confirms this.

School C a serves a large rural area in the Norfolk fens with no competition from local independent schools. The intake for 1992 is at the 32nd percentile of the national average, but there are enough higher ability pupils – 48 out of a total intake of 241 at the concrete generalisation level or above – to constitute three classes in the top band comparable with classes at School A. But 36.5 per cent of the pupils come in the range of the bottom 25 per cent of the national average, the group for which earlier discussion suggested the context-independent intervention of IE would be needed. This has obvious consequences for school organisation. There are in fact three broad bands and although it has been possible, with some adaptation, to use *Thinking Science* for the middle band of four classes with some success, the three classes in the bottom band all have a mean level at the early concrete (2A)/middle concrete (2A/2B) boundary, and present a severe problem.

Use of Feuerstein Instrumental Enrichment (IE) for two years with pupils from a special school (Shayer and Beasley 1987) showed that gains averaging 25 percentile points on Piagetian tests were possible. If we assume that the students were in the bottom 25 per cent of the ability range initially at age 12, it can be seen from Fig. 10.1 that by the end of year 8 this would bring them to the mature concrete (2B)/concrete generalisation level by the age of 14. Thus a possible solution to planning intervention for the bottom band of School C might be to start with use of IE on entry; continue this through year 7, and then at a strategic point in year 8 – perhaps about the end of February – begin the use of *Thinking Science* relying on 18 months use of IE to have brought the students within the cognitive range from which they can profit from the CASE approach. This would mean that the use of *Thinking Science*, for this band, would continue through to the end of year 9.

## St Mary's, Newcastle-upon-Tyne

It is good to be able to cite one example where the whole of the above recommendations, and more, are being implemented as a whole-school policy. St Mary's is a Catholic mixed comprehensive school with an intake a little below the national average (40th percentile of the CSMS survey), but not as far below as School C above. David O'Neill, the headteacher, is determined to raise both pupils' expectations for themselves and their actual achievement. A chemist in origin himself he – together with two other members of staff – has taken further training in IE and teaches English five lessons a week to a year 7 class within which he averages two IE lessons a week. Thus he and his school exemplifies a strong example of active involvement by senior management in the development of new professional expertise. Other IE teachers have as their main subjects mathematics and geography, so bridging to major school subjects is already initiated. IE is used only for the classes with pupils in the lower-ability range, and for them *Thinking Science* is delayed until Easter in year 8. The other classes get both *Thinking Science* in years 7 and 8, and also the *Somerset Thinking Skills* course (Blagg *et al.* 1988 – see ch. 3), used by various teachers in several subjects.

St Mary's did some preliminary intervention work which has already enhanced the achievement of the year 9 pupils, and has also shown up on Piagetian tests, but the main programme is now (1992/93) in the second year. A detailed monitoring of all the effects and problems of this school programme will be of great interest.

Remember that in all of these examples cited, the intervention programme takes only 20–25 per cent of time from one subject area. The rest of the curriculum time remains available for instruction in content matter, now defined by the National Curriculum. Our confident prediction is that the effect of the intervention activities will be to give all pupils greater access to this content as their enhanced processing ability increasingly enables them to handle the higher levels of concepts required by levels 5, 6, and above of the curriculum. Time is not 'lost' to intervention. The intervention programmes are like catalysts which greatly increase the efficiency of normal instruction.

## A FIVE-YEAR PLAN AND BEYOND

Here we will outline a possible timetable for a school which wishes to introduce a cognitive intervention programme, describing how intervention and instruction interact with one another. We have seen that teachers who have previously used an intervention procedure for over two years on their younger students begin in an informal way to add to their repertoire of teaching skills for their older students. This must mean that although they may love their subject no less they will begin to see in their students' learning two faces. On the one hand, there is an opportunity to learn more of the subject, but on the other, there may be chances for each and every student, and also for the learning group collectively, to go beneath the surface of what is being learnt to the underlying thinking skills required for any learning or higher-level practice. Perhaps some new life can be breathed into the old primary school cliché that one is teaching children not subjects.

In Chapter 9 it was emphasised that for intervention to be effective it has to be school policy. Let us assume that such a policy is in place, and that, as in the instance of St Mary's, Newcastle, a spectrum of approaches is used. We know already that both modes of intervention have an associated effect of making the learning process more obviously of individual value to the students: some of the work may be difficult, but they are rarely in doubt that it is worthwhile to them. So one can anticipate a change in the attitude of the students to learning – but what of the teachers? We described at the start of this chapter how teachers accommodate their instruction to their pupils. If the class is 'bright' then the corresponding learning opportunities they are given will be more demanding. Conversely, with a class of low ability it is often considered both kinder and more prudent not to expect too much of them. Sometimes teachers and students collude together in this process without recognising that in the long run it is disastrous for all. But where teacher and students have experienced together the discovery and creation of new and more powerful strategies of learning and thinking, then expectations of what is possible begin to rise, and the teacher will want and need to change the instructional goals for each year of school. Thus the presence of successful intervention teaching in a school will have effects on the instructional teaching which need to be anticipated and planned for. We offer a two-phase plan.

## Phase 1

Let us assume that school policy is set for a five-year plan, and that a group of the teachers have undertaken training in either context-delivered or context-independent intervention methods. One can then anticipate that during the first two years (a) only a minority of the teachers – those with responsibilities for year 7 and 8 teaching – will be involved in the new teaching skills, and (b) as with all new curriculum development those teachers will be gaining first-hand experience of the specifics, and so will be reluctant as yet to communicate to the rest of the staff. After one year, having taken one class through year 7 and into year 8, the teachers will then begin with a fresh year 7 class, having learnt from their previous year's experience. Only at this point will they begin to use the technical vocabulary specific to intervention teaching to discuss the teaching art with colleagues with similar experience. Only after one further year, having taken a class through two years of intervention, will they have the confidence to begin a dialogue with the rest of the staff.

At this point one can anticipate a further problem, to avoid which advanced planning is essential. Some staff will leave, in the natural course of promotion, and other staff will enter to take their place. Only a resolutely public style of communication within the school, and within departments, of a shared and evolving teaching expertise can preserve a 'steady state'. If the policy is to be maintained then induction of new staff must be planned and carried out just as with the initial training of the teachers already in the school. Further, a willingness to make a commitment to this should be part of the negotiations leading to the appointment of all new staff. In the case of a head of department it may even be necessary to specify prior experience.

In the third year of the five-year plan the first cohort of students will enter year 9 with two years of intervention teaching behind them. This is the point at which instruction will begin to evolve, even in the teaching of those not involved in the intervention teaching. If the school has a lower band in which the intervention teaching has been IE for two or three hours a week, then teachers will begin to find their pupils in year 9 resembling their previous middle band students in teachability. If the middle and upper bands have been receiving CASE in the context of science, then already their learning in science and mathematics will have been radically affected, and the evidence from the CASE II project suggests that the difference should be showing even in English. About half way through this year the second phase of evolution can start.

## Phase II

This is where all the staff need to be brought into the process of change explicitly. How this is done will depend on whether the students they teach in year 9 have had the context-independent approach of IE, or CASE delivered in the context of science. In both cases the pupils will have experienced many instances of bridging which will have helped them apply their new skills to some of the specifics of school learning.

For those students whose intervention has been mainly IE it is to be hoped that the work has been shared between departments in years 7 and 8, so that there will have been a departmental representative from each, for example, of English, mathematics and one humanity. Over a two-year period many opportunities will have arisen for bridging during the instructional lessons for which the subject teacher is responsible. These offer the medium of communication to the other subject specialists in the department both of what has been going on in these mysterious IE lessons, and what new instructional possibilities are present in year 9 because of the previous experience and vocabulary of the students. If students have been used to applying the cognitive functions listed in Table 3.2 (p. 46), then they will have a store of special context-related meanings of 'hypothetical thinking' or 'logical evidence', and so on (Table 3.2, II, 9 and 10, say) within their experience of English comprehension. This would be the point of entry for other English teachers (a) into the underlying style of IE, and (b) how to modify their year 9 teaching to take advantage of their students' familiarity with this metacognitive vocabulary.

For those students whose previous intervention experience has been with CASE the difference in teachability will be through inference from what has happened in science, so here it would be a matter of the science teachers showing the other subject teachers what have been the qualitative changes in their subject. On the one hand, they need to know how concrete preparation, cognitive conflict, and construction zone activity have been part of the teaching style in varied science contexts. On the other, they need to see how many of the students can handle the control of variables in experiments, and the disembedding of the salient variables from scientific evidence. Then in history, for example, by an imaginative leap they could infer how to present learning in a more challenging way than previously.

The learning and adaptation period for the staff during Phase II might take two years to bear fruit, which brings one to the end of the five-year plan, with the first cohort rewarding the school with feedback by taking their public exams at 16+ at the end of year 11 with demonstrably raised standards.

In the longer view still, it is important for school policy makers to monitor the five-year process, build in staff training, selection and promotion systems which value commitment to cognitive stimulation, and develop a public image for governors, parents, and prospective parents which gives due weight to the development of thinking as an essential element in the delivery of content objectives.

## PROFESSIONAL DEVELOPMENT

We have emphasised throughout that intervention methods demand a radical departure from normal teaching practice, requiring the development of skills designed to stimulate and stretch the student mentally which need a separate description as skills of intervention. Widespread adoption of such an art will require a substantial professional development programme for teachers.

In the CASE III project Shayer worked closely with teachers in three schools in order to gain more insight into the skills involved in the effective delivery of CASE. As teachers reflect on the CASE lessons they have taught they become able to use the methods (a) in planning the use of whatever time-line is available for the *Thinking Science* lessons they will teach next, and (b) to transform their other science lessons by seeing which of the CASE parameters is relevant. The task for the teacher concerned with raising the levels of thinking of his/her students becomes one of seeking out opportunities in all of their teaching and capitalising on them. A further consequence of three years' use of the CASE approach is that the science teachers have informally begun to modify their approach to instructional teaching in years 9 to 11. The change is largely in the teachers more readily spotting or anticipating their pupils' learning difficulties, and then modifying their lesson plans and class management strategies to give pupils the opportunity to recognise, discuss and modify their approach. It is not the case that keeping the development of cognition in mind will interfere with the instructional goals of the curriculum. Good instruction and the promotion of higher-level thinking can be integrated throughout the curriculum.

This is the point at which, to the benefit of the whole school, the simple-minded educational experiment breaks down as it is no longer possible to compare 'CASE classes' with 'control classes'. What can be done to reach this point generally in many schools across the country? In Chapter 9 it was argued that INSET practice was in need of the same kind of professionalisation as is taken for granted in management training for industry and commerce. A start has already been made with the programmes for CASE trainers run at King's College London. Given this growing pool of developing expertise what is then required is adequate funding for school-based professional development. It is not inconceivable that such funding could come from schools themselves but the signs in 1993 are not encouraging.

National- or local authority-based funding specifically targeted at the development of intervention methods seems to us to be the only way to ensure that schools will give it the necessary priority.

In parallel with school-based INSET, those responsible for pre-service training of teachers can be expected to place more emphasis on the process of cognitive stimulation. Here we must point out a difficulty with the current vogue (1994) in Britain for school-based pre-service training. If one was perfectly content with current teaching practice then there might be something to be said for inducting new teachers to the profession purely by apprenticeship in schools – but not much, for even then continual mimicking of practice without recourse to reflection on aims or consideration of learning theory must lead to ossification of methods: 'it's always been done like that' (see 'The sabre-tooth curriculum', Benjamin 1975). More importantly the removal of training from university departments completely obviates the possibility of introducing radical changes in methods which we have been advocating and so, we would claim, of bringing about the interventionist revolution which is the only possible route to raised standards.

## NATIONAL POLICY

Recommendations for school-based development of intervention methods and for professional development can be paralleled with suggestions for a national approach to raising standards through intervention in the cognitive development of the school age population. The first is simple enough: recognition of the value of applied research to the enterprise of continually improving the quality of education. Such research is almost bound to be a university-based enterprise since, as we have continually emphasised, a theoretical model is essential as a guide to the development of replicable practice and schools, concerned as they properly are with the practicalities of teaching, have neither the time nor (generally speaking) the academic background required to develop and prosecute research studies on the scale required. The anti-academic stance of many of the New Right, as of many of the Old Left, should become a source of shame to politicians really concerned with improving the educational system if raising standards is really their game. However, it needs also to be recognised that applied research takes time. CASE had a one-year feasibility study, took three years to develop and test, and a further three years to establish its long-term effects on general academic achievement. We recognise that this is a difficult time-scale for a democratic government to contemplate without uncharacteristic far-sightedness.

More specifically, we would urge the early commissioning of a long-term independent case study of a school such as the ideal described above in order to provide (a) confirmation or otherwise of the claims that have been made in this book, and (b) a more detailed characterisation of the nature of intervention teaching than our essentially quantitative studies have been able to provide. Such a study would be expected to shed extra light on the relation between good intervention and good instruction teaching skills, and also on all the administrative considerations which are found in practice to be needed to develop good practice. Given the usual time-cycle between completion of monitoring a case study and getting the detail digested and published, it can be seen that the earliest at which a policy report could be produced for Government is towards the end of year 6, with proper publication in year 7. So Government may get recommendations for trialing further ideas on school practice leading to further raising of standards early in the second five-year cycle, and at that point commission further applied research on their wider applicability and the necessary INSET.

There is also more work to be done exploring possibilities for other context-delivered intervention projects. At the time of writing proposals are in the pipeline for CASE-related interventions in the contexts of mathematics and history. Given the existing art in science, then the assumption is that a transmittable intervention teaching style in secondary mathematics could be worked out in principle in two years, and developed into a tested teaching programme in a further two. History may take five. Such projects have much to offer to the theory and practice of the teaching of these subjects as well as to the further development of general models of cognitive intervention.

## CONCLUSION

Perhaps only now are we in a position to be professionals in the art of teaching as distinguished, for example, from being professionals as historians and amateurs in the practice of teaching. A professional is not only a good practitioner but is one who has an internalised theory which allows him or her to modify practice in the light of feedback.

Today you cannot build cars efficiently using old machine tools and lots of manpower. Children will not be able to handle the high level and flexible thinking required in twenty-first-century employment using concrete operations. The new educational professionalism means that the development of flexible formal operational thinking for almost all is now as real a possibility as the re-tooling of a modern factory for automated, flexible, and low-labour production – and it is as necessary for any country that wishes to retain a prominent place in the world economic order. Of course investment is required, both in professional development and in applied research, but without investment the factory will no longer be able to compete and the education system will run down a tired lane of traditional instructional practice which is not working now and will become increasingly irrelevant to the social and economic needs of a technically sophisticated world.

You can raise standards substantially only by improving the quality of thinking. This can be done, and we have seen how raised levels of thinking open up opportunities to all children to benefit anew from good instructional practice. All that is required now is the professional and political will to make it happen.

# Appendix

# Added value

The concept of 'added value' is likely to become common currency in political discussions concerning education. The idea is that if the quality of a school is to be judged – particularly in comparison with others – then one wants to know primarily, for a given pupil, would he be better in the long run in *this* school rather than *that*. Even the politicians have begun to realise that this question cannot be answered just in terms of gross GCSE or A-level results. It may very well be that School A may have a higher proportion of A-level passes than School B simply because its intake is from a prosperous suburb. School B may be in an inner city area with relatively few professional class parents and for this reason not so many are able by the sixth form to undertake A-level studies. But the parent with a child, whose overall intelligence is just average for the British Isles, should want to know whether over a five or a seven-year period her child will learn more, and of a better quality, if she chooses school B rather than A. The only way she can decide this is by being provided with evidence of how children's' long-term achievement in the two schools relates to the general educational level of children when they enter the school.

This is the start of the notion of 'added value'. Given some measure of a child's educational level at entry to secondary school, then one needs to assess how much further in five years, how much further in seven years, the school adds to the child's overall achievement. For example, given a National Curriculum with definitions of achievement at 10 levels, when the Key Stage 2 test results are available for all children in their last year at primary school at age 11, one need only look at their Key Stage 3 test results at age 14 to be able to tell how many levels up the National Curriculum in science, mathematics, etc., each secondary school has added educational value to their students. If School A, with a Key Stage 2 intake of average level 5.2 has increased their students' average only to 6.2 by Key Stage 3, it will be no use their boasting of a Key Stage 3 mean of 6.2 if School B has taken an intake of average level 3.8 to a Key Stage 3 average of 5.4. For School A will only have added a value of 1.0 National Curriculum levels to their students in three years (6.2–5.2) while in the same time School B have added an average value of 1.6 levels to their students (5.4–3.6).

Several groups have already undertaken a limited 'added value' exercise to compare the quality of sixth-form teaching in different schools. In Carol Fitz-Gibbon's (1990) A Level Information System (ALIS), evidence of students' GCSE results at 16+ is related to their subsequent performance at A level in their chosen subjects. This only takes two years to collect and interpret the evidence, and the data is reported to the schools so that they can monitor the performance of individual departments. In ALIS the analysis obtained is confidential to schools but in principle the approach could yield better public information than the present government policy of publishing school's raw GCSE and A-level results. If students with GCSE C grades in School A only get D grade passes on average at A-level, whereas in School B they achieve B grades at A-level (given C grade at GCSE), then a parent and student will know which school is the better chosen, even if School A has more A-level results due to previous misguided parental choice in terms of School A's general reputation.

Of course *average* 'added value' is not the whole story. There is also the question of what statisticians call 'interaction'. Schools may differ in how well they treat children of different abilities. A notorious example of this were the students in 'D' streams of grammar schools in Britain, many of whom might have been the star performers of comprehensive schools had their parents made a different choice. But interaction can also act the other way. Some primary schools may do quite well for average pupils, but the teachers fail to recognise that their more able children are learning nothing by their own standards. In other cases there is an explicit school policy (a) to notice and then provide for the minority of more able pupils, and (b) to recognise when a child has special needs and to provide more specific professional skills to address them. In the long run the 'added value' concept has to include interaction.

## ADDED VALUE AND THE CASE PROJECT EVIDENCE

In the CASE project we used a version of added value as part of the research design. All students, both in control and experimental classes were given two Piagetian Reasoning Tasks (PRTs) at the outset of the research. The Piagetian tests serve as a general measure of the intellectual level of the student, and previous research (Shayer and Adey 1981) has shown that the tests have substantial predictive power for students' school achievement. Part of the reason for the use of the tests was, of course, to monitor the effect of the CASE intervention directly in terms of changes in cognitive development over the two-year period but subsequently they proved extremely valuable in applying the added value concept. Inspection of Fig. A.1 will show at once that there are problems involved.

For the preparation of Fig. A.1 only those students were selected whose initial 1985 PRT scores were in the concrete generalisation (2B*) range. In effect, this is a crude but limited way of controlling for differences in initial abilities of students, both between schools and between control and experimental classes within schools. The bars in the diagram mark the mean science GCSE grade of the students in 1989, and it can be seen that if the students in the control class of School 7 are compared

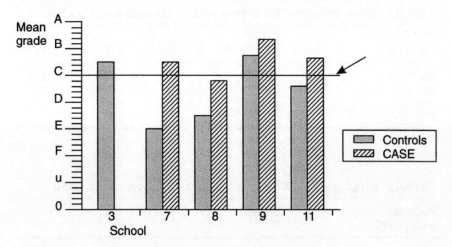

*Fig. A.1*   Mean grades in GCSE science obtained in five schools

with the control classes of School 9 there is a mean difference of about 2.5 grades attributable to the difference in schools alone. In addition, the experimental classes within the schools achieved even higher GCSE grades in every case than the controls. As a first approximation it can be said that, despite large inter-school differences, if a student was in a CASE class it did not matter which school he or she were in. The average prediction would still be C-grade or above, a level which in Britain is one of the major predictors of higher education achievement and is used as one of the selection instruments.

Because of the large inter-school effect it would not be valid to compare students in control classes of one school with students in an experimental class of another – comparing control students from School 7 with CASE students from School 9 would yield a wonderful effect, but likewise comparing School 7 CASE students with School 9 controls would argue for no effect whatsoever. Therefore the analysis has to be a more complex one in which students are compared with control class students as alike as possible to the same schooling as themselves.

In the Tables A.1–A.3 this mode of analysis is generalised by splitting the students in the control and CASE classes into four ranges in terms of their pre-test (1985) Piagetian Reasoning Task levels. Given students at the same cognitive level on entry into secondary school, one then compares the students four years later in terms of their GCSE science grades.

Table A.3 is derived from the first two by subtraction – for example, in the top left-hand cell the value of '1.25' is derived by subtracting the control 2B* mean value of 4.08 from the CASE 2B* mean value of 5.33.

Finally, the relation between ex-control and CASE students in their GCSE science grades is shown in the bar-charts in Fig. A.2. Note that the Piagetian pre-test

*Table A.1*   Mean grade in GCSE science 1989 for 12+ boys cohort: controls

| Piagetian level (1985) | School 7 | 8 | 9 | 11 |
|---|---|---|---|---|
| 2B* | 4.08 | 4 | 5.92 | 5 |
| 2B | 3.88 | 2.5 | 5 | 2.5 |
| 2A/2B | — | 1.8 | 4.5 | |
| 2A | 3 | — | 6.5 | |

*Table A.2*   Mean grade in GCSE science 1989 for 12+ boys cohort: CASE

| Piagetian level (1985) | School 7 | 8 | 9 | 11 |
|---|---|---|---|---|
| 2B* | 5.33 | — | 6.5 | 6 |
| 2B | 3 | 4.5 | 5.57 | 4.8 |
| 2A/2B | 2 | 2.25 | 6 | 1.5 |
| 2A | — | — | — | — |

*Table A.3*   CASE–controls differences in mean GCSE grades

| Piagetian level (1985) | School 7 | 8 | 9 | 11 |
|---|---|---|---|---|
| 2B* | 1.25 | — | 0.58 | 1 |
| 2B | –0.88 | 2 | 0.57 | 2.3 |
| 2A/2B | — | 0.45 | 1.5 | — |
| 2A | — | — | — | — |
| Means: | 0.12 | 1.23 | 0.89 | 1.65 |
| Grand mean: | **0.97** in favour of CASE classes | | | |

levels are on an equal-interval scale from 2A = early concrete through 2B = mature concrete, to 2B* = concrete generalisation.

Although this method of analysis keeps close to the raw data, it has its disadvantages. First, it loses some of the data – students who were outside the ranges selected in the three tables above. Secondly, many of the cells contained very few students – as low as 2 or 3 – and so chance variations in either of the test data cause very large changes in the means. Thirdly, although there is plenty of data, it can be seen that many of the cells cannot be compared because the other class had no members at that level. One needs a way of handling the data which uses all the information on the students.

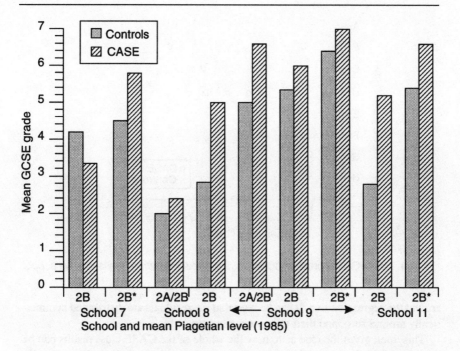

*Fig. A.2*   GCSE grades (1989) by school, class, and 1985 pre-test Piagetian test level

In Fig A.3 the GCSE grades obtained for the boys in School 11 in 1989 are plotted in relation to the students' 1985 pre-test Piagetian test levels. Several things can be seen on inspection of this figure:

- the control group was a little more able than the CASE group initially. There are relatively more students with the higher Piagetian levels, and there is no one with an initial level as low as 4.9, the level of the lowest pupil in the CASE class;
- there is substantial correlation between the pre-test levels for the control class and their subsequent GCSE science achievement ($r = 0.74$); and
- the general scatter of the CASE students' GCSE grades lies above those of the controls.

How then can we use all the information in the diagram to compare the CASE and control classes as validly as possible? In Fig. A.4 the data just for the control class is plotted, together with the regression line. When a linear regression is computed the line is placed so that the sum of the vertical differences – called the *residuals* – between any point and the line is just zero. In effect the regression line is a running average put exactly through the whole data-set, and enables the information to be summarised in two parameters: the slope of the line, and a constant on the predicted axis, in this case GCSE grade. In Fig. A.5 a histogram is plotted of the residuals

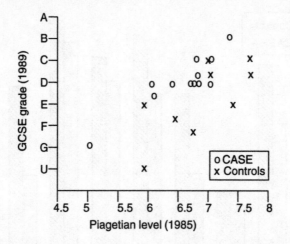

*Fig. A.3*   1989 GCSE grade against 1985 pre-test Piagetian levels for one school

around the regression line. It can be seen that the residuals are distributed symmetrically around zero, and their sum is exactly zero.

This, then gives the clue as to how the whole of the CASE class results can be compared with the whole of the control class results, despite their not being exactly comparable at pre-test in 1985. The CASE 1989 GCSE results are plotted on the same graph as was used previously for the controls, and then their residuals are inspected around the regression line previously computed for the controls (Fig. A.6). On average, if the CASE class have had comparable teaching in the school,

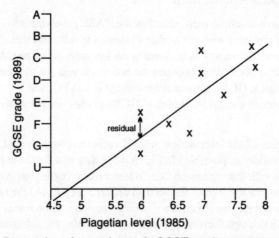

*Fig. A.4*   Regression of control group's GCSE grades on pre-test Piagetian levels

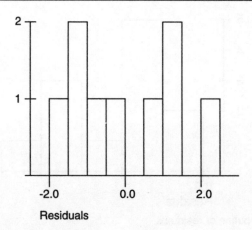

*Fig. A.5*   Distribution of the residuals

then, in relation to their 1985 Piagetian levels the sum of their residuals around the regression line should be zero like the controls'.

It can be seen that all the CASE class residuals are positive, and the histogram of their values is shown in Fig. A.8. The mean of the CASE class residuals is 1.59 grades. The meaning of this is that when allowance is made for individual differences between members of the two groups, on average the students in the CASE class did 1.59 grades better at GCSE science four years after their entry into the secondary school. Finally, the residuals for both classes are compared on the same diagram.

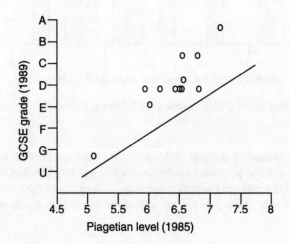

*Fig. A.6*   CASE data on regression line for controls

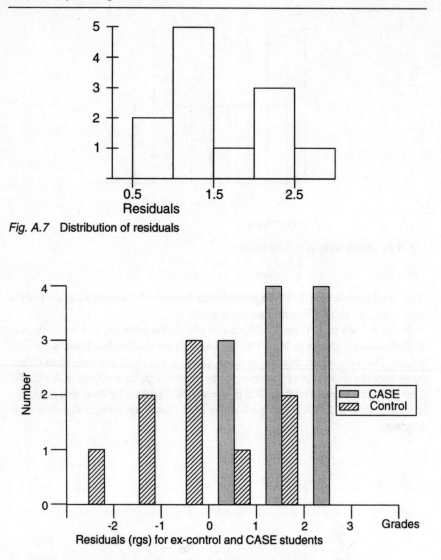

Fig. A.7   Distribution of residuals

Fig. A.8   Histogram of GCSE science rgs for boys, School 11

Since this method of analysis both uses all the data, and also allows students to be compared as far as possible exactly like for like by using the data from the same school, this is the preferred way of presenting the findings of the CASE project. In Fig. A.9 the whole of the data for the boys in the 12+ cohort are shown.

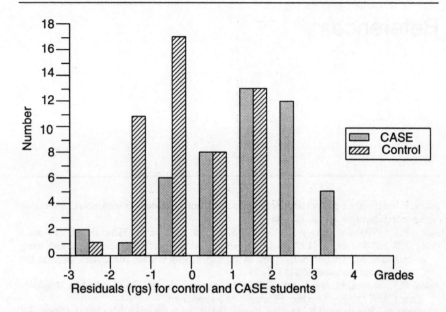

*Fig. A.9*   Histogram of boys 12+ GCSE science rgs for ex-control and CASE students

# References

Adey, P.S. (1988) Cognitive acceleration – review and prospects. *International Journal of Science Education*, 10, 2, 121–34.

Adey, P.S. (1993) *The King's–BP CASE INSET Pack*. London: BP Educational Services.

Adey, P.S. and Shayer, M. (1993) An exploration of long-term far-transfer effects following an extended intervention programme in the high school science curriculum. In press for *Cognition and Instruction*, 11, 1, 1–29.

Adey, P.S., Shayer, M. and Yates, C. (1989) *Thinking Science: The Curriculum Materials of the CASE Project*. London: Thomas Nelson and Sons.

Ahlgren, A., Roseman, J.E, McGee Brown, M. J. and Brantley, V. (1993) Using and evaluating Project 2061 benchmarks as a reform tool. Paper given at the American Association for the Advancement of Science Annual Meeting, Boston.

Ashby, R. and Lee, P. (1987) Children's concepts of empathy and understanding in history. In Portal, C. (ed.) *The History Curriculum for Teachers*. Lewes: Falmer Press.

Ausubel, D. (1965) An evaluation of the conceptual schemes approach to science curriculum development. *Journal of Research in Science Teaching*, 3, 255–64.

Ausubel, D. (1968) *Educational Psychology: A Cognitive View*. New York: Holt Rinehart and Winston.

Baddeley, A. (1990) *Human Memory: Theory and Practice*. London: Lawrence Erlbaum.

Bateson, G. (1983) *Steps to an Ecology of the Mind*. London: Paladin.

Beasley, F.P. (1984) An evaluation of Feurstein's model for the remediation of adolescents' cognitive deficits. PhD thesis, Chelsea College, University of London.

Beasley, F. and Shayer, M. (1990) Learning potential assessment through Feuerstein's LPAD: can quantitative results be achieved? *International Journal of Dynamic Assessment and Instruction*, 1, 2, 37–48.

Benjamin, H. (1975) The sabre-tooth curriculum. In Golby, M., Greenwald, J. and West, R. (eds) *Curriculum Design*. London: Croom Helm.

Biggs, J.B. and Collis, K.F. (1982) *Evaluating the Quality of Learning*. New York: Academic Press.

Blagg, N. (1991) *Can We Teach Intelligence?* London: Lawrence Erlbaum.

Blagg, N., Ballinger M. and Gardner, R. (1988) *Somerset Thinking Skills Course*. Oxford: Basil Blackwell.

Blagg, N., Ballinger M. and Lewes, R. (1993) Thinking and learning at work: a report on the development and evaluation of the Thinking Skills At Work modules. Sheffield: Department of Employment.

Blank, R. and Miller, J. D. (1993) America 2000: progress and possibilities. Paper given at the American Association for the Advancement of Science Annual Meeting, Boston.

Bolam, R. (1987) What is effective INSET? In *Professional Development and INSET*. Slough: NFER-Nelson.

Bond, T.G. (1976) *BLOT: Bond's Logical Operations Test*. Townsville: Townsville College of Advanced Education.

Bond, T.G., (1980) The psychological link across formal operations. *Science Education*, 64, 1, 113–17.

Bond, T.G., (1990) An investigation of the structure of the Piagetian formal operations stage: an application of Rasch analysis. PhD thesis, James Cook University of North Queensland.

Boole, G. (1854) *Investigations of the Laws of Thought*. London: Dover Publications.

Bridges, D. (1989) Evaluating the LEA Training Grant Scheme. In McBride, R. (ed.) *The In-service Training of Teachers*. Lewis: Falmer Press.

Brown, A.L. (1987) Metacognition, executive control, self-regulation and other more mysterious mechanisms. In Weinert, Franz and Kluwe, Rainer (eds) *Metacognition, Motivation and Understanding*. London: Lawrence Erlbaum.

Brown, A.L., Bransford, J.D., Ferrara, R.A. and Campione, J.C. (1983) Learning, remembering and understanding. In Mussen, Paul H. (ed.) *Handbook of Child Psychology*. New York: John Wiley.

Bruner, J. (1968) *Towards a Theory of Instruction*. New York: W.W. Norton.

Butler, J. (1992) From action to thought: the fulfilment of human potential. Fifth International Thinking Conference, Townsville.

Case, R. (1985) *Intellectual Development: Birth to Adulthood*. New York: Academic Press.

Champagne, A.B., Gunstone, R.F. and Klopfer, L. (1985) Effecting changes in cognitive structures amongst physics students. In West, L.H.T. and Pines, A. L. (eds) *Cognitive Structure and Conceptual Change*. Orlando: Academic Press.

Clarke, A.M. and Clarke, A.D.B. (1976) *Early Experience: Myth and Evidence*. London: Open Books.

CLISP (Children's Learning in Science Project) (1987) *CLIS in the Classroom*. Leeds: University of Leeds Centre for Studies in Science and Maths Education.

Cockcroft Committee of Inquiry into the Teaching of Mathematics in Schools (1982) *Mathematics Counts*. London: HMSO.

Coleman, J.S. (1966) *Equality of Educational Opportunity*. Washington, DC: US Department of Health, Education and Welfare.

Coles, M.J. and Robinson, W.D. (eds) (1989) *Teaching Thinking. A Survey of Programmes in Education*. Bristol; Bristol Press.

Collings, J. (1987) A study of the effects of field-independence training for early adolescents on science learning and cognitive development. PhD thesis, College of St Paul and St Mary, Cheltenham.

Cronbach, L. and Furby, L. (1970) How should we measure change, or should we? *Psychological Bulletin*, 74, 68–80.

de Bono, E. (1976) *Teaching Thinking*. London: Maurice Temple Smith.

de Bono, E. (1987) *CoRT thinking program: workcards and teachers' notes*. Chicago: Science Research Associates.

Demetriou, A., Gustafsson, J-E., Efklides, A. and Plastidou, M. (1992a) Structural systems in developing cognition, science and education. In Demetriou, A., Shayer, M. and Efklides, A. (eds) *Neo-Piagetian Theories of Cognitive Development*. London: Routledge.

Demetriou, A. Shayer, M. and Efklides, A. (eds) (1992b) *Neo-Piagetian Theories of Cognitive Development*. London: Routledge.

Demetriou, A. Efklides, A. and Platsidou, M. (1993) Experiential structuralism: a frame for unifying cognitive developmental theories. *Monographs of the Society for Research in Child Development*, 58, 5, Serial No. 234.

DES (Department of Education and Science) (1988) *Science for Ages 5 to 16: Proposals of the Secretary of State for Education and Science and the Secretary of State for Wales.* London: HMSO.

DES (Department of Education and Science) (1989) *National Curriculum History Working Group. Final Report.* London: HMSO.

DES (Department of Education and Science) (1991) *Science in the National Curriculum. Revised Order.* London: HMSO.

Dewey, J. (1933) *How We Think: A Restatement of the Relation of Reflective Thinking to the Educative Process.* Chicago: Henry Regnery.

Dickinson, A.K. and Lee, P.J. (1978) *History Teaching and Historical Understanding.* London: Heinemann Educational books.

Dignon, K. (1993) Integrating the principles of cognitive acceleration with a Key Stage 3 science curriculum. *School Science Review,* 74, 269, 113–20.

Donaldson, M. (1978) *Children's Minds.* Glasgow: Fontana.

Driver, R., Guesne, E. and Tiberghien, A. (eds) (1985) *Children's Ideas in Science.* Milton Keynes, Open University Press.

Edwards, J. (1991) The direct teaching of thinking skills. In Evans, G. (ed.) *Learning and Teaching Cognitive Skills.* Hawthorn, Victoria: Australian Council for Educational Research.

Eggleston, J. (1984) *An Evaluation of the PKG Inservice-Onservice Teacher Education Project.* Directorate of Secondary General Education, Ministry of Education, Indonesia.

Epstein, H.T. (1980) EEG Developmental stages. *Developmental Psychobiology,* 13, 629–31.

Epstein, H.T. (1986) Stages in human brain development. *Developmental Brain Research,* 30, 114–19.

Epstein, H.T. (1990) Stages in human mental growth. *Journal of Educational Psychology,* 82, 876–80.

Eraut, M., Pennycuick, D. and Radnor H. (1988) *Local Evaluation of INSET: A Met-evaluation of TRIST Evaluations.* Bristol: National Development Centre for School Management.

Falkner, F. and Tanner, J.M. (1986) *Human Growth: A Comprehensive Treatise. Vol. 3: Methodology: Ecological, Genetic and Nutritional Effects on Growth.* London: Plenum.

Fensham, P.J. and Kass, H. (1988) Inconsistent or discrepant events in science instruction. *Studies in Science Education,* vol. 15, pp. 1–16.

Feuerstein, R., Rand, Y. and Hoffman, M. (1979) The dynamic assessment of retarded performers: the Learning Potential Assessment Device, theory, instruments and techniques. Baltimore, MD: University Park Press.

Feuerstein, R., Rand, Y., Hoffman, M. and Miller, M. (1980) *Instrumental Enrichment: An Intervention Programme for Cognitive Modifiability.* Baltimore, MD: University Park Press.

Fitz-Gibbon, C.T. (1990) (ed.) Performance indicators: a BERA dialogue. Clevedon: Multi Lingual Matters.

Froufe, J. (1987) Feuerstein's theory applied to the school science curriculum. MA dissertation, King's College, University of London.

Fusco, E.T. (1983) The relationship between children's cognitive level of development and their responses to literature. PhD thesis, University of Hofstra.

Gagné, R.M. (1965) *The Conditions of Learning.* New York: Holt Rinehart and Winston.

Gardner, H. (1983) *Frames of Mind.* New York: Basic Books.

Gardner, P.L. (1974) Research on teacher effects: critique of a traditional paradigm, *British Journal of Educational Psychology,* 44, 2, 123–30.

Gauld, C.F. (1986) Models, meters, and memory. *Research in Science Education,* 16, 49–54.

Goossens, L. (1989) Training scientific reasoning in children and adolescents: a critical review and quantitative integration. Paper presented at the Third European Conference for Research on Learning and Instruction, Madrid.

Gulbenkian Foundation (1982) *The Arts in Schools*. London: Caloust Gulbenkian Foundation.

Hallam, R.N. (1967) Logical thinking in history. *Educational Review*, 119, 182–202.

Hart, K., Brown, M., Kerslake, D., Küchemann, D. and Ruddock, G. (1985) *Chelsea Diagnostic Tests*. Windsor: NFER-Nelson.

Hodson, D. (1990) A critical look at practical work in school science. *School Science Review*, 70, 256, 33–40.

Hudson, L. (1966) *Contrary Imaginations*. London: Methuen.

Hunter-Grundin, E. (1985) *Teaching Thinking: An Evaluation of Edward de Bono's Classroom Materials*. London: The Schools Council.

Huxley, A. (1932) *Brave New World*. London: Chatto and Windus.

ILEA (Inner London Education Authority) (1988) *Science in Process*. Marshall, D., Gilman, D., Halstead, L., Thompson, M. and Watson, J. (eds). London: Addison Wesley.

Inhelder, B. and Piaget, J. (1955) *De la Logique de l'Enfant a la Logique de l'Adolescent*. Paris: Presses Universitaires de France.

Inhelder, B. and Piaget, J. (1958) *The Growth of Logical Thinking*. London: Routledge and Kegan Paul.

Inhelder, B., Sinclair, H. and Bovet, M. (1974) *Apprentissage et Structures de la Connaissance*. Paris: Presses Universitaires de France.

Jensen, A. (1973) *Educability and Group Differences*. London: Methuen.

Jessup, G. (1991) *Outcomes: NVQs and the Emerging Model of Education and Training*. London: Falmer Press.

Joyce, B. and Showers, B. (1980) Improving inservice training: the messages of research. *Educational Leadership*, 37, 5, 379–85.

Joyce, B. and Showers, B. (1988) *Student Achievement through Staff Development*. New York: Longman.

Jurd, M. (1973) Adolescent thinking in history-type material. *Australian Journal of Education*, 17, 1, 2–17.

Karmiloff-Smith, A. (1991) Beyond modularity: innate constraints and developmental change. In Carey, S. and Gelman, R. (eds) *The Epigenesis of Mind*. Hillsdale, NJ: Lawrence Erlbaum Associates.

Karplus, R. (1979) Teaching for the development of reasoning. In Lawson, A.E. (ed.) *The Psychology of Teaching for Thinking and Creativity*. Columbus Ohio: ERIC-SMEAC.

Kessen, W. (1984) The end of the age of development. In Sternberg, R.J. (ed.) *Mechansisms of Cognitive Development*. New York: W. H. Freeman.

Kuhn, D. and Angelev, J. (1976) An experimental study of the development of formal operational thought. *Child Development*, 47, 697–706.

Kuhn, D., Amsel, E. and O'Loughlin, M. (1988) *The Development of Scientific Thinking Skills*. San Diego: Academic Press.

Landa, L.N. (1974) *Algorithmization in Learning and Instruction*. Englewood Cliffs, NJ: Educational Technology Publications.

Landa, L.N. (1976) *Instructional Regulation and Control: Cybernetics, Algorithmization, and Heuristics in Education*. New Jersey: Educational Technology Publications.

Larkin, J.H., McDermott, J., Simon, D.P. and Simon, H.A. (1980) Expert and novice peformance in solving physics problems. *Science*, 208, June, 1335–42.

Lawson, A.E., (1989) Research on advanced reasoning: concept acquisition and a theory of science instruction. In Adey, P., Bliss, J., Head, J. and Shayer, M. (eds) *Adolescent Development and School Science*. London: Falmer Press.

Lawson, A.E. and Nordland, F.H. (1976) The factor structure of some Piagetian tasks. *Journal of Research in Science Teaching* 13, 5, 461–6.

Lawson, A.E. and Snitgen, D.A. (1982) Teaching formal reasoning in a college biology course for preservice teachers. *Journal of Research in Science Teaching*, 19, 233–48.

Lawson, A.E. and Wollman, W.T. (1976) Encouraging the transition from concrete to formal cognitive functioning – an experiment. *Journal of Research in Science Teaching*, 13, 5, 413–30.

Light, P.H. and Butterworth, G.E. (eds) (1992) *Context and Cognition: Ways of Learning and Knowing*. London: Harvester Press.

Lipman, M., Sharp, M. and Oscanyan, F. (1980) *Philiosophy in the Classroom*. 2nd edn. Philadelphia: Temple University Press.

Longeot, F. (1978) *Les stades operatoires de Piaget et les facteurs de l'intelligence*. Grenoble: Presses Universitaires de Grenoble.

Lovell, K. and Shields, J.B. (1967) Some aspects of a study of the gifted child. *British Journal of Educational Psychology*, 37, 201–8.

Lynn, M.C. and Kyllonen, A. (1981) The field-independence construct: some, one, or none. *Journal of Educational Psychology*, 73, 261–73.

McPeck, J.E. (1990) Critical thinking and subject specificity: a reply to Ennis. *Educational Researcher*, 19, 4, 10–12.

Mehl, M. (1985) The cognitive difficulties of first year physics students at the University of the Western Cape and various compensatory programmes. PhD thesis, University of Cape Town.

Meisels, S.J. and Shonkoff, J.P. (1990) *Handbook of Early Child Intervention*. Cambridge: Cambridge University Press.

Miller, G.A. (1956) The magic number seven plus or minus two: Some limits on our capacity for processing information. *Psychological Review*, 63, 81–97.

Monk, M. (1990) A genetic epistemological analysis of data on children's ideas about DC electrical circuits. *Research in Science and Technological Education*, 8, 2, 133–43.

Monk, M. (1991) Genetic epistemological notes on recent research into children's understanding of light. *International Journal of Science Education*, 13, 3, 255–70.

Neimark, E. (1975) Intellectual development during adolescence. In Horowitz, F.D. (ed.) *Review of Child Development Research*, Vol. 4. Chicago, Il.: University of Chicago Press, pp. 541–94.

Nelson, T.O., Dunlosky, J., White, D.M., Steinberg, J., Townes, B.D. and Anderson, D. (1990) Cognition and metacognition at extreme altitudes on Mt Everest. *Journal of Experimental Psychology*, 119, 4, 317–34.

Newell, A. and Simon, H.A. (1972) *Human Problem Solving*. Englewood Cliffs, NJ: Prentice-Hall.

Newman, D., Griffin, P. and Cole, M. (1989) *The Construction Zone: Working for Cognitive Change in School*. Cambridge: Cambridge University Press.

Newport, E.L. (1991) Contrasting conceptions of the critical period for language. In Carey, S. and Gelman, R. (eds) *The Epigenesis of Mind*. Hillsdale, NJ: Lawrence Erlbaum Associates.

Nickerson, R.S., Perkins, D.N. and Smith, E.E. (1985) *The Teaching of Thinking*. Hillsdale, NJ: Lawrence Erlbaum Associates.

Nisbet, J. and McGuiness, C. (1990) Teaching thinking: the European scene. *Teaching Thinking and Problem Solving*, 12, 3, 12–14.

Norman, D.A. and Shallice, T. (1986) Attention to action: willed and automatic control of behaviour. In Davidson, R.J., Schwarts, G.E. and Shapiro, D. (eds) *Consciousness and Self-regulation: Advances in Research and Theory*. New York: Plenum.

Olby, R.C. (1967) *Origins of Mendelism*. New York: Schoken Books.

Osborne, R.J. and Freyberg, P. (1985) *Learning in Science: The Implications of Children's Science*. Auckland: Heinemann.

Pascual-Leone, J. (1969) Cognitive development and cognitive style: a general psychological integration. PhD thesis, University of Geneva.

Pascual-Leone, J. (1984) Attention, dialectic and mental effort: towards an organismic theory of life stages. In Commons, M., Richards, F. and Armon, C. (eds) *Beyond Formal Operations: Late Adolescent and Adult Cognitive Development*. New York: Praeger.

Pascual-Leone, J. (1988) Organismic processes for neo-Piagetian theories: dialectic causal account of cognitive development. In Demetriou, A. (ed.) *The Neo-Piagetian Theories of Cognitive Development: Towards an Integration*. Amsterdam: North-Holland.

Peel, E.A. (1967) Some problems in the psychology of history teaching I: Historical ideas and concepts and II: The pupils' thinking and inference. In Burston, W.H. and Thompson, D. (eds) *Studies in the Nature and Teaching of History*. London: Routledge and Kegan Paul.

Peel, E.A. (1971) *The Nature of Adolescent Judgement*. London: Staples Press.

Perkins, D.N. and Salomon, G. (1989) Are cognitive skills context-bound? *Educational Researcher*, 18, 1, 16–25.

Perret-Clermont, A.-N. (1980) *Social Interaction and Cognitive Development in Children*. New York: Academic Press.

Phelps, C. (1993) The formative evaluation of a school based curriculum development project in science. PhD thesis, University of London.

Piaget, J. (1949) *Traité de logique: Essai de logistique opératoire*. Paris: Colin.

Piaget, J. and Inhelder, B. (1974) *The Child's Construction of Quantities*. London: Routledge and Kegan Paul.

Piaget. J. and Inhelder, B. (1976) *The Child's Conception of Space*. London: Routledge and Kegan Paul.

Polya, G. (1957) *How to Solve it*. 2nd edn. New York: Doubleday.

Ramadas, J. and Driver, R. (1989) *Aspects of Secondary Students' Ideas about Light*. Leeds: Children's Learning in Science Project.

Rand, Y., Mintzker, R., Hoffman, M.B. and Friedlender, Y. (1981) The Instrumental Enrichment programme: immediate and long-term effects. In Mittler, P. (ed.) *Frontiers of Knowledge: Mental Retardation,* Vol. 1. Baltimore: University Park Press.

Renner, J.W., Stafford, D.G., Lawson, A.E., McKinnon, J.W., Friot, F.E. and Kellogg, D.H. (1976) *Research, Teaching, and Learning with the Piaget Model*. Norman: University of Oklahoma Press.

Resnick, L.B. (1987) *Education and Learning to Think*. Washington, DC: National Academy Press.

Resnick, L.B., Bill, V. and Lesgold, S. (1992) Developing thinking abilities in arithmetic class. In Demetriou, Andreas, Shayer, Michael and Efklides, Anastasia (eds) *Neo-Piagetian Theories of Cognitive Development*. London: Routledge.

Rose, C. (1985) *Accelerated Learning*. Aylesbury: Accelerated Learning Systems.

Rosenthal, D.A. (1979) The acquisition of formal operations: the effect of two training procedures. *Journal of Genetic Psychology*, 134, 125–40.

Rousseau, J.-J. (1762) *Emile*. Paris, Duchesne. English edition, 1911. London: Dent.

Salomon, G. (1988) Two roads to transfer; two roads of transfer. Paper delivered at the Annual Meeting of the American Educational Research Association, New Orleans.

Salomon, G., Globerson, T. and Guterman, E. (1989) The computer as a Zone of Proximal Development: internalising reader-related metacognitions from a reading partner. *Journal of Educational Psychology*, 81, 4, 620–7.

Schoenfeld, A.H. (1985) *Mathematical Problem Solving*. New York: Academic Press.

Shayer, M. (1972) Piaget's work and science teaching. M.Ed., University of Leicester.

Shayer, M. (1978) A test of the validity of Piaget's model of formal operational thinking. PhD thesis, University of London.

Shayer, M. (1979) Has Piaget's construct of formal operational thinking any utility? *British Journal of Educational Psychology*, 49, 265–7.

Shayer, M. (1981) How to make cognitive level matching valid. Consultant's report to Shoreham School District, Long Island, New York.

Shayer, M. (1987) Neo-Piagetian theories and educational practice. *International Journal of Psychology*, 22, 5/6, 751–72.

Shayer, M. (1988) Neo-Piagetian theories and educational practice. In Demetriou, A. (ed.) *The Neo-Piagetian Theories of Cognitive Development: Towards an Integration*. Amsterdam: North-Holland.

Shayer, M. (1989) Hewers of wood and drawers of water. In Adey, P., Bliss J., Head, J. and Shayer, M. (eds) *Adolescent Development and School Science*. London: Falmer.

Shayer, M. (1991) Improving standards and the National Curriculum. *School Science Review*, 72, 260, 17–24.

Shayer, M. (1992) Problems and issues in intervention studies. In Demetriou, Andreas, Shayer, Michael and Efklides, Anastasia (eds) *Neo-Piagetian Theories of Cognitive Development*. London: Routledge.

Shayer, M. and Adey, P.S. (1981) *Towards a Science of Science Teaching*. London: Heinemann Educational.

Shayer, M. and Adey, P.S. (1992) Accelerating the development of formal thinking II: postproject effects on science achievement. *Journal of Research in Science Teaching*, 29, 1, 81–92.

Shayer, M. and Adey, P.S. (1993) Accelerating the development of formal operational thinking in high school pupils, IV: three years on after a two-year intervention. *Journal of Research in Science Teaching*, 30, 4, 351–66.

Shayer, M. and Beasley, F. (1987) Does instrumental enrichment work? *British Educational Research Journal*, 13, 2, 101–19.

Shayer, M., Demetriou, A. and Pervez, M. (1988) The structure and scaling of concrete operational thought: three studies in four countries. *Genetic, Social and General Psychological Monographs*, 114, 3, 309–75.

Shayer, M. and Williams, J. (1984) Sex differences on Piagetian formal operational tasks: where they went and how to find them. In Turner, C.J. and Miles, H.B. (eds) *The Biology of Human Intelligence*. Driffield, Hull: Nafferton Books.

Shayer, M. and Wylam, H. (1978) The distribution of Piagetian stages of thinking in British middle and secondary school children. II – 14- to 16-year-olds and sex differentials. *British Journal of Educational Psychology*, 48, 62–70.

Shipstone, D.M. (1984) A study of children's understanding of electricity in simple d.c. circuits. *European Journal of Science Education*, 6, 2, 185–98.

Siegler, R., Liebert, D. and Liebert, R. (1973) Inhelder and Piaget's pendulum problem: teaching adolescents to act as scientists. *Developmental Psychology*, 9, 97–101.

Smith, L. (1987) A constructivist interpretation of formal operations. *Human Development*, 30, 341–54.

Smith, L. (1992a) *Necessary Knowledge: Piagetian Perspectives on Constructivism*. London: Lawrence Erlbaum.

Smith, L. (1992b) Personal communication.

Smith, L. (1993) *Necessary Knowledge: Piagetian Perspectives on Constructivism*. London: Lawrence Erlbaum.

Somerville, S.C. (1974) The Pendulum problem: patterns of performance defining developmental stages. *British Journal of Educational Psychology*, 44, 3, 266–81.

Stenhouse, L. (1975) *An Introduction to Curriculum Research and Development*. London: Heinemann Educational Books.

Strang, J. and Shayer, M. (1993) Enhancing high school students' achievement in chemistry through a thinking skills approach. *International Journal of Science Education*, 15, 3, 319–37.

Tanner, J.M. (1978) *Foetus into Man: Physical Growth from Conception to Maturity*. London: Open Books.

Tizard, J. (1975) Race and IQ: the limits of probability. *New Behaviour*, 24 April, 6–9.

Tobin, K., Kahle, J.B. and Fraser, B.J. (eds) (1990) *Windows into Science Classrooms*. Basingstoke: Falmer Press.

Tomlinson-Keasey, C. (1976) Can we develop abstract thought (ADAPT) in college freshmen? One year later. Paper presented at AERA Annual Conference.

Tomlinson-Keasey, C. and Eisert, D. (1977) Doing and thinking: their relationship in college freshmen. Paper delivered at AERA Annual Conference.

von Wright, J. (1992) Reflections on reflection. *Learning and Instruction*, 2, 1, 59–68.

Vygotsky, L.S. (1978) *Mind in Society*. Cambridge, Mass. : Harvard University Press.

Vygotsky, L.S. (1981) The genesis of higher mental functions. In Wertsch, J.V. (ed.) *The Concept of Activity in Soviet Psychology*. Armonk, NY: M.E. Sharpe.

Wason, P.C. and Johnson-Laird, P.N. (1972) *Psychology of Reasoning: Structure and Content*. London: Batsford.

Webb, R.A. (1974) Concrete and formal operations in very bright 6 to 11-year-olds. *Human Development*, 17, 292–300.

Weinert, F. (1987) Executive control. In Weinert, Franz and Kluwe, Rainer (eds) *Metacognition, Motivation and Understanding*. London: Lawrence Erlbaum.

Weller, K. and Craft, A. (1983) *Making Up Our Minds: An Exploratory Study of Instrumental Enrichment*. London: Schools Council Publications.

Wertsch, J.V. (ed.) (1985) *Culture, Communication, and Cognition: Vygotskyan Perspectives*. Cambridge: Cambridge University Press.

White, R.T. (1988) *Learning Science*. Oxford: Basil Blackwell.

Woolnough, B.E. and Toh, K.A. (1990) Alternative approaches to assessment of practical work in science. *School Science Review*, 71, 256, 127–31.

Zeichner, K.M. and Tabachnick, B.R. (1991) *Issues and Practices in Inquiry-Oriented Teacher Education*. Lewes: The Falmer Press.

# Name index

Adey, P.S. 6, 32–3, 54–5, 80, 95–6, 103, 104, 122, 123, 135, 152, 162–3, 184
Ahlgren, A. 167
Angelev, J. 57–8
Ashby, R. 138
Ausubel, D. 5, 14, 122, 123–4

Baddeley, A. 125
Bateson, G. 70–1
Beasley, F. 47, 48–9, 90–1, 153–5, 156, 174, 176
Benjamin, H. 181
Biggs, J.B. 25, 135, 139
Blagg, N. 48, 54, 147, 153–4
Blank, R. 166
Bolam, R. 149
Bond, T.G. 24, 117
Boole, G. 115
Bridges, D. 149
Brown, A.L. 69–70, 74
Bruner, J. 8, 123, 156
Butler, J. 158
Butterworth, G.E. 15

Case, R. 71, 124
Champagne, A.B. 121
Clarke, A.D.B. and A.M. 120, 127, 166
Cockcroft Committee 31
Cole, M. 8
Coleman, J.S. 168
Coles, M.J. 39
Collings, J. 132–3
Collis, K.F. 25, 135, 139
Craft, A. 48, 54, 153–4
Cronbach, L. 93

de Bono, E. 7–8, 40–3, 46, 51, 146
Demetriou, A. 16, 24

DES (Department of Education and Science) 10
Dewey, J. 158
Dickinson, A.K. 138
Dignon, K. 131–2
Donaldson, M. 68, 117–18
Driver, R. 121, 123

Edwards, J. 41, 42
Egglestone, J. 152
Epstein, H.T. 11, 140–1, 143
Eraut, M. 149

Falkner, F. 11
Fensham, P.J. 63
Feuerstein, R. 8, 9–10, 11, 12–13, 21, 45–54, 60–1, 68, 72, 120, 155
Fitz-Gibbon, C.T. 184
Freyberg, P. 121
Froufe, J. 52
Furby, L. 93
Fusco, E.T. 21, 25, 135–6

Gagné, R.M. 5, 145, 168
Gardner, H. 15
Gardner, P.L. 150
Gauld, C.F. 123
Goossens, L. 54–5
Gulbenkian Foundation 140

Hallam, R.N. 25, 138
Hart, K. 137
Haywood, C. 48
Hodson, D. 130
Hudson, L. 42
Hunter-Grundin, E. 41
Huxley, A. 165

# Subject index